Youth, Crime, and Justice

Youth, Crime, and Justice

A Global Inquiry

CLAYTON A. HARTJEN

RUTGERS UNIVERSITY PRESS

NEW BRUNSWICK, NEW JERSEY, AND LONDON

LIBRARY OF CONGRESS CATALOGING-IN-PUBLICATION DATA

Hartjen, Clayton A., 1943–

Youth, crime, and justice: a global inquiry / Clayton A. Hartjen.
    p. cm.
    Includes bibliographical references and index.
    ISBN-13: 978-0-8135-4321-5 (hardcover : alk. paper)
    ISBN-13: 978-0-8135-4322-2 (pbk : alk. paper)
    1. Juvenile delinquency—Cross-cultural studies. 2. Juvenile
corrections—Cross-cultural studies. I. Title.
    HV9069.H324 2008
    364.36—dc22   2007033608

A British Cataloging-in-Publication record for this book is available
from the British Library.

Visit our Web site: http://rutgerspress.rutgers.edu

Manufactured in the United States of America

For Don C. Gibbons
Scholar, Mentor, and Friend

CONTENTS

ILLUSTRATIONS

ACKNOWLEDGMENTS

I am indebted to S. Priyadarsini, wife, colleague, and collaborator, for her assistance with all aspects of this effort. Without her the book would never have been written.

INTRODUCTION

This volume provides a summary and assessment of criminological research on youth crime and juvenile justice that has been carried out in countries around the world. My purpose in doing so is threefold. First, by drawing upon a wide range of criminological research and data from diverse societies, I hope to provide a global, as opposed to a country-specific, portrait of the misbehavior and victimization of young people and how different societies respond to problems concerning their young. Second, global inquiry can advance criminological knowledge by not only increasing our database but also providing a forum for testing theory, refining our understanding of patterns and trends, and expanding the horizons of our inquiry. Third, and more significant, by viewing youth crime and justice from a global perspective, criminology may be in a better position to cast light on what is becoming a problem of increasing international scope and on how societies might best respond to this challenge.

In this regard, United Nations and other data (United Nations 2004a, 2004b; UNICEF 2006c) indicate that juvenile delinquency, as well as the abuse and exploitation of children and juveniles, and societies' efforts to deal with these matters, have become issues of international concern. As discussed in the chapters to follow, there is good reason to believe that the problem of youth crime is on the rise throughout much of the world, especially in countries undergoing economic and political transition. Three forces that will increasingly impact the world in the present century—population dynamics, widespread economic deprivation and political oppression, and Westernized globalization—suggest that in the decades to come youth crime and juvenile justice will increasingly become topics of global concern. Although these matters will continue to be confronted as national issues, they are rapidly being recognized as international problems affecting most, if not all, of the world's societies.

In part, the present and emerging global problem of youth crime and justice is a reflection of the demographic transformation that occurred in 2000 when more than one half of the world's population was reported to be below age fifteen (United Nations 2000). Given that crime has always been a largely young male phenomenon, in the opening decades of the twenty-first century a substantial portion of the world's population will have reached its most crime-prone years (late teens to early twenties). Of equal significance is the fact that the vast majority of these young people live in the economically developing societies of Asia, Africa, and South America. Many exist in abject poverty, under totalitarian regimes, and/or in societies confronted with endless war and conflict (United Nations 2000, 2004a). Although in much of the world many infants will never live to see age five, the demographics of the world's population are such that in the early decades of this century a very large segment of the people who inhabit our globe will not only have reached their most crime-prone ages but will also be destitute, desperate, and without hope (United Nations 2004b). That they might become involved in crime, either as offenders or victims, should surprise no one.

These facts have significant implications for societies throughout the world. Large numbers of young people at peak crime ages will increasingly strain the resources of already floundering societies. In addition, all manner of criminality involving them could directly and indirectly impact individual societies, many ill-equipped to deal either with growing dependent populations or the substantial rise in youth crime and delinquency associated with their increasing numbers. As such, youth crime and the question of how to deal with it will no longer be problems specific to individual societies or particular types of societies.

In addition to actual and potential increases in youth crime in individual countries, transnational criminality involving the young, both as participants and as victims, is also likely to proliferate (Reichel 2005a). Even now millions of children and young people participate in, are victimized by, or have their lives impacted by international criminal activities that permeate the world. The distribution of drugs and pornography, the recruitment of children and juveniles into prostitution, slave labor, and organized criminal gangs, as well as their victimization by every other form of theft, exploitation, fraud, and abuse are increasingly becoming global and not simply local problems.

As in past centuries, economically desperate people, and those fleeing oppression of every kind, seek refuge in largely European or North American societies. Thousands of single young males seeking opportunities, as well as the marginalized children of migrants who cannot or are not allowed to integrate into the host population, become ripe reservoirs for all manner of criminality and exploitation, from petty theft to the spread of gangs and organized criminal networks. Or else they become objects of suspicion, fear, and targeted action by host populations and authorities. As the numbers of desperate young people multiply in largely third-world countries, host countries will face increased pressure from those migrating across their borders. In many host societies the real or imagined criminality attributed to the young people of displaced populations is

likely to be increasingly seen as matters of national concern and subject to coer-
cive action.

At the same time, clashes of cultures across and within societies around the
globe are being produced by the contravening pressures of cultural homogenization stemming from globalization—largely dominated by, reflecting, and based on
Western (primarily American) foundations—and conservative reaction to change
from those fearing the demise of traditional values and power structures. As a
result, family and social arrangements that traditionally prevented and controlled
youthful misconduct in many societies are becoming ineffective or arcane. In
diverse societies new conceptions of personal freedom, the rights of children, and
changes in responsibilities for and limitations on their control have eroded traditional practices as well as established legal systems. Thus, both the behavior of
young people and how to deal with it are becoming matters of public policy and
political dispute in countries across the globe.

But, to be sure, the growth in the youth-crime problem is by no means universal or uniform. Data from individual societies indicate that often countries
experience unique aspects of the problem—such as increased gang activity,
changes in drug abuse patterns, unusual levels of violence, or child-sexual
exploitation. And, while many societies may report rising levels of youth crime
and delinquency, others, even neighboring countries, may demonstrate specific
or general declines. Thus, as the problems of youth crime and juvenile justice
are generally intensifying across the globe, in individual societies there may be
little apparent reason to be concerned with such matters at all. Criminology has
yet to investigate why these differences may exist.

As the potentially real and perceptual problem of youthful misconduct
grows in the world's societies, the question of how to respond to youth crime
has also become ever more significant. Standards on how to treat youthful
offenders have been established by the United Nations, the Human Rights Convention, and such organizations as Amnesty International. Almost all countries
are signatories to international agreements specifying ages of responsibility,
conditions of confinement, legal rights and protections of young people
accused of offenses, as well as a host of related issues. Often these provisions
have simply been ignored, implemented in name only, or, where in force, meet
the bare minimum of humane and civil treatment. Nevertheless, these agreements provide leverage that can be used to pressure offending nations and, to
some extent, provide opportunities to protect the young from abuse and injustice. They also serve as guides to assess juvenile justice operations in specific
parts of the world (Winterdyk 2005).

The ways in which offending and other young people are viewed and treated
across the globe are as dynamic and variable as is the misconduct of the world's
young. Research on the juvenile justice systems discussed in this volume reveals
that countries around the world have created a remarkable array of mechanisms

and procedures in dealing with young people suspected or accused of misconduct and/or are victimized or subject to danger. In many societies, often those that are already facing a growing problem of youth crime, little has been done in addressing the issue beyond recognizing that there is one. Elsewhere concerted action is being taken to combat offense behavior and/or to structure just or effective systems to deal with young people.

As discussed in this volume, two dominant approaches characterize how individual countries have responded to their youth-crime problems. In some countries children's rights are primary, combined with nonpunitive mechanisms as the preferred ways of dealing with young people. In some of these countries truly innovative and potentially remedial solutions are being tried, often providing models for other jurisdictions to emulate. On the other hand, an apparently growing number of societies have implemented get-tough crackdown strategies as the preferred approach in responding to young miscreants. In these countries a culture of control appears to have come to dominate official responses to the perceived menace of youthful criminality.

Considering societal reactions to youth crime from a global perspective, Muncie and Goldson (2006) suggest that four trends appear to dominate juvenile justice in much of the world today. First, in many countries there has been a clear movement away from an approach oriented to the best interests of the child to a more punitive strategy directed to the best interests of society. Second, a growing tendency is dominating juvenile justice in many places to treat juveniles as adults, with an emphasis on deterrence over that of care. Third, in spite of wide disparities, many countries are increasing the use of incarceration as a way to deal with young offenders or would-be offenders. And, fourth, there is evidence of a growing worldwide fear of increased immigration along with conservative politics oriented toward a crackdown on the perceived misbehavior of immigrant youth in host countries, generating a concomitant disproportionate rise in official reactions to young offenders, generally, and minority youth, specifically. The concept of the "best interests of the child" has been replaced with terms such as "risk management" and "public safety." Fighting crime, not securing juvenile justice, has become the goal.

Criminology has yet to fully investigate this trend or document its impact. But, in the opening decade of the twenty-first century, it appears that in many of the world's societies we may be witnessing a turnabout in the perception and treatment of young people as significant as that which occurred at the beginning of the twentieth century, when the notion of juvenile justice was first implemented. The idealized "nonpunitive," "best interests of the child," approach initiated at the beginning of the last century is being challenged, either in fact or in rhetoric, by a "due-process," "crime-control," approach. And, as indicated throughout this volume, in much of the world even the notion of justice, particularly for juveniles, is itself an illusion.

Criminologists have some ideas as to how differences in youthful offense behaviors and rates may be patterned. But explaining these differences on an international scale presents a challenge yet to be met by criminology. And, although important variations in both its scope and dimensions may exist in individual societies, essentially everywhere people and governments have, or are beginning to, become aware that criminality involving young people, and the question of what to do about it, are matters that require more complete understanding than we have as yet gained from traditional criminological inquiry. As criminologists, how we look at or attempt to deal with the behavior of young people cannot continue to remain matters of localized concern or study. As a truly international science of crime and justice, criminology must investigate these matters from a broader perspective than has been common to the discipline.

The scientific study of delinquency, including the behavior of young people and societal reaction to it, largely remains parochial in character. Criminology has produced a mountain of research, theory, and information on these phenomena from individual countries. Most of that knowledge centers on the Untied States, Canada, the United Kingdom, various European countries, and, to a lesser extent, Australia, New Zealand, and Japan. Information from other parts of the world is available from the United Nations and reports of other organizations, as well as a few studies by native or visiting criminologists. While comparatively wanting next to the substantial volume of information we have for countries such as the United States and a handful of other societies, during the past twenty-five years criminological inquiry has produced a sizable and growing body of comparative or international literature on youth crime and juvenile justice in diverse societies (see, e.g., Booth 1991; Brusten et al. 1984; Bullock 1992; Hackler 1991c; Hartjen and Priyadarsini 2004; Junger-Tas 1994; Mehlbye and Walgrave 1998; Muncie and Goldson 2006; Shoemaker 1996b; Winterdyk 2002). Even so, our base of knowledge is extremely limited, if not nil, for much of the world. Very simply, as far as research on crime and delinquency is concerned, much of the world remains an unknown quantity, an information black hole. In this regard, any statements we might make about worldwide trends in, or even the present dimensions of, youth crime and victimization or societal responses to these phenomena must be considered speculative.

Even though we know relatively little about many of the world's societies, the existing literature offers criminologists enough information to begin to develop a global understanding of youth crime and justice. We now have, if not firm conclusions, adequate data to make some informed speculations about these matters for countries across the globe. It is the purpose of this book to attempt to do just that.

It is, of course, important to understand the problems of youthful misconduct and victimization and possible solutions to these problems in one's own society. And criminological inquiry will undoubtedly continue to remain largely a country-specific enterprise. But, a global perspective on delinquency is worthy for its own sake, in order to better map and hopefully understand similarities and variations in the criminal behavior and victimization of young people, as well as the nature and impact of different strategies societies use in dealing with these issues. And, in the end, any such study also helps us to better understand ourselves (Hartjen 1998).

This book, therefore, is a survey of what we know (and, consequently, what we do not know) about youth crime and victimization, and how various governments around the world have chosen to deal with the misbehavior and exploitation of their young. Unlike most books on the subject that provide chapters on country A, country B, country C, and so forth, my intent here is to draw upon the existing body of international literature and information on delinquency, juvenile justice, and related phenomena produced by scholars and organizations from around the world. Given the availability of data, however, much of what is discussed in this volume is derived from research on relatively few countries. While not a random or even necessarily representative sample of the world's societies, the summary and assessment provided in this volume is based on as diverse a sampling of the literature as was reasonably accessible.

Individual chapters address a variety of specific topics germane to understanding youth crime and justice. In taking a global approach, we begin by looking at some aspects of delinquency laws and the definition of "delinquent." Then, with emphasis on the universal explanatory ability of existing etiological theory, the question "Why do young people offend at all?" is examined. That discussion is followed by an analysis of similarities and variations in measured rates of such behavior and our ability to explain these variations. This is followed by a look at a variety of forms of offense behavior committed by young people around the world. The different strategies adapted by countries across the globe to deal with delinquents and predelinquents are then addressed at some length. A more specific comparative look is offered by examining the judicial processing systems found in several countries and the similarities and differences among them. The question of "correcting" offenders is then addressed. As a distinctive issue in its own right, a final chapter highlights some aspects of the worldwide victimization of young people.

The descriptions of delinquency or juvenile justice throughout this book are based on research conducted at the times cited. Both the behavior of young people and how that conduct is reacted to by authorities in any society are dynamic and subject to change. Even recently published research may not be totally accurate in describing the current situation. Thus, the examples cited should be considered illustrative rather than definitive.

In discussing youth crime and justice from a global as opposed to a country-specific perspective, the reader will discover that much has been left unsaid. Representation, not exhaustive coverage, was my goal in selecting specific topics and examples for this volume. The real problem facing a truly comprehensive understanding of young crime and justice is what remains unknown. It is with some hope that this volume can help stimulate inquiry, shrinking the size of that "unknown."

Youth, Crime, and Justice

1

Law

All human societies recognize generational distinctions among persons of varying ages. Typically, elders are venerated and excused from full community participation. Other adults are expected to participate in the activities of the tribe, clan, or community and are accorded the power and authority of their maturity and position. Children, or young members, are expected to be deferential to their elders, to acquire the skills and knowledge deemed necessary for future adult participation, and, to a more or less limited extent, contribute to the well-being of the group. Usually, the transitions between the generational stages recognized by the group are marked by rituals and ceremonies—often elaborate and sometimes painful for the neophytes. But, everywhere, age has been a significant criterion for categorizing societal members into groupings. Of these life stages, the transition between childhood and full adult status is usually most socially significant. Moreover, it is the meaning this transition has that has been a matter of considerable debate and consternation for the administration of justice in modern world societies.

As all societies recognize social distinctions between generational groups, all also have different expectations regarding the behaviors, responsibilities, and privileges of members of various age groupings. While all members are expected to follow the norms and customs of the group, both the extent to which persons of differing age status are required to adhere fully to these standards and/or the consequences that apply for violation may not be uniform. Similarly, while some norms apply to all, some age groupings may be subjected to additional standards or rules not required of others.

Throughout most of human history, and among many societies in contemporary times, these age generational standards and expectations have been grounded in custom and tradition (Aries 1962; Empey 1979b; Gillis 1981). As law and legal structures emerged over the millennia, primarily in Western societies

1

or those under their colonial authority, these customs became increasingly codified in law in the form of proclamations, statutes, or judicial decisions or common law. From what is known historically, children and the very young have rarely been subjected to the full force of expectation or sanction when it comes to violations of law or custom (Krisberg and Austin 1978; Sanders 1970). As the notion of mens rea became firmly established as a grounds for culpability, in the case of crimes, following custom, children and infants were increasingly accorded legal exclusion from criminal sanction on the grounds that they were by virtue of their age incapable of forming criminal intent and, therefore, could not be held accountable for their actions—at least to the same extent that adults were accountable. Some such notion probably was behind the protection from criminal sanction that historically and universally has been accorded the very young. By the end of the nineteenth century, this concept became the foundation for a full-fledged legal revolution and the invention in Western nations of the notion of delinquency and establishment of separate legal systems and procedures to dispense what has come to be called juvenile justice (Empey 1979b; Platt 1969; Sussman 1959; Tappan 1960).

All societies recognize that the young cannot, and should not, be held accountable for their behavior to the same standards as adults, nor should they be subjected to the same penalties for violating these standards. However, this recognition alone has by no means resolved a number of thorny questions that have plagued the pursuit of justice for juveniles everywhere in the world since the beginning of the twentieth century. Of these, four issues are most perplexing for modern societies around the globe: the age of culpability, and responsibility; jurisdiction; the forms of behavior prohibited or required of the young; and the legal rights of juveniles. Different societies have formulated a large variety of responses to these four concerns. In the following, we explore some of these responses in a global investigation of juvenile law and approaches to juvenile justice.

Age of Responsibility

Probably the laws and prevailing customs of all societies have used biological age as the standard for determining at what point in life individuals can be held responsible for their behavior and subjected to the penalties that others suffer for violating the group's rules (Aries 1962; Gillis 1981; Sanders 1970). Typically, these ages corresponded with socially recognized biological development from infancy to childhood to adulthood.

Virtually everywhere, infants and children (usually persons below ages four, five, six, or seven) have been considered to be beyond the pale of legal sanction of any kind for their misconduct, although even then infants and children could come under legal jurisdiction for their protection or well-being.

In the contemporary world almost all societies mandate some minimum age for criminal culpability below which no individual, regardless of offense, can be subjected to criminal punishment for his or her conduct. What that age may be is by no means uniform, nor necessarily something that can be mandated, given variations in custom and social systems (Dünkel 1991; Johnson 1995; Sagle-Grande 1991). In an effort to do just that on a global scale, in 1985 a United Nations resolution stated that signatory states should establish minimum ages below which it would be presumed that children did not have the capacity to infringe the penal law. But not all countries, even some signatories to the UN resolution, have established minimum-age laws, nor do countries agree on what that age should be. Recognizing the likely impossibility of mandating a specific minimum age that would be acceptable to all countries, the United Nations commented that "the modern approach would be to consider whether a child can live up to the moral and psychological components of criminal responsibility; that is, whether a child, by virtue of her or his individual discernment and understanding, can be held responsible for essentially antisocial behavior. If the age of criminal responsibility is fixed too low or if there is no age limit at all, the notion of responsibility would become meaningless" (United Nations 1986, 6). Thus, although a global, uniform age of culpability does not exist, or is likely to in the foreseeable future, it seems to be widely accepted that age as such is a reasonable criterion for determining who may or may not be subject to some kind of legal proceeding and potential punishment for misconduct by the authorities of the state. Virtually everywhere, by law or custom, persons below some recognized age cannot, under any circumstances, be subjected to punishment or other treatment for engaging in forbidden behavior. Generally, societies agree that older youths may be treated differently from adults. But, to what extent and at what age they may be subject to this differentiation is by no means a settled question.

If societies agree that (1) young people can only be subjected to any kind of corrective action once they have reached a specific age (however varied that age may be globally) and that (2) for some period beyond this age they are not to be subject to the full standards of law and correction, then an issue of major concern throughout much of the world is at just what age individuals can be held fully accountable and/or accorded the full measure of criminal procedure and justice for their misdeeds. It is this "age of full responsibility" that has been most perplexing for legal authorities, and the cause of much controversy among jurists around the world.

When the juvenile courts were established in the United States and elsewhere at the turn of the nineteenth century, one of the compelling concerns for the founders was the question of at what age should persons above the minimum age of culpability be considered adults, held responsible for their behavior, or, more broadly situation in life, and be subject to the full weight of criminal

procedure and sanction. In this regard, as far as their misconduct was concerned, in creating systems of juvenile justice, rather than simply raising the age
of culpability, the founders of juvenile justice systems sought to protect young
people by creating a new age category (that of "juvenile") by establishing an age
below which offenders were to be excluded from the scope of the penal law and
criminal justice system, but would still be subject to some kind of societal intervention should they misbehave. Persons engaged in misconduct who were
above the legal/customary age of culpability but still not considered responsible
as adults could be dealt with by authorities of the state. But, they would be
excluded from the purview of the criminal law or at least protected from the
harshness of its penalties (Bensinger 1991; Bernard 1992). A pressing issue then
and today became determining this new age of criminal, as opposed to legal,
responsibility.

Intellectual and emotional maturity is generally associated with physical
maturity—something that normally takes place in the mid to late teens. This age
usually marks the end of compulsory schooling and the acquisition of privileges
(e.g., right to vote, operate a motor vehicle, drink alcohol) and responsibilities
(e.g., military service) in modern societies. Therefore, the age of physical maturity for most individuals has almost universally been set as the age of legal
responsibility as far as criminal matters are concerned. In primitive societies or
premodern times, a kind of "old enough" arbitrary standard was probably used
to assess when someone had transited from child to adult and was therefore eligible not only for adult privileges but adult consequences as well. No such arbitrary standard will do in societies governed by the rule of law. Law demands
precision. Thus, definite demarcation lines (ages) must be drawn to determine
just when an offender is to be considered eligible for criminal punishment or to
be treated in some other way. All modern societies have established these demar-
cations primarily using biological age as the standard. The only issue, however,
has been "What age?" Winterdyk (1997a) compiled ages of criminal responsibility
for a variety of countries. Table 1.1 depicts both the similarities and wide disparities he found in the ages for which young people could be held legally
accountable as criminals for their miscount in countries throughout the world.

It is probably accepted universally that infants and young children cannot
be expected to comport themselves as adults and thus should not be punished
as adults would be if they misbehaved. For how many specific years thereafter
offenders are to be tolerated, excused, given special consideration, or deemed
less than competent is neither universal nor a matter for global consensus.
If the ability to reason, which provides the basis of modern penal law, is somehow contingent on intellectual and emotional maturity, and if that emotional
and intellectual maturity is somehow correlated with physical maturity, the
question remains "Is one's age of legal responsibility to be established by one's
biological development alone?" People mature biologically at similar, but not

TABLE 1.1

Ages for Youth and Criminal Justice Jurisdiction for Selected Countries

Country	Minimum–maximum ages	Alternatives
Egypt	?–18	Youths segregated by age: 12 and under; 12–15; 15–18
Singapore	?–12	
Cuba	6–16	
United States	7–15+	Varies by state, most = 17
India	7–16/18	Girls = 16; Boys = 18
Cayman Islands	8–17	8–14 = young persons; 14–17 = juveniles
Philippines	9–15	15–18 = young offenders
Australia	10–16/17	Varies by jurisdiction
Canada	12–18	
England	12–18	
Netherlands	12–18	
France	13–18	
Israel	13–18	
Poland	13–17	16–17 = responsible based on moral and mental ability
New Zealand	14–17	10 if mens rea proved
Germany	14–17	18–20 transferable to juvenile court
Hungary	14–18	
China	14–25	Partial responsibility to 18
Italy	14–18	
Japan	14–20	
Russia	14–18	
Norway	15–18	
Austria	14–19	
Sweden	15–20	15–17 special consideration
Finland	15–21	Under 18 = child; under 21 = juvenile

(Continued)

TABLE 1.1

(Continued)

Country	Minimum–maximum ages	Alternatives
Switzerland	15–18	7–15 = children; 15–18 = adolescent; 18–25 = young adult
Argentina	16–18	
Scotland	?–16	18 if under supervision
Hong Kong	16–20	7–15 = juvenile

Source: Adapted from Winterdyk 1997, xxiv–xxvi.

identical, ages. Thus, is someone who is biologically mature at age thirteen to be considered legally culpable as a criminal while another is excused until his or her biological maturity takes place at, say, age fifteen? If not, where should we draw the line? The United Nations' guidelines on this question are just that, guides, not strict rules. Within some reasonable limits, signatories of the convention were left free to establish their own exact age standards. A quarter of a century later the United Nations is still having disputes with a number of countries that have set age limits lower than those the UN considers reasonable.

As suggested by table 1.1, considerable variability exists as to just when different countries feel individuals have reached the age or responsibility and, therefore, fall under the realm of adult criminal law. Indeed, even within some counties the age at which young people can, or must, be excluded from adult court jurisdiction can vary considerably. As indicated by table 1.2, laws concerning age limits in the United States are by no means uniform across jurisdictions.

Under the presumption of doli incapax (presumption of incompetence) common to law generally (Nicol 1995), it has been recognized that the ability to reason (mens rea) is not inexorably linked to physical maturity. Realizing that unless one establishes separate tests for every individual to determine when and if they have reached mental/emotional maturity (presuming thereby that they possess mens rea), the realities of administering justice based on the criterion of age alone have led many societies to, in effect, fuzzy the picture. Thus, for example, it may be established that anyone below age four is to be excluded from criminal-like jurisdiction of any kind and that children between the ages of four and seventeen are to be accorded a different set of standards, treatment, and processing from those who are older. But, the question that remains (besides

TABLE 1.2

Statutory Ages for Juvenile Court Jurisdiction in the United States

State	Minimum age[a]	Maximum age	Extended age	Minimum transfer age[b]
Alabama	None	17	20	14
Alaska	None	17	18	None
Arizona	8	17	20	None
Arkansas	10	17	20	14
California	None	17	24	14
Colorado	10	17	Full disposition	12
Connecticut	None	15	20	14
Delaware	None	17	20	None
District of Columbia	None	17	20	None
Florida	None	17	21	None
Georgia	None	16	20	None
Hawaii	None	17	Full disposition	None
Idaho	None	17	20	None
Illinois	None	16	20	13
Indiana	None	17	20	None
Iowa	None	17	18	14
Kansas	10	17	22	10
Kentucky	None	17	18	14
Louisiana	10	16	20	14
Maine	None	17	20	None
Maryland	7	17	20	None
Massachusetts	7	16	20	14
Michigan	None	16	20	14
Minnesota	10	17	20	14
Mississippi	10	17	19	13
Missouri	None	16	20	12
Montana	None	17	24	12
Nebraska	None	17	18	None

(Continued)

TABLE 1.2

(Continued)

State	Minimum age[a]	Maximum age	Extended age	Minimum transfer age[b]
Nevada	None	17	20	None
New Hampshire	None	16	20	13
New Jersey	None	17	Full disposition	14
New Mexico	None	17	20	15
New York	7	15	20	13
North Carolina	6	15	20	13
North Dakota	None	17	19	14
Ohio	None	17	20	14
Oklahoma	None	17	18	None
Oregon	None	17	24	None
Pennsylvania	10	17	20	None
Rhode Island	None	17	20	None
South Carolina	None	16	20	None
South Dakota	10	17	20	None
Tennessee	None	17	18	None
Texas	10	16	20	14
Utah	None	17	20	14
Vermont	10	17	18	10
Virginia	None	17	20	14
Washington	None	17	20	None
West Virginia	None	17	20	None
Wisconsin	10	16	24	None
Wyoming	None	17	20	13

Sources: Data from http://www.ncjj.org/stateprofiles/overviews/lowerage.asp; http://www.totalcriminaldefense.com/who_is_a_juvenile.asp; http://www.pbs.org/wgbh/pages/frontline/shows/juvenile/stats/states.html.

[a] If no age is specified, common law or case law may be used to decide jurisdiction.

[b] Individual state laws may place special age restrictions on criminal trial and/or specify conditions for transfer.

what exact ages should be used) is "Should everyone between ages four and seventeen be treated the same, regardless? Or, should exceptions be made? And, if so, how should these exceptions be determined?" Most modern societies have opted for exceptions. What seems to differ from country to country and even within some countries is the grounds for and procedures to invoke these exceptions. That raises the question of jurisdiction.

Jurisdiction

The idea behind a separate system of juvenile justice was a belief that all culpable youths below some designated age would be excluded from the jurisdiction of the adult criminal court, yet subject to intervention of some kind. These individuals, called juveniles, instead would be processed in a special court designed and designated just for them.

However, concepts of the juvenile, and fear and intolerance of their misconduct, have changed over time or have varied from place to place. Accordingly, efforts have been made to exempt some offenders from the jurisdiction of the juvenile court and to place them under the authority of some adult (or adultlike) criminal jurisdiction, or to modify the kinds of treatment the juvenile court traditionally accorded offenders. Normally these exemptions are based on age and/or offense, so that persons of a certain age and/or accused of a serious offense would be transferred or waived to adult criminal jurisdiction. Commenting on the legal changes that have taken place in English juvenile justice in recent years, Fionda (2001, 88) nicely summarizes the jurisdictional issue:

> Childhood . . . technically runs from the age of ten to seventeen in the youth justice system, with just a few concessions made between the ages of eighteen and twenty to acknowledge that full maturity may only be reached at twenty-one. However, to some extent childhood in criminal justice terms is dependent on the gravity of the offense. The commission of a (very) serious offense can mean that a child essentially transcends their own childhood— they have committed an adult act and therefore are treated as an adult on that basis. This might alternatively be seen in more emotive terms as the withdrawal of the privilege of childhood for the most serious offenders.

Essentially, a biologically incompetent person somehow suddenly becomes competent if the offense in question is grave enough, even if the person's ability to reason remains immature.

As with other age-based criterion, these standards for exemption and the procedures to invoke them vary considerably among jurisdictions around the globe. In recent decades, the conditions for exempting youths from juvenile jurisdiction have been matters of much debate and controversy (Albrecht 1997; Bishop 2000; Coalition for Juvenile Justice 1994; Justice 1996; Sebba 1986).

Where separate juvenile justice systems exist, juveniles deemed worthy of adult sanction may be transferred or waived to the adult authorities for trial and disposition. Most typically, older youths accused of serious crimes face waiver. However, in some places specific age categories have been established for the differential treatment of offenders.

Tiered and Alternative Court Systems

Generally, in attempting to implement differential treatment for youths in specific age categories, some countries have established two-tiered juvenile justice systems wherein youths of different ages can be processed in different courts depending on the nature of the offense in question. In Germany, for example, all juvenile cases are under the jurisdiction of courts of ordinary jurisdiction; but depending upon the seriousness of the offense, the composition of the court can vary. For minor offenses, a single juvenile judge (*Jugendrichter*) tries the case and can impose an incarceration sentence of up to one year. A mixed tribunal (*Jugendschöffengericht*) made up of a professional and two lay judges hears more serious cases, while a *Jugendkammer* consisting of three professional judges presides in major and capital crimes (Wolfe 1991, 1996). Similarly, in Greece three different types of juvenile courts try cases. As described by Petoussi and Stavrou (1996), these consist of "one-judge juvenile courts" that try petty violations and can impose reform, therapeutic measures, and incarceration for up to five years. "Three-judge juvenile courts" try misdemeanor cases for which a youth could be incarcerated for over five years. A three-judge juvenile appeals court hears appeals from the three-judge trial court. The vast majority of juvenile cases in Russia appear before the Commissions on Juvenile Affairs (CJAs), established in 1918, which operate very much like family courts in that they hear and dispose of a host of cases involving juveniles. Youths age fourteen to sixteen who commit serious crimes, however, are subject to arrest and can be brought before the criminal court following a procurator's decision to relinquish the case to adult authorities (Finckenauer 1996).

Alternatively, some countries have established alternatives to both the regular juvenile or adult criminal courts in which some cases may be heard. In the United States, for example, what are often called teen or youth courts are found in some jurisdictions in which first offenders may be handled rather than having the case adjudicated in a normal juvenile hearing. Four types of such courts may be found. Adult judge courts have an adult serve as judge, but all other participants are juveniles. In youth judge courts all participants are juveniles. Tribunals consist of courts wherein juvenile attorney's present cases before a panel of juvenile judges, similar to the tribunal system found in normal European criminal justice systems. Peer jury systems are similar to the American grand jury in that individuals of any age can present cases before juries made up of juveniles who are allowed to ask questions directly (see Butts et al. 1999; Godwin 1998). Similarly, specialized courts to hear cases involving drugs, traffic violations, or other matters may be found in the United States and many European countries.

Both the proceedings and potential sanctions for offenders can be quite different for youths depending on the court reviewing their case. In two-tiered systems, age at time of the offense typically is itself the standard for determining which court hears the case. Although, even here, a waiver or waiverlike procedure may also be available to transfer jurisdiction and subsequent possible consequence.

Waiver Hearings

In the case of transfer between juvenile and adult criminal courts the common mechanism is a waiver hearing. How waiver is administered varies considerably, although usually the state must make an application to send the case (juvenile) to the adult court, subject to approval by the presiding juvenile jurist. Most often this is an affirmative procedure, with the burden on the state to give adequate justification to the juvenile court to relinquish its jurisdiction. In some instances waiver is automatic (mandated by law) for certain offenses or offenses committed by certain offenders (usually determined by age at the time of offense). In Canada, for example, a youth age fourteen or older charged with an indictable (felony) offense can be transferred to adult court. In making the transfer decision, the juvenile court judge uses specified criteria: severity of offense, age and character of the offender, prior record, ability of the juvenile versus adult system to deal with the case, youth treatment or correctional resources, and any other factors the judge deems relevant (Corrado and Markwart 1996, 39). According to Fagan and Zimring (2000), in the United States waiver decisions are ideally based on two criteria: amenability to treatment and a judgment that the youth is not a fit subject for the juvenile justice/corrections system. Debatable as even these criteria might be in deciding whether to send a juvenile offender to the adult system, Fagan and Zimring (2000, 3) argue that "the reality is that most decisions about transfer standards are made on an ad hoc basis without any reference to general notions about the competence or limits of the juvenile courts. Decisions are made as an aspect of policy toward crime, but not as a self-conscious act of constructing or elaborating a theory of juvenile justice." It is unknown to what extent this is generally true of waiver decisions wherever mechanisms exist to transfer jurisdiction of juvenile cases across the globe. Broad international research on the issue is simply not yet available.

Competency Tests

A third procedure is used in some jurisdictions, in conjunction with a two-tiered or a juvenile-to-adult transfer procedure, where the legal competency of the accused is assessed before the case is waived. In such cases, competency is typically determined in terms of the youth's ability to distinguish right from wrong and to understand that the conduct of which they are accused was wrong (not merely bad or naughty). Much like an insanity proceeding in criminal courts, the burden of proving competency or incompetence can be on the state or the defense, depending on jurisdiction, and can rely on testimony and evidence that would usually be excluded from a criminal trial. Again, age and type (seriousness) of offense are the criteria occasioning the need for a competency hearing. In Australia, for example, anyone under the age of fourteen years cannot be held criminally responsible unless competency can be proved. The Queensland Criminal Code Act of 1899 illustrates this idea: "A person under the age of 14 years is not criminally responsible for an act or omission, unless it is proved that at the time of doing the act or making the omission the person had capacity to know that the person ought not to do the act or make the omission" (Urbas 2000, 3–4).

Diversion

Unless jurisdiction is waived to adult authorities or mandated by specific statute as outside their scope, generally in modern societies across the globe juvenile authorities, typically in the form of judicial bodies, have legal authority over all persons included within their jurisdictional ages. It is the juvenile court judge who has the final say in disposing of youths accused of delinquency and other conduct. However, in keeping with the informality and nonpunitive ideals of the original juvenile courts, various countries have developed a number of innovative ways to deal with youths in an informal, nonjudicial, manner.

There are a host of ways to spare youths from formal court intervention. Often beginning as early as police contact and extending through court hearings, diversion programs have been developed to keep young people out of the hands of officialdom and to protect them from the stigma and possible punitive treatment of court processing. While retaining its ultimately legal authority, the court in these cases has essentially delegated its jurisdiction and decision-making responsibility to nonjudicial bodies.

In England, the informal and long-standing practice of police warning mild offenders rather than subjecting them to arrest and formal processing was formalized as "police cautions." With this approach, youths detected or accused of misconduct are issued a formal caution by the chief inspector in charge of the juvenile bureau rather than face prosecution and a court hearing. Both the juvenile's parents and the victim or complainant must consent to accept the caution notice rather than proceed with the formal judicial process (Farrington and Bennett 1981). Similarly, The Young Offenders Act in Canada stipulates a policy of minimum interference in processing and sentencing youths accused of isolated and nonserious crimes. The law mandates that, rather than formal charges, police cautions and various alternative measures (diversion options) be relied upon (Corrado and Markwart 1996). Although the juvenile court holds ultimate authority, in many countries ways to delegate jurisdiction over juvenile cases to administrative and other agencies have been established, thereby avoiding judicial processing.

Other Approaches

Many countries have incorporated tradition and custom into the more formal authority of the legal system, either as a part of or as adjunct to, the use of courts and judges to deal with young people accused of minor offenses. In the Philippines, for example, local community units known as *barangays* have been formalized (Shoemaker 1996a). Besides serving as local administrative bodies, under the direction of elected officials called "captains," *barangays* are recognized, and in some cases mandated, to mediate certain offenses and disputes. Indeed, according to Shoemaker (1996a), the Child and Youth Welfare Code specifically identifies the *barangay* as a body important to the prevention of delinquency. If unable to handle the matter himself, the captain is assisted by a mediating panel of three people called a *pangkay,* although it is rarely used in practice. Under law, *barangay* matters must be amicably settled. Legal assistance is forbidden. Instead offending juveniles are represented by family or responsible friends.

A similar approach has long existed in India under the auspices of the village *panchayat.* This traditional local administrative body of prestigious elders has considerable informal authority throughout India (Hartjen and Priyadarsini 1984). Parents commonly still bring misbehaving children before the local *panchayat* for discipline, and the body may be called upon to arbitrate matters when youths have committed any manner of offense. Without legal judicial authority or control, to what extent *panchayats* are fair or evenhanded in dealing with such matters remains an open question.

Perhaps the most extensive use of officially recognized informal authority in dealing with juvenile offenders are help and education teams in China and the family group conference procedure adapted in New Zealand, parts of Australia, and other countries. These bodies have been legislatively created to mediate and resolve delinquency and other matters in ways that are both reflective of tradition or political ideology and seek a restorative rather than a punitive outcome.

According to Reichel (2005a), in China some three thousand special agencies (juvenile courts) hear criminal cases involving juveniles (generally persons under eighteen) but are required to uphold a policy of education, reform, and rehabilitation in dealing with offenders (Hewitt, Hickey, and Regoli 1991). Instead of a formal judicial process, in China "the preferred response to juvenile offenders uses the 'help and education team' system. With the close cooperation of government agencies and private citizens, young people are placed under the constant care of the help-education teams until they are reformed.

Each help-education team has three to five members who take responsibility for helping one individual. Team members can represent teachers, parents, police officers, neighbors, government officials, or other interested citizens" (Reichel 2005a, 355).

The family group conference (FGC) approach that was developed in New Zealand represents a unique blend of the formal application of law and an informal deliberative procedure. The 1989 Children, Young Persons and Their Families Act in New Zealand sought to promote the well-being of young people and their families (Morris and Maxwell 1991, 1993). Its primary goal was to assist families in caring for their young and to repair disruptive relationships. To do so a special quasi-judicial procedure was implemented based on established custom and a restorative versus a punitive approach to juvenile offending. In an FGC, the offense, need, family situation, and other issues are discussed among participating parties, with the state acting only as an arbitrator to facilitate and enforce whatever resolution of the matter is agreed upon by the participants (including the offender). Although a juvenile court can be involved in cases of delinquency, the FGC is at the heart of New Zealand's juvenile justice system, either as an alternative to formal judicial processing or as an integral part of that procedure itself.

It appears to be a universal and historically grounded fact that young people should be accorded different expectations from adults regarding their conduct and not be subject to the awful consequences that could follow accusations of wrongdoing under criminal law. Few, for example, would want to see any child executed, even if the crime they committed was quite horrific. And, most people probably feel that even serious offenders of tender age can somehow be salvaged or redeemed for a future life. The problem has been where to draw the line, both to be reasonable in the treatment of young offenders and just for victims and offenders alike. Age has seemed to be a reasonable standard by which to draw this line. However, law demands uniformity and definitive criteria for its administration. Thus, determining what age and how rigorously to adhere to it have become perplexing problems for societies around the world. The diverse ways in which these questions have been addressed are as varied as the systems that have been invented to deal with them.

Forms of Behavior

In creating a new body of law and system of justice for juveniles, the founders of the first juvenile courts were concerned with more than mitigating the harsh treatment young offenders could expect in adult criminal courts. Their primary concern was to save youths from lives of crime and degradation (Empey 1979b). Not only were the new courts to take a different form and follow procedures radically different from adult criminal courts, but the scope of the court's authority was to be sweeping. Under the guise of *parens patriae,* the court would act as a super parent for all children within its jurisdiction, looking after their well-being and welfare in addition to their behavior. To provide for this, laws were written giving courts jurisdiction over three categories of juveniles: juvenile criminal offenders; status offenders; and dependent, neglected, and abused juveniles.

Crimes

Virtually all juvenile authorities (courts) throughout the world now have jurisdiction over youths accused of violating the criminal code of the jurisdiction in which they are located. The specific court or authority that may deal with youths accused of various kinds of criminal offenses, and how they are to be handled, may vary from place to place. Examples can be found in societies across the globe.

The Child and Youth Welfare Code for the Philippines, for instance, defines a "youthful offender" as a person between ages nine and eighteen accused of committing felonies and is processed through the formal machinery of juvenile justice (Shoemaker 1996a, 41). In Poland, the law provides that the juvenile court has jurisdiction over "cases involving punishable acts in relation to persons between the age of 13 and 17 years who have committed such acts" (Krukowski 1987, 115). Similarly, in the Netherlands, within the district court, jurists appointed as children's judges try all criminal cases against youths designated to be minors under the law; although, for those juveniles between age sixteen and eighteen the case can be waived to be tried by the criminal court instead (Carlie 1997, 133). Tribunals for juveniles in various East and Central European countries deal with offenses committed by juveniles in violation of the criminal code and other statutes (Selih 1996, 175).

Status Offenses

In addition to criminal acts, the courts established at the turn of the twentieth century, and in most countries of the world today, also have the authority to deal with juveniles accused of committing a host of acts not prohibited of adults. These so-called status offenses include such things as truancy, underage drinking, and running away from home—acts thought to endanger the well-being of the juvenile and potentially expose the youth to crime and other dangerous activities. The criminal-act jurisdiction of juvenile courts is essentially ubiquitous and largely undisputed. But both the kinds of behavior specifically prohibited or required of youths and the scope of the court's authority to deal with youths regarding these activities are variable across the globe and are often matters of contention. In Poland, for example, family tribunals deal with various noncriminal forms of youthful misbehavior. The law gives these tribunals jurisdiction over youths showing "signs of demoralization," defined as "breach of social coexistence principles, commission of an unlawful act, systematic evasion of obligatory school or vocational training attendance, use of alcoholic liquor or other means of intoxication, prostitution, vagabondage, association with criminal groups" (Krukowski 1987, 115). Neighboring countries such as the Czech Republic and Hungary relegate these matters to administrative agencies (Selih 1996, 175). The sweeping nature of these special prohibitions common to the laws of many countries is exemplified by Ohio state law, which defines an "unruly child" as "beyond control by reason of being wayward or habitually disobedient; is truant from home or school; so deports self as to injure or endanger the health or morals of self or others; attempts to marry without parental consent; found in a disreputable place; visits or patronizes a place prohibited by law; or associates with vagrant, vicious, criminal, notorious, or immoral persons; engaged in occupation prohibited by law, or is in a situation dangerous to life or limb or injurious to health or morals of self or others; has committed status offense" (Community Research Associates 1987, 16–17). Other U.S. states typically have similar, and similarly vague, laws. Some countries, such as France and Belgium, enacted legislation during the twentieth century that created entire legal systems explicitly designed as comprehensive welfare institutions encompassing all civil as well as criminal matters involving juveniles (Blatier 1999; Christiaens 1999; Hackler 1991a, 1991b; Humphris 1991).

Singling out persons by age for additional, special, legal prohibition is not without its detractors (Collins and Kearns 2001; Wardhaugh 1991; Zimring 1979). Curfew laws aimed at preventing delinquency by forcing juveniles to be at home or otherwise under supervision at specific hours exemplify the kind of controversy one can meet in legislating the behavior of a specific age-related class of people. Besides some doubt as to the effectiveness of such laws to actually curb delinquent behavior (Adams 2003; Fried 2001), in a number of countries considerable concern has been voiced by some that such laws unreasonably or unconstitutionally violate the civil rights of juveniles (e.g., Drakeford and Butler 2001; Hemmens and Bennett 1999). This issue points to the very heart of the controversy over the purpose and nature of juvenile justice itself.

Dependent and Neglected Children

Originating as an authoritative agency (at a time when few alternative mechanisms existed) to look after the well-being and welfare of young people, juvenile courts still often have responsibility over youths not accused of any offense but who, nonetheless, are in some kind of need or danger. Everywhere, judicial or judicial-like mechanisms exist to care for needy or dependent children. In premodern or tribal societies these mechanisms may be informal and governed by custom. In countries governed by formal rules of law, the care of such children is normally under the jurisdiction of juvenile court authorities, often with other agencies also involved in such matters.

In Bangladesh, for example, a caseworker or probation officer can forward a juvenile to the juvenile court if the youth is "shelterless, floating having no means for livelihood to lead an honest life, or is engaged in begging, or juvenile is neglected or tortured by his guardians or is living in a brothel coming in contact with an organized gang." And parents can also refer a child they feel is beyond control (Bhuiyan 1990, 94). Similarly, the 1986 Juvenile Justice Act in India defined a neglected youth as any juvenile who:

(i) is found begging; or
(ii) is found without having any home or settled place of abode and without any ostensible means of subsistence and is destitute;
(iii) has a parent or guardian who is unfit or incapacitated to exercise control over the juvenile; or
(iv) lives in a brothel or with a prostitute or frequently goes to any place used for the purpose of prostitution or is found to associate with any prostitute or any other person who leads an immoral, drunken or depraved life;
(v) is being or is likely to be abused or exploited for immoral or illegal purposes or unconscionable gain. (Ministry of Law and Justice 1986, 4; also see Hartjen 1995)

The laws of most states in the United States have some kind of provision to deal with youths who are "termed 'dependent,' 'abused,' 'deprived,' 'neglected,' and/or 'children in need of care' or, 'services,' or 'assistance,' that is, destitute, homeless, abused, neglected, abandoned, without proper parental care or control, and/or not receiving ordinary proper care and attention" (Community Research Associates 1987, 17). Typically referred to as JINS, MINS, or PINS (juvenile, minor, or person in need of supervision), it is the guardianship foundations of juvenile justice that include these individuals under the jurisdiction of juvenile authorities in many countries.

Besides deeming persons of designated ages to be in need of special attention in criminal matters, countries around the world, to varying degrees and in different but similar ways, have sought to provide legal umbrellas for these persons concerned not only with their criminal-like behavior but also with their conduct and situations in life generally. It is the criminality of youth that has engendered much concern and attention around the globe. But, it is probably the petty misconduct and problematic situations young people encounter that consumes much of the real day-to-day work of juvenile authorities.

Rights

In 1967 the Supreme Court of the United States rendered a crucial decision in the case of *in re. Gault* (Weinstein and Mendoza 1979). In that case the Supreme Court, for the first time, recognized that juveniles before the juvenile court accused of delinquency should be accorded at least some of the rights enjoyed by adults accused of crime in criminal courts. Other major decisions were soon to follow. In the United States prior to *Gault* juveniles had virtually no due process rights when brought before juvenile authorities. Since the juvenile court was considered not to be a criminal court and since the purpose of the court was the protection and well-being of the juvenile, not his or her punishment, it was originally believed that due process protections did not apply to juvenile proceedings. Moreover, formal trial procedures would be detrimental to the *parens patriae* ideals of the court. In practice, however, those ideals were rarely met and some sixty years after its founding, juveniles accused of offenses and processed in American juvenile courts have come to receive most, but not all, the due process rights of adults. That development also marked a transformation of juvenile justice from a largely protective to a much more punitive (from a welfare to a legalistic) enterprise by the last decades of the twentieth century. Debate regarding the impact on young people and the desirability of this transformation continues to reign in American jurisprudence to this day.

To greater or lesser extent the American example has been duplicated wherever systems of juvenile justice have been established around the world. Of course, where no special laws and system of justice exist for juveniles the issue is mute. Juveniles have the same rights as adults similarly confronted with criminal processing. In some countries, regardless of the due process status of juveniles, no noticeable issue regarding their rights or the lack of them has surfaced, for whatever reasons. But, much of the world grapples to some extent with the same issues faced by American jurisdictions: To what extent should juvenile proceedings resemble adult proceedings and, as such, to what extent should children receive the same protection and suffer the same consequences for misconduct as adults? Some countries lean quite clearly toward an adult-type legalistic approach. Others still retain much of the original welfare-protective foundations of juvenile justice. Still others combine the idea of separate, nonpunitive, juvenile court processing with specific rights for juveniles that are explicitly articulated. And, many jurisdictions have sought some middle ground vacillating between welfare versus a punitive approach in how they deal with young offenders. These different approaches comprise models of juvenile justice that are largely differentiated in terms of their legal/welfare ideals.

Procedural Rights

That juveniles who are accused of misconduct do have, or should be accorded, procedural protection has today become generally acknowledged. Rule 7 of the United Nations Standard Minimum Rules of the Administration of Juvenile Justice, for instance, specifies that "basic procedural safeguards such as the presumption of innocence, the right to be notified of the charges, the right to remain silent, the right to counsel, the right to the presence of a parent or guardian, the right to confront and cross-examine witnesses and the right to appeal to a higher authority shall be guaranteed at all stages of proceedings."

Further, in rule 8 the UN stipulated that "the juvenile's right to privacy shall be respected at all stages in order to avoid harm being caused to her or him by undue publicity or by the process of labeling" (United Nations 1986, 7).

Both as specified by the United Nations and as contained in the procedure codes of many countries, regardless of the specific orientation of the juvenile justice system in place in some societies, procedural safeguards of some kind are typically accorded juveniles accused of crimes and status offenses. Rarely are juveniles granted all the due process rights accorded adults in criminal courts—unless, of course, they are transferred to such courts. Nevertheless, even in the most welfare-oriented systems the protectionist ideals of the original juvenile courts that negated both the need for or desirability of due process protections have given way to due process safeguards of some kind and extent just about everywhere.

Generally these safeguards are detailed in one or another code, as exemplified in Article III of the Brazilian Statute of the Child and Adolescent:

   I. full and formal knowledge of the imputation of an infraction by arraignment or equivalent means:
  II. equality in the procedural relationship, with the right to confront victims and witnesses and produce all the proofs necessary to his or her defense;
 III. technical defense by a lawyer;
  IV. free and full legal assistance to those in need, according to the law;
   V. the right to be personally heard by the competent authority;
  VI. the right to request the presence of his or her parents or guardian in any phase of the proceedings. (Leal 1996, 23)

In some instances juveniles may even enjoy greater rights than adults. According to Corrado and Markwart (1996, 39), the much contested Young Offenders Act of 1982 in Canada, for example, actually gave juveniles "a more complete set of rights than adults, and case law since 1984 has effectively confirmed and even expanded these rights." And, in China the Juvenile Protection Law "elucidates juvenile offenders' rights, such as the confidentiality of juvenile cases, private court proceedings, and separate pretrial detention for juvenile offenders." In addition, the law "defined more legal obligations for adults to be accountable in caring, supervising, educating, or instigating and corrupting minors" (Ren 1996, 62).

It is increasingly common to find procedural rights for juveniles accused of offenses (especially criminal offenses) specifically articulated in national statutes. Although, this is not always the case. And, it is often difficult to identify if, or to what extent, juveniles have any or all of whatever rights might be accorded adults accused of crimes in some country. Where identifiable, juveniles in delinquency proceedings typically have most, if not all, the rights accorded adults and, sometimes a few rights not articulated for adults, such as a right to a separate trial (or hearing apart from that of adults) and greater privacy protection from the press and security of records. Where they are even used, the right to a jury trial is not always enjoyed by juveniles, and the right to appeal judgments or dispositions may be denied to them. Generally, however, even though the protectionist ideals of early-twentieth-century juvenile justice still exist in even the most punitive/legalistic systems, the idea that the state cannot interfere in the lives of young people without some kind of procedural safeguards has become nearly universal in the contemporary world.

Civil Rights

Procedural rights are not the only issue when it comes to juvenile rights. Frank Zimring (1979, 315) distinguished between "rights for children" versus the "rights of children." Due process protections essentially concern the legal rights of children, as with adults, to protect them from arbitrary, capricious, and unduly harsh treatment by agencies of the state. Regardless of the issue, or alleged offense, recognition that children, as with adults, warrant such protection has become a more or less generally accepted premise throughout the world (or, at least, in those places where such rights are accepted). Countries differ as to what specific rights children and adults receive or how they are implemented in the criminal process. Few today would argue that due process of any kind is not something a juvenile facing possible punishment should not receive. What is of much more debatable concern in many parts of the world is whether, or to what extent, juveniles should or should not have full legal rights as adults.

In part, as an outgrowth of the post-World War II due process revolution for juveniles that took place in the North America and Western Europe, a large and sustained children's rights movement emerged. This movement challenged not only the numerous age-specific prohibitions and duties young people must adhere to but also the universally imposed restrictions on their self-determination.

Some argue that to deny anyone all the rights accorded anyone else simply because of age is fundamentally discriminatory, akin to racism, sexism, and the like. Children, it has been argued, should enjoy the same rights to self-determination as any adult. Others argue that children are simply too immature, too inexperienced, too powerless to be granted such total freedom. They would be easy prey for others. Rather than rights, children need the care and protection that various restrictions and laws provide them until they are old enough, mature enough, to fend for themselves (Farson 1979). The issue is nicely expressed by Empey (1979a, 381–382): "In order to quarantine them from evil, they were stripped of all power, denied a sense of personhood, and confined in an age-segregated prison. But one wonders whether . . . that, in order to liberate children, they should be empowered against their adult oppressors, that the only way to really protect them is to grant them all the constitutional protections afforded adults, and that anything that is legally permissible for grownups should be permissible for children."

Only the most ardent would argue that a five-year-old should have the right to marry, possess a firearm, drive a car, or do any of a number of things reserved for adults in just about any society. Nor would many be opposed to child-labor laws and protection from sexual and other exploitation. The issue in modern societies is where and when to draw the line. As with all other aspects of juvenile crime and justice, little agreement can be found around the world on either matter. And, while proclaiming children's rights, the United Nations offers vague guidance on the questions (see United Nations 1989). Thus, while marginally related to the problem of delinquency and administration of justice for juveniles, the questions of the rights of children reflects its central concern—whether or to what extent the young should be treated differently from adults and for how long they should be so treated (Farson 1979; Queloz 1991; Short 1979; Skolnick 1979; Woodhouse 2001).

Rights versus Responsibilities

In the contemporary world, the fundamental issue facing how we deal with young people accused of criminal or statuslike offenses is drawing a balance between their rights and their responsibilities. If juveniles are incompetent and therefore lack legal responsibility, the question of their rights is largely irrelevant—except insofar as they, as anyone, are to be protected from unwarranted interference. Whether today juveniles are increasingly seen in much of the world as responsible and therefore punishable because societies have increasingly granted them due process and, to a limited extent, social rights is an open question. Perhaps changing ideas of the nature of childhood and adolescence has itself reshaped public ideas of the extent to which young people can be held responsible and granted rights. Historical analyses of the twentieth century in years to come may cast light on this second revolution in juvenile justice.

What remains in doubt for the twenty-first century, however, is the very continuation of juvenile justice as an institution itself, at least in much of the world. Especially when it comes to older offenders, those near the border age of legal responsibility, the increased use of waiver procedures, the legalization of juvenile justice procedures, the willingness to impose punitive sanctions and widespread intolerance of misconduct may not lead to the actual abolition of the juvenile court. Worldwide trends in youth crime and punitive policies will surely transform the court in many places. At no other time has a global perspective and understanding for delinquency and juvenile justice been more compelling.

Conclusion

The terms "juvenile delinquent" and "delinquency" are legal constructs of the early twentieth century. They are products of emerging ideas about the nature of young people and a newfound faith in social engineering (Empey 1979b).

Young people and children have always engaged in acts in violation of societal norms. And while such individuals were rarely treated the same as their adult counterparts, it was not until the turn of the twentieth century that nations around the globe began to establish separate systems to explicitly deal with young offenders and/or those deemed vulnerable to such a fate. Today anyone would know what is meant when one uses these terms. Both in science and law, however, the concept of "juvenile delinquent" remains an elusive entity, one that lacks both the precision and universality one may hope for to pursue a global understanding of either delinquency or juvenile justice.

Except in the broadest terms, little unanimity can be found around the world in just who may fit the category of juvenile delinquent. This applies both to what age categories and what exact behaviors are included in the designation. Indeed, in many countries neither the term "juvenile" nor "delinquent" (nor their equivalents) are to be found in law. Thus, while everyone may know what is meant by the term, for scientific purposes a universally applicable definition of "juvenile delinquent" can be an ideal-type construct. In that regard, our working definition of "juvenile delinquent" as anyone younger than eighteen who commits a crime or status offense as defined by the laws of the individual's society should be understood as just that—a working definition that may or may not correspond to any legal designation in specific countries.

As this lack of precision may complicate, if not negate, our global inquiry of the phenomenon in question, the very ambiguity and variability of our subject matter opens up numerous possibilities for criminological inquiry and, more important, for the pursuit of justice and reasoned public policy. Young people in all societies engage in disapproved conduct. However, youth in different societies may offend in different ways and with different frequencies. Why? What explains offense behavior at all? All societies respond to young offenders in ways likely to be more caring and less harsh than is typical for older offenders. Many have formalized and institutionalized this difference. Others follow traditional and customary practices in their differential treatment of children and youth, with no age-related distinctions articulated in law. Some societies are very punitive in how young offenders are treated, locking up many in secure facilities and even reserving the death penalty in some cases. Others appear extremely benevolent and forgiving of youthful misconduct, even serious offense behavior. Why is the reaction different among different countries? With what consequences?

Lack of precision in any global definition of the term "delinquent" may make findings answers to questions such as these less than scientifically satisfactory. It is this very ambiguity that makes such inquiry both meaningful and exciting. As we explore these matters in the pages that follow, we may find that understanding how the nations of the world define and treat their young casts light on the human situation and ourselves.

2

Explaining Delinquent Acts

Perhaps the most frequently asked question in criminology, and by the public at large, is "Why do they do it?" The amount of criminological research and speculation regarding the causes of crime and delinquent behavior would probably fill a small library and would take the life work of any one person to read and digest. Much of this inquiry is highly repetitive, testing or disputing tests of one or more aspect of a handful of criminological theories. The bulk of this research has been conducted on samples of American youths, with a handful of studies carried out in other countries, primarily Canada, the United Kingdom, and some Western European countries. Aside from the explanatory validity of any of these theories, a major question for a global understanding of youth crime and delinquency is the extent to which any of these ideas provides a universal and valid explanation of this behavior. While the consistency of the findings produced from this research is suggestive, we actually do not know the extent to which theories of delinquent behavior can explain the behavior of young people across the globe.

In this chapter, we explore some of these ideas and the research testing them. In so doing, we get a glimpse of the delinquent conduct young people commit and what universally may account for such behavior. It is not my purpose here to provide an exhaustive recitation of explanatory theory, nor do I seek to evaluate the validity of various arguments. An extensive literature already exists in this regard (see, e.g., Cote 2002; Crutchfield et al. 2000; Ellis and Walsh 2000). Instead, I seek to explore several major ideas and their applicability to understanding the etiology of delinquent behavior among youths everywhere.

Major Theories

Since the beginnings of criminological inquiry, numerous ideas, both specific and general, have been put forward to account for why juveniles commit crimes.

Although almost all of the research devoted to testing any of these ideas focuses on juveniles, few of these arguments specifically target offense behavior on the part of juveniles. Most are actually quite vague as to just what populations or offense behaviors are, or are not, included in the scope of the explanation.

Generally, criminologists would agree that there are three major theoretical perspectives offering viable explanations of delinquent conduct: social learning theories, control theories, and life-course or developmental theories. Efforts to integrate or incorporate these competing ideas, or aspects of them, into broader explanatory forms have met with mixed success and considerable debate (see Bernard and Snipes 1996; Elliott et al. 1979; Messner et al. 1989), although Agnew's (2005) recent general theory of crime may have succeeded where past efforts have failed.

Two major theoretical traditions have dominated criminological thinking as to why individuals offend at all—social learning theories and control theories. These traditions represent polar extremes as far as their typically implicit assumptions about human nature, the forces responsible for human behavior, and the focus of causal explanation are concerned. Often incorporating aspects of one or both of these traditions within the explanatory framework, life-course theories depart from learning and control theories insofar as they are oriented to a somewhat different explanatory question.

Why do some individuals engage in offense behavior over a life course while others descent from offending after a brief period of time? The common theme of all such arguments is the central role social factors such as interpersonal relationships, life events, social or economic situations, and the like play in the explanatory framework. In some arguments, allusions to psychological or psychobiological factors may be embedded in the theory. But contemporary criminological explanations of criminal/delinquent behavior are overwhelmingly sociological in tone.

The idea that delinquent and criminal behavior, or propensities to engage in such conduct, is socially acquired through a process of learning, as opposed, for example, to being merely a function of some biological or psychological defect, was first articulated by Sutherland (Sutherland and Cressey 1955) in his theory of differential association. Later restatements of this theory, most notably Burgess and Aker's (1965) differential association-reinforcement argument, have elaborated on specific aspects of Sutherland's idea. However, generally, they all contend that youths become delinquent through some kind of interpersonal relationships with others.

While learning, and virtually all other theories, ask what causes youths to offend, assuming they would not were these causal conditions absent, control theories, on the other hand, take a different approach. These theories start from the premise that human beings normally would offend unless they are somehow prevented (or controlled) from doing so. Most noted of these arguments at present are Hirschi's (1969) social control argument and Gottfredson and Hirschi's (1990) self-control theory, both of which seek to answer the question "Why not?"—"Why *don't* youths offend?" In answer to that question, these theories imply that offending youths lack something that allows their natural proclivities to offend to be acted upon.

Both learning and control perspectives are primarily concerned with the act. That is, they address why youths do or do not commit a delinquent act. The question of why some youths commit such behavior only once or infrequently, while others do so extensively for extended periods of time is largely unaddressed. That problem is the central focus of life-course theories. Five such theories have been identified by Farrington (2003): a social development model proposed by Catalano and Hawkins (1996), an age-graded informal social control argument offered by Sampson and Laub (1996), the life-course-persistent versus adolescence-limited theory by Moffitt (1993), LeBlanc's (1997a) multilayered control theory, and the interactional argument of Thornberry and Krohn (2001). In addition, Farrington (2003) offers his own integrated cognitive antisocial potential theory. While differing in specifics, according to Farrington, all these arguments are primarily concerned with accounting for within-individual changes in offending throughout life. To some extent, they all, as with learning and control theories, may help us understand why offense behavior occurs at all and why some people become offenders and others do not.

The results of research testing aspects of specific expression of these various arguments have been mixed. Generally, however, support for all three approaches has been found so that it is likely that, ultimately, a full understanding of why youths offend and continue to do so or not will involve some more general articulation of all these ideas. All but three of these theories have been formulated by American criminologists. One is authored by criminologists from New Zealand (Moffitt), a second from Canada (LeBlanc), and the third (Farrington) from the United Kingdom. All clearly echo American criminological thought.

Besides the empirical validity of any explanation, the scientific significance of any theory also depends on its universality—that is, the extent to which the theory explains what it seeks to explain everywhere under all conditions. A theory that explains the delinquent behavior of American boys and girls, for example, but cannot account for the behavior of youths in other social-cultural settings may be valid, but it is not a theory of delinquent behavior as such. The authors of the dominant criminological theories may have had some universal idea of offenders and/or offense behavior in mind while formulating the various arguments. Moreover, given the existing research, each of them appears to have some claim to explanatory validity. The extent to which any of these ideas is a general or universal explanation of offense behavior among young people everywhere, however, remains an empirically unexplored question. A mountain of research exists testing the validity of these various claims. However, the bulk of that research is on samples of American youths, or youths in similar socio-cultural environments (e.g., Canada, Western European societies). Hardly any such inquiry has been conducted on youths in diverse societies. What little data is at hand is promising, but it is simply still too early to say whether or to what extent any of the existing criminological explanations of "Why they do it" apply to youths universally.

Peers and Delinquency

It is practically certain that the bulk of the misconduct committed by youths everywhere in the world is in some way related to their involvement with peers. The evidence is clear that most of the offense behavior individuals up to their early twenties commit occurs with others. Some young people may engage in offense behavior in association with, under the direction of, or as a consequence of exploitation by adults. In addition, a few aberrant youths in any society may engage in isolated, or "lone wolf," acts of often bizarre or very serious misconduct. As would be predicted from learning theories, the overwhelming majority of the delinquency and crime youths find themselves involved with is committed in association with other youths—which certainly has something to do with "why they do it."

Learning theories argue that it is through associations that individuals come to acquire the sentiments, skills, and motivations to commit delinquent acts. Therefore, we could assume that in lacking these associations the vast majority of youths would not become involved in delinquent acts. Considerable research seems to support this conclusion. Little of this research actually directly tests specific propositions of any of the major learning theories. Thus, it is still not known if or to what extent differential association, or differential association-reinforcement, or other learning arguments offer definitive explanations of delinquent and criminal conduct. Further, it is not clear if delinquent orientations follow involvement with delinquent peers or if such orientations lead one to become associated with similarly oriented persons. However, criminologists generally would not contest the idea that peer relationships and delinquent involvement or noninvolvement go together.

This argument makes perfect sense in a society and historic time such as twentieth-century America, where such arguments were proposed. Young people in post–World War II America have been heavily peer oriented and peer involved. The separation of generations into age-graded groupings almost necessitated that adolescents turned to other youths for support and influence. But what about societies where family, clan, or tribe are one's center of existence, where adults, rather than other teenagers, are the authority, role models, sources of influence, support, and guidance? Do juveniles in these societies also acquire pro-criminal sentiments, skills, and motivations from others in the way American and Western European youths appear to do? If it is not the influence of peers that is behind the delinquency of youths in such societies, what is?

Little research on the matter exists in the literature, but a few examples from inquiries conducted around the world are illuminating. In one study comparing middle-class Danish and American youths, Arnett and Jensen (1994) found differences in the offense patterns and socialization experiences of the two groups. A study in Stockholm (Sarnecki 2001) found that while the vast majority of the most delinquent youths in Stockholm were drawn together in a central network, organized youth gangs of the type found in North America were absent. A study of Dutch youths corroborated some of the central propositions of differential association theory (Bruinsma 1992). Specifically, it was found that the greater youths' contact with friends, the stronger the impact of their friends' deviance on their pro-offending sentiments and offense-related skills. A study of homeless adolescents in Toronto (McCarthy 1996) found that tutelage in delinquency by other adolescents was an important ingredient in the self-reported offending of these youths. Baron and Hartnagel (1997) made a similar observation in their report that the criminal behavior of peers was one of the main contributing factors for offending among street youths in Canada. A study in Cologne, Germany, concludes that peers and time spent with peers had the major effect on delinquency (Oberwittler et al. 2001). And Fenwick (1983) concluded that, due to the breakdown of informal social controls and relationships in traditional Japanese society, increased attachment to peers was probably responsible for the increased delinquency observed in that country. Research also reports that juvenile offenders in Japan had more friends outside of school who were prone to delinquency (Kobayashi et al. 1988). That associates other than delinquent peers can contribute to a youth's offending behavior was reported from a study of Iranian juveniles in Tehran (Nakhshab 1979). Research by Hartjen and Priyadarsini (2003) on a sample of youths in rural France found that scales measuring aspects of differential association theory alone explained the bulk of the variance in all measures of delinquent behavior among both boys and girls. In addition, in a study comparing the delinquency of Indian and American youths, Hartjen and Kethineni (1996, 126) concluded that "involvement with peers who are, or are not, engaged in delinquent activity is closely associated with an individual's similar involvement/non-involvement, regardless of cultural setting."

The information available does indeed suggest that the actions, beliefs, and orientations of peers and others similarly influence youths everywhere with whom they associate. As such, those who come to engage in delinquency probably do so as a consequence of these associations. This, in turn, may help explain why offense rates vary among the populations of youths in different societies, given that both the extent and kinds of associations young people have with others vary across the globe. Quite simply, as societies differ in the extent to which their young, and especially those in their adolescent years, are cast together and largely excluded from direct and meaningful participation in the world of adults, we can expect variations in the rates of offenders and offending behavior the youth of these societies commit.

Lack of Control

The two dominant control theories in contemporary criminology, social control theory (Hirschi 1969) and general theory of crime (self-control theory) (Gottfredson and Hirschi 1990) differ substantially. However, both assert that those people who come to engage in delinquent or criminal behavior do so because they lack a strong bond to conventional society (social control) or the restraining force of self-control (general theory). In either case, the central question for criminology is not "Why do they do it?" but "Why don't people engage in crime?" The assumption behind this question is that people would engage in crime were they not adequately controlled. Neither theory, however, attempts to explain why some people lack social or self-control, freeing them to deviate.

Both theories have generated considerable attention and controversy in Western criminology, along with a large number of studies attempting to test various aspects of each theory. Almost all of this research has involved samples of American youths, although the results have been published from a handful of investigations in other societies. While generally supportive of one or the other argument, findings from these inquiries are somewhat mixed in contrast to findings from research on learning theory. Nevertheless, the idea that a lack of social and/or self-control lies behind involvement in offense behavior has gained many adherents in criminology generally.

In societies such as that found in contemporary America, the idea that delinquent youths are somehow lacking in control—and it is therefore this lack of control that must be responsible for their misconduct—makes some sense. In societies where traditional social networks, such as the family, seem weak and ineffectual, where individualism and nonconformity are valued, where juveniles are relegated to a marginal status, and where opportunities to escape from the constraints of parents or other authority abound, the idea that delinquent people are uncontrolled people seems like a reasonable explanation of their behavior. In addition, such arguments have implications for public policy as far as reducing offense rates that often lead to the conclusion that such behavior can be prevented or reduced by the reassertion of usually formal forms of control—policies that seem to have gained appeal, as is evidenced by the increased use of official authority in dealing with offenders in American and other Western societies in the last decades of the twentieth century.

But, is lack of control a culturally relative explanation of crime and delinquency? Can these arguments help explain the delinquency of youths in more structured societies, societies where individuals are more embedded and constrained by broad social-economic networks? As with learning theory, if control theories provide explanations of offense behavior universally, we should find support for such arguments wherever they are tested. Even though very limited, the research that has been conducted on these ideas across the globe seems to suggest that they might.

A series of studies by LeBlanc (1993, 1997b) in Canada found support for aspects of both social and self-control arguments. More recently, LaGrange and Silverman (1999) found support for self-control theory on a sample of secondary school children in Canada. Research in the Netherlands (Junger-Tas 1992; Junger and Marshall 1997) similarly found that aspects of the social bond identified in social control theory explained increases in offense behavior, and cross-ethnic differences, in such conduct among Dutch youth. In Japan researchers have found that aspects of Hirschi's social bond argument help account for delinquent conduct among large samples of youth (Hoshino 1989; Nishimura et al. 1982). In Taiwan, Sheu (1988) argues that control theory is the most appropriate explanation of both the origins and increases in delinquency in that country. Torstensson (1990) reports that involvement in delinquency among Swedish youth varies with the strength of the social bond. A similar conclusion was reached in a study of kibbutz children in Israel (Cohen and Zeira 1999).

As with research on American samples, some studies in other countries cast some doubt on the explanatory or predictive ability of specific aspects of control theory. However, as limited as the research may be, it appears that youths who lack social and/or self-controls are more likely to commit delinquent acts compared to those more controlled. As societies or groups differ in the extent to which their young are bonded to the society and/or inculcate self-control, one would expect that rates of delinquency would vary among societies.

International research can tell us whether, or to what extent, control of any kind is related to individual involvement in misconduct. Criminology, however, has yet to begin investigating how societies or groups might differ in the nature and extent of their social or self-controls. Research by Vazsonyi (1996, 2001) is suggestive of what might criminologists might do in this regard. In one study, he compared the delinquency of youths in Switzerland with the behavior of youths in the United States and concluded that differences in the observed rates of offense behavior found in these two societies could be accounted for by family socialization differences relating to self-control factors. A second, broader inquiry comparing four countries revealed that different elements of self-control theory explained different amounts of the variance in offense behavior. In short, accounting for variations in self-control among different population groups may help explain why they exhibit different rates of delinquent behavior.

The verdict is still out as to the ultimate answer to the question of "Why do they do it?" Undoubtedly both learning and control perspectives give us part of the answer, even though they proceed from totally opposite conceptions of the nature of human beings and the opposed explanatory question that they feel need to be answered. Existing theories reflecting either tradition are, if not invalid, overly simplistic and somewhat simpleminded explanations of human behavior, criminal or otherwise. Nor do they tell us why some youths are chronic, as opposed to being one-time, offenders.

One-Time versus Chronic Offenders

The issue of explaining careers in delinquency (persistence or dissonance from offending) has been a major, if until recently a secondary, concern for criminological theory. Given the concern with nipping delinquency in the bud, preventing a life of crime, and similar articulations voiced by the public and authorities, this is a bit surprising. Everyone recognizes that there is a considerable difference between the teenager who, on a dare with a group of friends, swipes something from a store and the youth who systematically and repeatedly engages in such conduct with a band of others. Some juveniles seem to be constantly in and out of trouble, while for most such conduct is a rare or a singular event. Some children start regular involvement in offense behavior quite young. Others become involved, frequently or occasionally, in late adolescence. The same forces or circumstances might explain why youths may or may not offend at all, but what explains differences in the frequencies or patterns of such behavior over a life course?

To address just that issue, criminologists have formulated several life-course theories of crime. Research testing aspects of several of these theories has begun to accumulate, even if the volume of this research is comparatively sparse. Once again, beyond the borders of North America little empirical work has been done on any of these arguments. In part, this lack of research is a consequence of the very nature of these theories. Research to test any life-course theory would normally require longitudinal studies involving the testing, following up, and retesting of an extensive sample over a substantial period of time. Criminological research of any kind is hard to come by in societies that have few resources or interest in conducting it. It is very unlikely, therefore, that funding to carry out extensive longitudinal research to test a criminological theory would be found in most societies, no matter how promising the theory to be tested may be.

So far, Moffitt's (1993) argument that there are two types of juvenile offenders is the only such theory that has been empirically tested in more than one society. In addition to the extensive research conducted by Moffitt and her colleagues derived from the large-scale survey of youth in Dunedin, New Zealand (Bartusch et al. 1997; Wright et al. 2001), several studies on samples of American youth have been carried out (Cernkovich and Giordano 2001; Piquero et al. 2005). And, one study based on a survey of Dutch youth testing an aspect of this theory have been reported (Donker et al. 2003). Combining elements of both psychology and sociology, Moffitt's theory essentially proposes that juvenile offenders are of two basic types—what she calls "life-course-persistent" and "adolescence-limited" offenders. Life-course-persistent offenders are proposed to suffer from various neuropsychological defects that predispose them to engage in long-term, chronic offense behavior that is either impeded or facilitated by a variety of contingencies of life that are outlined in the theory. Adolescence-limited offenders, on the other hand, resemble the "made a mistake," "got in with the wrong crowd," "youthful experimentation," "bad situation" offender that most people envision as the typical "good kid" doing something "bad" or "stupid" but otherwise being "OK." The offense behavior of such individuals is likely to be short term but can also be extended and increased or nipped in the bud by various life-course events that the theory describes. Research on the Dunedin sample, and the single Dutch study, basically support various aspects of Moffitt's arguments. Research on American youths has also been supportive, although on occasion also calling for modification of some aspects of the theory (see, e.g., Piquero and Brezina 2001).

LeBlanc's study of Canadian youth, on whom he tested his version of life-course theory, supported the argument (1997b, 1997c). Limited research on Catalano and Hawkins's theory also suggests that it too may have explanatory validity (Catalano and Kosterman 1996). The two arguments by American criminologists Sampson and Laub, and Thornberry and Krohn, have both been subjected to much scrutiny using samples of American respondents. While specific questions may be raised regarding specific arguments of each, both have also found empirical support (e.g., Sampson and Laub 2003; Thornberry 1996). The theory proposed by Farrington (2003) has not, as of this writing, received explicit empirical scrutiny.

Given the intrinsic similarities of these apparently competing ideas, it is not surprising that all, in spite of specific differences, have been supported by the research. They each probably have explanatory validity in accounting for the known facts of offense patterns of individuals over the course of their lives—from early adolescence to later adulthood. Undoubtedly, some combined modified version of these theories will ultimately provide an explanatory model of why people come to or cease to offend over time.

However, again, it remains highly speculative as to whether any of these theories, or some variation of them, will provide a valid understanding of offense patterns in diverse social/cultural settings. Indeed, it remains to be seen to what extent the offense patterns such theories seek to explain are in fact universal. We might very well speculate that they are universal and that the same kind of life-course forces that stimulate or impede the onset and continuation of delinquency in societies like Canada, New Zealand, the United States, and England exist and operate in the same way in Indonesia, North Korea, South Africa, and Saudi Arabia. The only way to know if this is true or not, however, is to go and see.

A sizable body of longitudinal research from diverse European countries adds weight to the plausibility of life-course theories as viable explanations of the onset and persistence/cessation of delinquent behavior. None of this research was designed to test any specific theory. But, the findings from these inquiries often are consistent with what one or another of the theories would predict (see Thornberry et al. 2003; Weitekamp and Kerner 1992). For example, an extensive longitudinal study in Sweden produced findings consistent with much of what one would predict from Moffitt's theory, in that a subgroup of young offenders exhibiting attention difficulties tended to become violent offenders (Eklund and af Kinteberg 2003). Research in Germany found that early onset disruptive behavior disorders predicted continued delinquency and crime in adulthood (Lay et al. 2001). One study in Puerto Rico also found onset ages and offense rate patterns consistent with those predicted from life-course theories generally (Nevares et al. 1990). Finally, Wong (2001) argues that, consistent with findings in the United States and United Kingdom, an interactional theory model best explains the onset, escalation, and withdrawal from delinquency among youths in Hong Kong and China.

Other Ideas

The theories that were briefly addressed earlier reflect the dominant ideas in contemporary criminology. They by no means, however, exhaust scientific arguments proposed to explain delinquency—rates, acts, or offenders. A host of factors have been investigated as plausible correlates of delinquency, although explicit theories explaining why and how these various factors are responsible for delinquency are hard to come by. In addition, while this research is voluminous, little cross-national inquiry assessing the generalizability of ideas relating to these factors is practically nonexistent.

Psychological Dimensions

For example, there exists an extensive literature on research carried out by scholars in diverse societies on various psychological dimensions thought to be responsible for delinquency (Jones and Heaven 1998; Moffitt et al. 1994; Ward and Tittle 1994). Research in Russia reports that youths with different temperaments are at a greater or lesser risk of disruptive behavior that could lead to alcohol and drug abuse in adolescence (Ruchkin et al. 2002). The role of various personality traits in problems of social adjustment linked to delinquency was investigated in Spain (Osuna et al. 1992). In Sweden, Dalteg and Levander (1998) studied the possible relationship between delinquency and attention deficit hyperactivity disorder among a sample of incarcerated youths. An extensive study in Finland examined the association between delinquent behavior and various psychosomatic symptoms (Kivivuori 2000). And, a study in Australia confirms the importance of the relationship between self-concept and delinquency (Levy 1997).

This body of research suggests that delinquents everywhere are more likely than others to suffer from various personality, emotional, or neuropsychological problems. Ideas such as these have long been a part of criminological thinking. At present, however, no biological, psychological, or bio-psychological theory on the causes of offense behavior has gained criminological prominence. Additionally, cross-national tests of any of these ideas are practically nonexistent. More sophisticated inquiry along these lines may ultimately find that there is a universal biological or bio-psychological dimension related to offense behavior, at least among some categories of offenders (e.g., life-course persistent). However, we have little reason to assume that some magic line exits among young people across the globe separating them in to delinquents and non-delinquents and that offending youth in one society are as different from nonoffending youth in any other society as they are from nonoffenders in their own society.

Family Factors

A host of other factors that are assumed to be linked in some way to delinquent conduct have also been investigated in diverse settings. Prominent among these are investigations of family-related factors. For example, a study in Sweden investigating a number of these variables and their effects on delinquency concluded that, rather than direct, the effects of such factors as family structure, mother's attitudes toward child rearing, and the like on delinquency were probably greater due to the interaction among such factors than the impact of any such factor individually (Smith 1991). Investigations of delinquency and right-wing extremism among German youths suggest that, in part, family nurturing and monitoring reduced such behavior (Boehnke and Bergs 2002; Boehnke et al. 1998). A study in Spain found that youths in Spanish training schools reported a high incidence of interfamilial pathology (Osuna et al. 1992a). Zhang and Messner (1995) found that family deviance was positively related to juvenile delinquency in China. In the Philippines, Maxwell (2001) found that a familial dynamic was driving both minor and serious forms of antisocial behavior among children and adolescents. In contrast to findings reported from much of the research in North America and Western Europe, a study in Saudi Arabia found no relationship between family structure and delinquency (Airomaih 1993), while a Swiss survey found few differences in the delinquency of youths from broken and nonbroken homes (Aebi 1997). In a test of power-control theory among Russian youths, Finckenauer et al. (1998) concluded that the family and gender variables in that theory had virtually no explanatory power, although, as learning theory would predict, the influence of peers had a strong effect on delinquency.

Schools

Similar kinds of research have been done in diverse countries on schooling and delinquency. For example, in an early study of the relationship between school competitiveness and delinquency among Australian youths, Braithwaite and Braithwaite (1976) found no support for the idea that less competitive school environments reduce strains that create delinquency. However, Kouvonen (2001) found that part-time work among school children was associated with more frequent reports of problem behavior among Finnish youth.

Other Theories

Other, although very limited, research has sought to test several other theories of crime that may have explanatory power as far as delinquency is concerned. For instance, a multinational study testing aspects of the routine activities theory of Cohen and Felson (Cohen and Felson 1978; Felson and Cohen 1980) concluded that the theory applies across national borders. And two studies testing Agnew's general strain theory, one in China (Bao et al. 2004) and another in Canada (Baron 2004), report findings consistent with the theory.

At best, the research on theories or ideas purporting to explain the etiology of delinquent behavior forms a patchwork of largely unrelated inquiries of varying sophistication and rigor. Extensive information has been produced from these inquiries. But, a systematic body of findings has yet to be assembled from this research, so it is premature to make any definitive statements about what the data show.

Conclusion

Any theory of delinquent behavior that helps us understand delinquency's origins and causes is likely to have universal applicability—unless, of course, the theory is specifically restricted to some population group. That conclusion, however, is not foretold by tests of a theory's validity in one country or even among samples of youths in a handful of countries. Broad criminological research employing diverse samples of youths across the globe is necessary before one can say with confidence that theory X is, in fact, a general theory of delinquent behavior, a theory that is equally valid among all groups in all social/cultural/economic settings. To date, no such research exists for any etiological theory in criminology. At best, one can only assume that any of the theories so far produced by the discipline may be universal. Scientific appraisal must remain a matter of faith.

The research available on which to base that faith, however, does support a potential conclusion that the causes of delinquency are universal. That is to say, the immediate conditions that would lead or propel youths into offense behavior, or facilitate or impede its continuation, may vary, differing from one society or historical epic to another. Youth in a poor society, for instance, may steal out of economic necessity, while similarly aged youth in a more affluent society may commit the same activity out of a dare, to obtain status among peers, or simply for excitement. Nevertheless, the general kinds of situations (e.g., association with delinquent peers, poor parenting, societal rejection, etc.) that specific theories may identify as the root causes of or conditions behind such behavior may very well apply everywhere. If, for example, learning theory has universal explanatory merit as at least part of an explanation of delinquent behavior, one would expect that youths who become involved in delinquency in any society would exhibit associations with peers that are delinquency promoting. The exact composition of those peer associations, however, need not be the same. In some societies, "kids on the block" may constitute the relevant peers, whereas in others it could be extended family members, classmates at school, or some other culturally relevant group. Similarly, children everywhere who lack proper parental or adult supervision are probably more likely than others to become involved in delinquent activities, regardless of the social/cultural environment in which they live. However, structural and/or cultural variations in the relative or interactive effects of causal conditions that may account for delinquent behavior universally are to be expected, as research testing some of these ideas has already revealed. For example, in a sample of Swedish youths, Svensson (2003) found that the interaction effect between parental monitoring and peer deviance varied by gender. Research comparing Korean and American black and nonblack youths found that the effects of social bonds on delinquency were stronger for Koreans than for either group of American respondents (Lee 1993).

As criminology expands its database by testing causal arguments in diverse societies across the globe, such research may help us also better understand the similarities and differences in the patterns of delinquency exhibited by youths in various societies. If associating with delinquency-promoting peers, for instance, helps explain the etiology of delinquent behavior among boys and girls in diverse countries, why rates of that behavior vary among these youths may reflect differences in the extent to which youths in these societies are immersed in peer networks or the kinds of peer-group associations that are available to them. Differences in the rate of delinquency would be a function of differences in social/cultural structures producing differences in peer relations among youths around the globe, not differences in what is responsible for the etiology of that behavior in the first place.

3

The Global Extent and Distribution of Delinquency

How much delinquency exists in the world? This and a host of similar questions refer to the epidemiology (as opposed to the etiology) of delinquent behavior—the frequency, changes in, and relative distribution of delinquent behavior across and within populations.

Delinquent behavior is probably universal. What may vary, however, is how many youths in various societies commit such behavior, how often they do it, and what kinds of misconduct they engage in. Assessing these facts is a task that criminologists and the world's societies have yet to seriously grapple with. Explaining differences and similarities in the behavior of juveniles across the world's societies remains a little-pursued challenge. Answers to both problems, however, are fundamental to understanding such conduct and finding meaningful ways of dealing with it.

Measuring Rates

Criminologists typically rely on two measures of crime/delinquent behavior to assess the extent and distribution of its occurrence: prevalence and incidence. Ideally, measures of prevalence reflect the proportion of some population (country, gender group) engaged in delinquent behavior at all, or of some kind, at some point in time, or over some time period. Measures of incidence count the relative number of offenses, or frequency of such conduct, exhibited by a population at some point in time or over some time period.

The two may be related, as some assert, although this is yet to be demonstrated on a global basis. However, they are in fact measures of quite different things. Prevalence is a measure of the number (proportion) of delinquent persons in a population. Incidence is a measure of the number (frequency) of delinquent acts committed by members of that population. Two countries with equally high incidence rates could still be quite different. In one, for example, a large proportion (high prevalence) of its young population could be engaged in infrequent offense behavior, while in the other a small group of highly chronic delinquents could be engaged in such conduct with considerable frequency. The delinquency problem faced by the two countries is, thus, quite different, possibly requiring quite different strategies to deal with it. Lacking other information, a comparison of incidence rates for the two countries could be very misleading, as would a simple comparison of prevalence rates. Criminologists and shapers of public policy often overlook this simple realization, but it is important to keep in mind when making any assessments of the global extent and distribution of delinquency.

There is no way to determine how many people commit delinquent acts, and how many times. We simply cannot observe and record every illegal act committed by every person on every occasion. Thus, we will never know the true rate of delinquency, or how many juveniles are truly delinquents. At best, we can construct ways to estimate these rates. But, these measures have an unknowable relationship to the thing we are trying to measure. The various tests of validity and reliability constructed by criminologists notwithstanding, the actual rate of delinquency or the true number of offenders in any population can only be estimated.

Three ways of estimating delinquency (offense/offender) rates are typically relied upon in criminological research to support policy initiatives by agencies of government: official counts (statistics) of arrests, convictions, and incarcerations; self-reported delinquency surveys; and victimization surveys. Criminologists have subjected each to considerable debate and assessments of their validity, accuracy, reliability, and interpretation. Unsatisfactory as these measures are, they are routinely used with the understanding that they are the only and therefore best we have (Hindelang et al. 1981; Tracy 1996). With considerable effort we might make reasonable judgments of just how valid and reliable our proxy measures of delinquency might be when trying to measure the epidemiology of delinquency within a particular society. Nevertheless, assessing the extent and distribution of delinquency on a global scale presents a different kind of problem altogether.

Problems with Measures

Official Data

Assessments of a country's, or to a limited extent the world's, delinquency problem are based on official statistics provided by government agencies—most typically counts of arrests, prosecutions, convictions, or sentences. Criminologists have long been aware of the limitations of such information as measures of the amount and distribution of delinquent behavior. At best, these counts can only be used as measures of relative prevalence rather than incidence, since they normally count the number of persons being arrested or otherwise subjected to official action and not the number of offenses for which arrests and the like were made. An unknown number of offenses/offenders never come to the attention of authorities, and even many of those that do are filtered out before any formal action is taken. Thus, official statistics grossly underestimate the true rate of both the number of offense behaviors and persons engaged in them. In that regard, one might argue that official statistics are better understood as measures of criminal justice activity than of criminal behavior, for which they are commonly used (Hartjen 1978). The problem for determining global rates is that countries differ greatly in the composition and operation of their criminal justice agencies and practices. Thus, to what extent a high official rate in one country, compared to a low rate in some other, reflects real differences in the delinquency of their youth or differences in criminal justice activity is nearly impossible to determine at this point. However, such data do have some advantages over alternative measures. In many cases, besides being the only such data available, where reported, they provide the only consistent way to calculate delinquency trends over time. Secondly, they are usually the only countrywide and, in a limited way, worldwide count of delinquency to be found.

While official statistics may be useful in computing delinquency rates in individual countries, basing any firm conclusions about the global extent and distribution of delinquency on these data is problematic. This is so because many countries simply do not collect or report such information and, even where information is provided to an agency such as the United Nations, the data for many countries is highly suspect, either with regard to its truthfulness or accuracy. More basic, comparing rates across political borders or compiling information to form a global picture is nearly impossible since the governments that provide these statistics do not do so in a common, consistent manner using the same offense categories at the same level of official processing. Nor do they report information in the same format. Thus, even trying to determine what proportion of country A's and B's juveniles are subjected to arrest can be a matter of guesswork based on the information at hand. Finally, countries probably vary greatly in how they respond officially to youthful misconduct or record the actions of officials in public records. Thus, the processing filter that distorts all official crime data is an unknown quantity in using this kind of information in international comparative research (United Nations 1992). Compare, for example, the figures in table 3.1 showing the percentages of minors represented among the number of known offenders for different countries. From these data it is reasonable to assume that less than 2 percent of all offenders in the countries of Georgia and Ireland are minors, whereas in France and Switzerland more then 20 percent of all offenders are of similar age.

Victimization Surveys

A second, semi-official measure of delinquency rates is found in a handful of victimization surveys (e.g., Sampson et al. 1981; Van Kesteren 2000). These inquiries ask persons if they or members of their households were victims of

TABLE 3.1

Percentage of Minors among Offenders, by Country, in 1999

Country	Criminal offenses (total)	Traffic offenses	Intentional homicide (total)	Intentional homicide (completed)	Assault	Rape	Robbery	Theft (total)	Auto theft	Burglary (total)	Domestic burglary	Drug offense	Drug trafficking
Albania	13.5		8.6	7.8	16.8	2.4	19.7	27.0	5.1	33.1	37.7	4.2	
Armenia	6.0				6.4			16.3	16.2			0.2	
Austria	16.0	6.2	4.9		17.0	13.8	37.5	30.4	40.6	33.3	29.6	29.0	15.0
Belgium													
Bulgaria	12.0	2.3	4.2	4.0	2.4	13.3	16.7	9.6	73.0	12.3		14.4	
Croatia	9.5	2.3	2.9	1.8	8.2	7.9	13.2	20.6	12.2	26.7	28.8	14.8	1.2
Cyprus													
Czech Republic	13.7		1.9		9.4	11.9	27.0	16.4	23.2	35.0	31.7		
Denmark													
Estonia	16.3	1.4	7.6	8.3	6.6	19.4	23.1	23.1		28.6		8.2	9.3
Finland	11.7	5.4	5.1	4.3	14.3	4.2	32.2	19.6	27.0	19.7	16.6	9.1	
France	21.3		7.5	6.6	15.5	20.5	39.9	33.3	40.5	33.7	33.0	19.9	12.8
Georgia	1.2	1.8	0.9	1.2	1.8	8.9	3.5	1.3	6.3			0.8	0.2

(Continued)

TABLE 3.1
(Continued)

Country	Criminal offenses (total)	Traffic offenses	Intentional homicide (total)	Intentional homicide (completed)	Assault	Rape	Robbery	Theft (total)	Auto theft	Burglary (total)	Domestic burglary	Drug offense	Drug trafficking
Germany	19.3		7.6		20.1	11.1	40.1	32.8	42.4	34.0	32.7	17.3	6.7
Greece	16.7	32.1	9.6		4.6	18.2	28.5	29.2	33.8	26.9		24.1	
Hungary	8.4	1.5	4.4	5.8	7.4	13.1	28.5	14.6	15.1	18.0	16.6	17.7	22.8
Ireland	1.5	6.5	0.0	0.0	0.5	0.0	1.1	1.9		1.9		4.4	
Italy	2.8	0.7	2.7	2.7	2.6	6.0	6.7	8.9	6.4	4.9	18.6	5.2	
Latvia	6.5	0.6	5.8	0.0	3.1	7.0	7.8	6.8	8.4			1.3	
Lithuania	13.3		7.0	7.7	5.1	17.3	36.6	21.1	26.4		25.9	3.6	
Luxembourg													
Malta	5.5												
Moldova	13.8	1.4	5.6		6.0	12.7		21.5		23.2		10.8	
Netherlands	17.9	2.2			18.0	16.5	32.5	23.1		26.5		3.6	
Norway	14.8	6.6	3.7	6.3	14.7	24.6	47.7	29.9	32.8	22.0	18.3	11.2	8.3
Poland	14.5	1.9	7.1		20.9	10.0	26.7	28.6	15.0	33.6		19.1	12.7
Portugal													

Romania	6.3	2.9		12.7	7.8	19.9	16.2				6.8	
Russia	10.7	5.5		6.1	14.3	19.5					5.7	
Slovakia	19.5	4.4										
Slovenia	16.6	5.4	12.0	9.9	5.5	38.7	29.6	14.6	31.6	36.2	15.3	12.8
Spain	12.6	4.5				22.8	27.3	16.8				5.8
Sweden	11.8	2.6	2.4	14.5	4.9	21.8	18.4	21.3	14.9	15.6	4.1	3.8
Switzerland	28.8	6.0		16.4	8.0	38.4	26.6	25.7			11.8	6.0
Turkey												
Ukraine												
U.K.:	11.2	2.0	7.9	18.2	9.0	42.3	31.2	45.3	34.4	29.9	12.6	5.3
England/ Wales		7.3										
UK: Northern Ireland												
UK: Scotland												

Source: Adapted from Council of European Committee on Crime Prevention 2003, 66–67.

crime during some specified period of time. Theoretically, data from these surveys would cast some light on the extent to which juveniles are victimized, in what ways, and which of these victimizations involved juvenile perpetrators. Ideally, this information would also provide some measure of both prevalence and incidence, counting the number of victims/victimizations and offenders/offenses. In individual countries, such as the United States and Canada, criminologists have found victimization surveys to be a useful addition to the limited repertoire of measures. They are not, of course, without limitations that are well known to criminologists as ways of assessing rates of juvenile offenses/offenders.

As a way to measure global delinquency rates, however, victimization data is sorely lacking. For one, very few such surveys have ever been conducted, much less are routinely so, in the vast majority of the world's countries. The single global survey sponsored by the United Nations is extremely limited generally and of practically no value as far as delinquency is concerned because of the broad age categories used to report findings, categories that range from mid-teens to mid-twenties, negating any way to determine purely juvenile victimizations, much less offender rates. Thus, although victimization data may help shed some light on rates and distributions of offenses and offenders, they are at this point of only supplemental value for global inquiry.

Self-Report Surveys

The third way to estimate delinquency rates is by means of self-reported delinquency surveys. These surveys ask respondents if and how often they engaged in a list of offense behavior over some time period. In addition, detailed demographic information and responses to questions designed to test theoretical dimensions may be included. As far as youthful misconduct is concerned, criminologists have found these surveys to be extremely useful and, generally, have concluded they are valid and reliable measures of behavior. The data presented in table 3.2 exemplifies the kind of information obtained from self-report research.

Self-report surveys are not without limitations. While quite good at tapping much of the petty misconduct of juveniles that may not find its way into official statistics, how well inquiries of self-admitted serious activity is counted by them is questionable (Cernkovich et al. 1985). Many serious, repetitive offenders, for instance, may be excluded from such research. More important, with a very few exceptions, self-report surveys are of limited value in accessing trends over time. Most self-report surveys have been of the one-shot (cross-sectional) variety. They give a picture of delinquency committed by a sample of respondents at one point in time, as opposed to longitudinal research where respondents are followed and resurveyed over a number of years. Moreover, most of this research has been conducted on relatively small, non-national samples, leaving doubts as to how representative the findings are of a country's young population in general. Of primary importance in measuring the global dimensions of delinquency is the fact that

TABLE 3.2

Self-Reported Delinquency Prevalence Rates in Italy

Type	Ever n	%	Last year n	%
Stealing from telephone booths/automata	7	0.7	5	0.5
Shoplifting	179	17.7	66	6.5
Stealing at school	34	3.4	21	2.1
Stealing at home	68	6.7	44	4.4
Stealing from work	8	0.8	7	0.7
Stealing bike/moped/motorbike	5	0.5	3	0.3
Stealing car	0	0.0	0	0.0
Stealing from car	7	0.7	5	.05
Pickpocketing	0	0.0	0	0.0
Snatching purse/bag	0	0.0	0	0.0
Burglary	0	0.0	0	0.0
Stealing other	9	0.9	7	0.7
Buying stolen goods	125	12.4	74	7.3
Selling stolen goods	19	1.9	12	1.2
Prevalence property offenses	307	30.4	169	16.7
Graffiti	138	13.7	94	9.3
Vandalism	177	17.5	77	7.6
Prevalence violence against objects	257	25.5	141	14.0
Carrying a weapon	52	5.2	34	3.4
Threatening someone	0	0.0	0	0.0
Engaged in riots	150	14.9	105	10.4
Arson	33	3.3	14	1.4
Beating up family	8	0.8	1	0.1
Beating up nonfamily	43	4.3	21	2.1
Hurting with weapons	3	0.3	1	0.1
Prevalence violence against persons	203	20.1	133	13.2
Using soft drugs	89	8.8	63	6.2
Using hard drugs	4	0.4	3	0.3
Selling soft drugs	7	0.7	4	0.4

(Continued)

TABLE 3.2

(Continued)

Type	Ever		Last year	
	n	%	n	%
Selling hard drugs	0	0.0	0	0.0
Prevalence drug offenses	90	8.9	64	6.3
Fare dodging tram/bus/metro	802	79.5	497	49.3
Fare dodging train	117	11.6	68	6.7
Driving without license/insurance	228	22.6	170	16.8
Prevalence other youth-related offenses	825	81.8	571	56.6
Overall prevalence delinquent behavior	860	85.2	652	64.6
Without alcohol and problem behavior				
Truancy	453	44.9	316	31.3
Running away	26	2.6	11	1.1
Prevalence problem behavior				
Without alcohol use	457	45.3	319	31.6

Note: Offense category prevalence rates are derived from composite scales and are not necessarily summary rates of the individual offenses presented above each scale.

Source: Gatti et al. 1994, 279.

relatively few of these studies of any kind have been carried out, especially in countries outside North America and Western Europe. Indeed, only one international self-reported delinquency survey has ever been undertaken (Junger-Tas et al. 1994). As revealing as this enterprise was, it was hardly international, in that it only focused on Western European countries, involved unmatched samples (city populations vs. national samples, for example), and employed different survey methodologies. For much of the rest of the world, either no self-report studies have been conducted or they have involved very small, often nonrandom, samples. Thus, at this point, we are limited in drawing any conclusions about the global misconduct of young people from self-report research.

Lack of Data

The major problem in drawing any empirically substantiated conclusions about the delinquency of young people in the world's societies is the lack of information of any kind for much of the world. Although a few efforts have been made by the United Nations and other agencies to gain a comprehensive picture of the global extent and nature of delinquency, they are of disappointing value, limited in the information provided, and of questionable validity in any case. The simple fact is that we know virtually nothing about the behavior of juveniles in most of the world. No information of any kind exists. Either it has not been collected or it has not been made public. This is particularly true of almost all of Africa, South America, and Asia. There is copious information on youth in North America and many of the countries in Western Europe. Very sketchy, piecemeal, and limited data of one sort or another exists for a few scattered countries in other parts of the world. However, for most, there is nothing at all. Anyone who makes authoritative assertions about the extent of delinquency across the world's populations or makes claims about invariance in rates or differences between race, class, gender, and other large groups simply has no empirical grounds on which to base such claims. We cannot in this volume, nor can anyone as yet, draw authoritative conclusions about the extent and distribution of delinquency in the world's juvenile population.

Global Rates of Delinquent Behavior

Keeping in mind the limitations of the information currently available to criminology, it is not impossible to draw a picture of delinquency rates around the world. Although we can only describe these rates in a broad sense, the accumulated data we now have and the consistency of the image these data present can provide some illumination. As the database continues to grow, our knowledge of the true extent and distribution of juvenile misconduct throughout the world may be refined.

Extent and Forms

Delinquent behavior is ubiquitous. No country yet investigated is free of misbehavior on the part of its young people, and every country on which some information exists registers some involvement by at least some juveniles within its borders in acts that might legitimately be called delinquent or criminal behavior. In that regard, delinquent behavior is common throughout the world. It is a natural, normal phenomenon. What vary are the relative extent, seriousness, and forms of such conduct (Hartjen and Kethineni 1996).

Self-report studies conducted in diverse societies across the globe, for example, suggest that most juveniles everywhere engage in an extensive list of relative petty forms of misconduct primarily consisting of nuisance or mischief activities and status-types of behaviors (e.g., Barberet et al. 2004; Junger-Tas et al. 1994). Most of the world's youth readily admit to acts such as skipping school, cheating on tests, smoking, drinking alcohol, defying parents, curfew violations, and similar forms of conduct. Minor forms of criminality, such as mild vandalism, petty theft, fighting, sexual experimentation, and the like are also common. Although prevalence and incidence rates of such conduct vary between societies and among groups within specific societies, youthful misconduct appears to be normal, common behavior for young people everywhere. The responses to the self-report survey depicted in table 3.2 are typical for such inquiries, regardless of locality.

Self-report and official crime statistics also reveal that more serious forms of criminality are also frequently committed by young people everywhere. Compared to mild forms of misconduct, there is considerably more variability in these rates (due, in part, to organizational factors influencing official statistics). Serious forms of criminal activity are by no means restricted to one kind of country or certain categories of young people within countries. In a global survey, the United Nations asked participating countries to report on the numbers of juveniles and adults brought into formal contact with their criminal justice system by being arrested, questioned, and detained. Rates per 100,000 inhabitants for responding countries are presented in table 3.3.

Countries record extremely disparate contact rates, both for adults and juveniles—with a low rate of 3.63 for Côte d'Ivoire to a high rate of 836.85 for Germany. Does this wide disparity reflect real differences in the extent of criminal behavior by juveniles in various countries? Or, more likely, do the numbers reflect differences in the operation of criminal justice systems in these countries and the proclivity of authorities in various societies to officially respond to and record misconduct on the part of their citizenry? Whatever the case, it is clear that no society is free of juvenile crime and delinquency (see United Nations 2004a).

Self-report research and, especially, official statistics show that rates of overall criminal activity and the extent to which youth in various societies engage in specific forms of such behavior vary across societies. However, it appears that the criminality of young people throughout the world is very similar in terms of broad offense categories. Primarily, young people appear to engage in property offenses. Most of this conduct consists of direct-predatory acts that involve little skill and low levels of organization, such as strong-arming schoolmates, shoplifting, residential burglary, purse snatching, and the like. Relatively less frequently, juveniles are engaged in more sophisticated property crimes or offenses requiring organization and coordination, such as hijacking, business burglary, auto theft for profit, and armed robberies. In some cases juveniles are partners with or exploited by adults in carrying out criminal acts. Crimes such as fraud, embezzlement, organized gambling and the like are rare for juveniles, especially on their own, largely because young people are rarely in a position to carry out such criminality. A study conducted on juvenile violence in the United States, for example, shows that of the comparatively few youths arrested in 1994, a minuscule number were arrested for violent crimes

TABLE 3.3

Rate of Persons in the Criminal Justice System

Country	Juveniles (per 100,000)	Adults (per 100,000)
Azerbaijan	6.92	137.07
Belarus	77.69	604.56
Bulgaria	70.65	659.72
Canada	368.82	1,408.77
Chile	444.22	4,181.64
Colombia	17.76	352.95
Côte d'Ivoire	3.63	50.03
Czech Republic	172.85	1,091.55
Denmark	107.46	875.54
Estonia	140.25	831.04
Finland	787.44	5,964.23
Germany	836.85	2,245.83
Hong Kong	186.76	415.42
Hungary	110.81	1,116.85
Iceland	134.52	1,508.19
Italy	24.93	964.80
Japan	104.20	139.62
Korea, Republic of	302.36	3,709.08
Kyrgyzstan	34.85	440.51
Latvia	136.05	630.86
Lithuania	96.83	581.00
Macedonia, FYR	262.88	702.02
Malaysia	25.02	110.92
Mauritius	315.22	2,153.12
Moldova, Republic of	66.91	360.65
Netherlands	296.61	1,390.01
New Zealand	817.69	3,957.22
Norway	148.54	613.76
Pakistan	0.00	6.68
Qatar	31.63	1,063.62

(Continued)

TABLE 3.3

(Continued)

Country	Juveniles (per 100,000)	Adults (per 100,000)
Romania	73.71	999.25
Russian Federation	121.82	1,070.95
Singapore	39.77	403.43
Slovenia	147.74	791.70
Spain	68.65	663.01
Sri Lanka	56.07	1,542.92
Sweden	129.36	847.72
Thailand	44.66	1,804.75
Tunisia	76.61	1,347.75
Ukraine	59.83	564.53
Uruguay	424.54	1,667.97
Venezuela	10.89	54.30
Zambia	8.38	285.23

Source: Adapted from United Nations 2004a, 93–94, 99–100.

(Snyder et al. 1996). Indeed, only 6 percent of all American juveniles were arrested in that year, and of those only 7 percent (less than 1 percent of total juvenile population) were arrested for a violent crime. In other countries these numbers and proportions would typically be even smaller.

To an unknown extent, young people are involved in sexual misconduct. Sexual activity of all kinds is probably fairly common among the world's youth, with widely varying estimates being reported even within specific countries. Even if prohibited, sex-related behavior appears to be a normal part of the maturation process everywhere—although, again, it is most likely that actual rates of this behavior vary considerably because of social control and opportunity factors. Of periodic concern is the exploitation of children and young people in organized prostitution and pornography. How extensive this phenomenon may be is unknown, although evidence indicates that in some parts of the world it is widespread and the sexual exploitation of children is an emerging worldwide problem (International Tribunal for Children's Rights 2006). It is only of late, however, that any serious criminological research on the matter has been undertaken.

TABLE 3.4

Percentage of U.S. Population Reporting Illicit Drug Use

	Ever used	*Past year*	*Past month*
Total population	37.7	11.3	5.5
12–17 years old			
White	16.9	12.1	6.1
Hispanic	17.6	12.7	7.1
Black	15.1	9.9	6.2
18–25 years old			
White	56.3	28.7	13.7
Hispanic	39.2	20.0	10.2
Black	42.3	22.2	12.1
26–34 years old			
White	65.7	19.1	10.6
Hispanic	44.3	15.1	7.8
Black	51.4	18.1	10.3
35 and older			
White	28.7	5.3	2.2
Hispanic	20.7	4.1	1.3
Black	28.7	5.8	3.5

Source: Adapted from U.S. Department of Health and Human Services 1993, 20–21.

Contrary to the widespread media and law enforcement attention given to the matter in some countries, drug abuse behavior appears to be far less prevalent among the world's juveniles than one might conclude from the attention it receives. Surveys in the United States, for example, show rates far below those commonly assumed by the public. Some international surveys indicate that this could be even more so in much of the rest of the world. Moreover, the findings from these inquiries indicate that youths engaged in such behavior primarily abuse marijuana and synthetic products rather than hard drugs.

Table 3.4, for example, shows estimated prevalence rates for any illicit drug use in the United States by age and race. Table 3.5 showing the results of self-reported drug use surveys in various countries provides another picture. In reviewing table 3.5, keep in mind that the data in this table are abstracted from studies

TABLE 3.5

Self-Reported Drug Use by Youths in Various Countries

	Soft drugs (%)	Hard drugs (%)
France 2000	24	3
Greece 1992	9	<1
Finland 1992	13	<1
India 1987	1	1
Kenya 1995	8	2
Norway 1999	16	5
Portugal 1992	2	<1
United Kingdom 1992	30	2
United States 1978, 2005	31	3

Sources: France: Hartjen and Priyadarsini 2003; Greece Spinellis et al 1994; Finland: Aromaa 1994; India: Hartjen and Kethineni 1996; Kenya: UNODC 1999; Norway: Pape and Rossow 2004; Portugal: Gersão and Lisboa 1994; United Kingdom: Graham and Bowling 1995; United States: Elliott et al. 1979 and USONDCP 2005.

conducted in different years, using diverse methodologies based on samples that are not matched.

Trends

Making any conclusive statements about trends in the world's delinquency rates is highly speculative. We are limited by often questionable official statistics and few measures of actual prevalence/incidence rates over time within countries, and most of those are for fairly short-term duration. Thus, any claims that delinquency around the globe is getting worse or better should be read as expressions of usually uninformed opinion—not scientific facts. There is a general consensus among criminologists that offense rates probably did increase in the decades after World War II, and that the forms of offense behavior committed by young people are somewhat more serious and violent. However, this conclusion could be a function of better law enforcement and attention to, or reporting and recording of, delinquent behavior than any real change in the behavior of the world's young. One comprehensive study by Estrada (1999) used multiple sources of data to evaluate trends in delinquency in postwar Europe. Contrary to other findings, this research suggests that trends in many countries increased initially but then leveled off.

Keeping the limitations of official statistics in mind, it does appear that delinquency has become a problem of global proportions and is increasing in much of the world. Many countries in recent years have registered extensive concern, and even alarm, over the seemingly pervasive, serious, and often vicious criminality of their young. Consequently, many societies have taken a variety of steps (often punitive) to try to curb what is perceived to be a growing problem (United Nations 2004a). With globalization, modernization, and Westernization of countries around the world, this concern may have some basis in fact. This problem will become increasingly substantiated as the young of many countries emulate the behavior of youths in the United States and Western Europe (Bennett 1991; Hartjen and Priyadarsini 1984; Shelley 1981).

Distribution: Age, Gender, Race, and Class

Statistics regarding rates of delinquency normally focus on four demographic variables—age, gender, race, and social class. As with other data used to measure offense rates, breakdowns in terms of these variables are not always presented, nor are the categories themselves consistently defined. This is especially perplexing when trying to make cross-national comparisons or draw globally relevant conclusions. In spite of these drawbacks, some significant observations about the relative distribution of delinquent conduct in various societies around the world may be tentatively drawn from the information we have.

AGE. A common graphical depiction of relative involvement in crime and delinquency takes the form of an extenuated normal curve distribution. Criminologists have generally found that rates of such conduct tend to increase steadily from adolescence through late teens into young adulthood, peaking in the early to mid-twenties and then sharply declining thereafter. Referred to as the maturing-out process, it appears that late teens and early adulthood are the peak ages for criminal activity of all types, although offense-specific patterns of offense behavior by age seem to vary considerably (Farrington 1986; Graham and Bowling 1995).

Given the lack of age-specific data, to what extent this age-crime pattern is universal is unknown. But, since similar curvilinear patterns are reported in numerous studies on diverse populations, one can presume that it is. What varies is the relative frequency of offending and ages of offenders. While similar in overall pattern, the rate of offense behavior at specific ages may differ from society to society or group to group. Specifically, there is reason to believe that the age of onset, the age at which juveniles typically begin to commit noticeable delinquent acts, may differ across societies. In some societies this age may be several years later than in other countries. This could depress that society's overall delinquency rate and have different implications for strategies to deal with the country's delinquency problem. Why these differences in age may exist is yet to be understood by criminologists.

GENDER. Compared to girls, boys in all countries are more delinquent and they are more seriously delinquent in terms of the frequency and kinds of criminality they commit. This, so-called gender-gap is not only universal but also exists at all age levels from childhood through adulthood—although, the magnitude of the gap may increase with age so that young male and female offenders are more alike than are older ones. Data from a self-reported delinquency survey carried out in India exemplifies the kind of results typically found from such surveys conducted anywhere in the world (see table 3.6). As suggested by this research, what tends to differ is the magnitude of the male/female ratios found, overall or for specific offense forms.

The gender-gap has been a matter of much debate and research (Berger 1989; Chesney-Lind 1997). Largely missing from that debate, however, is an observation one might make from cross-national research on gender-related offense rates across countries. Specifically, all studies have found that males have higher rates than females, regardless of how these rates are measured. However, cross-national data also suggest that males are not equally more delinquent than females. Indeed, males of the same age in one country compared to females of the same age in another country may actually be less delinquent than the females. For instance, research by Hartjen and Kethineni (1996) comparing Indian and American boys and girls found this was indeed the case. Within each country, boys are typically more delinquent. However, the self-reported and official delinquency of Indian boys is often equal to or less than that of American girls (Hartjen 1997). Less systematic comparison of age-specific offense rates by gender across various countries suggest this finding may not be an anomaly (D'Unger et al. 2002; Hartjen and Priyadarsini 2003). In that regard, the gender/crime relationship may be tempered by social-system or cultural variables and not simply reflect some as-yet-unknown gender-related cause of delinquency.

RACE. Considerable debate has centered on whether offense behavior varies by race—or, more generally, ethnicity—and whether there is some kind of connection between race and crime (Fergusson et al. 1993; Huizinga and Elliott 1987; Jánson and Wikström 1995; Junger 1990). In virtually all societies one is likely to hear variations of expressions referring to "those kinds of people" and "their" behavior. In Europe and elsewhere the author frequently encountered sentiments that attributed local crime to "Gypsies," "Arabs," "Easterners," or, typically, some non-Caucasian racial group or disparaged ethnic group. Offenders from within their own community (racial group) were described as being somehow "different," "peculiar," "unfortunate," or otherwise abnormal to have committed such behavior. And, where available, if one looks at the official arrest and processing statistics of any country one inevitably finds wide disparity in arrests by a usually predominant minority population, causing some to conclude that those people are, indeed, somehow more criminal than others.

TABLE 3.6

Self-Reported Delinquency Rates for Indian Youths

Offense behavior	Boys (n = 1,328)	Girls (n = 1,233)	Ratio
Assault	11	2	6
Gang fight	12	3	4
Hit parent	5	5	2
Extortion	9	4	2
Concealed weapon	10	3	3
Major theft	8	4	2
Moderate theft	6	1	6
Petty theft	8	4	2
Breaking and entering	13	5	3
Steal from family	27	9	3
Steal from school	21	7	3
Vehicle theft	2	1	2
Joyride	12	2	6
Stolen property	12	2	6
Avoid payment	34	10	3
Vandalism	23	11	2
Throw objects	21	6	4
Disorderly conduct	16	5	3
Runaway from home	17	2	9
Lie about self	37	20	2
Drunk in public	4	1	4
Begging	6	2	3
Truancy	39	20	2
Cheated on test	47	40	1
Sold soft drugs	1	<1	2
Sold hard drugs	1	<1	2
Drank alcohol	18	5	4
Used soft drugs	4	1	4
Used hard drugs	2	1	4
Mean percent/ratio	15	6	3

Source: Adapted from Hartjen 1997, 295.

A large body of country-specific research questions this association. Self-report research generally finds little actual difference in offense rates when other variables are controlled (e.g. Huizinga and Elliott 1987). Some differences in the types of conduct likely to be committed by members of different racial groups, or the contexts in which that behavior occurs, therefore, may explain the wide disparity in official rates by race, rather than actual differences in a race or ethnicity-based proclivity to commit criminal acts.

Indeed, cross-national comparisons suggest that the apparent relationship between race/ethnicity and crime may be quite different from what single-society research would lead one to conclude. For example, in the United States and other predominately white societies, black youths are found in official arrest statistics considerably more frequently than their proportion of the population. This could lead to a possible conclusion that blacks are more criminal than whites, and therefore there is something about being black that increases one's likelihood of committing crimes. However, if that were the case, offense rates for predominantly black countries (African nations) would be higher than those found for predominantly white societies (European countries). This, however, does not appear to be the case. In fact, just the opposite may be true. Similar statements can probably be made about any racial/ethnic-crime relationship. Comparable data to test this possibility would do much to cast light on commonsense conclusions.

SOCIAL CLASS. Juveniles caught up in the arms of the law are overwhelmingly drawn from the lower economic strata of any society. Considering official statistics, one might conclude that delinquency is somehow a function of being in a lower social class. Indeed, images of the criminal classes that were popular in earlier centuries are by no means bygone ideas in modern societies. Yet, where class has been measured, the findings of self-report research cast doubt on a class-crime causal connection, although there is some reason to believe that the forms and settings (e.g., public vs. private) of offense behavior may vary by social class. In part, this may explain why much of the behavior committed by lower-class individuals comes to the attention of authorities to be counted in official rates (Weis 1996).

Nevertheless, as with race and gender, the conclusions about the class-delinquency association found when viewing individual countries might be quite different when one compares different countries. Specifically, offense rates and self-reported delinquency rates in poorer countries are almost uniformly lower than those of more affluent societies. Indeed, the highest offense rates are consistently found in the United States, the United Kingdom, Australia, Canada, and various Western European societies (see Ortega et al. 1992; Shelley 1986; Shichor 1990). If being poor in itself were responsible for delinquent behavior, we would expect countries like India, Columbia, Romania, and

Sri Lanka to be hotbeds of delinquent conduct. The United States and similar societies would be relatively free of such activity. They are not.

Ideas such as "relative deprivation," "culture of poverty," and the like may help account for this disparity because they seek to explain why the poor in any specific society seem to have higher official offense rates than the well-to-do. In part, this may simply reflect differences in reporting rates than any actual differences in crime rates (Soares 2004). Efforts to explain the apparent class-crime relationship need to account for the fact that, on a global scale, it is relative wealth, not relative poverty, which seems to breed delinquency. Why this may be the case is yet to be adequately addressed in criminology. If true, the implications will be profound as countries across the world modernize and Westernize.

Explaining Rates

All juveniles are delinquent, but some are more delinquent than others. In that respect, delinquent behavior is universal, but the problem of delinquency is not. A central issue for criminology is determining why crimes rates vary across populations. Why do some juveniles engage in more delinquent conduct more often, or in more serious acts, than other juveniles in their own countries or other countries?

In a simplistic answer to these questions one might propose that there is something about some youths that leads them to exhibit higher rates of offense behavior than other youths. They are somehow different or abnormal from other youths. From a commonsense perspective this idea is compelling—"Their (more delinquent) kids are not like our (less delinquent) kids!" However if we were to accept such an argument, we would have to acknowledge that American youths, for example, are somehow different or abnormal from the rest of the world's population, since Americans have routinely exhibited the highest offense rates of any society. Most people, of course, would find that idea patently absurd on a number of grounds, and few criminological arguments would even entertain such an idea. By why, then, don't children everywhere behave the same way?

Social Conditions

A number of constructs to explain differences in offense rates have focused on differences in the social, economic, and cultural situations in which youths find themselves. Early versions of these arguments, in the form of anomie and social disorganization theories (Durkheim 1951; Merton 1957, 1964) sought to explain the high rates of delinquency (crime) found in some communities, or historic times, in terms of various adverse social/economic conditions. More specific variants of these kinds of arguments—arguments that predate the advent of self-report research—attempted to explain the seemingly intractable higher rates of delinquency found in American lower-class, typically minority, neighborhoods of inner cities. Focusing on one or another aspect of the life situation faced by economically deprived youths, these theories attributed their high delinquency rates to such things as a value clash between lower- and middle-class groups (Cohen 1955); blocked access to legitimate opportunities (Cloward and Ohlin 1960); or peculiarities in the "focal concerns" (cultural values) of lower-class people engendered by their economic situation (Miller 1958). Although such arguments have found little empirical support, in part because of the difficulty of testing the arguments, they fostered a host of antidelinquency programs that survive in various forms to this day.

Other theoretical arguments, such as radical (cf. Inciardi 1980; Lunch and Groves 1986), conflict (Muncie 1999), or so-called labeling theory (Paternoster and Iovanni 1989) have received even less empirical support, basically due to the vagueness and/or all-encompassing scope of the arguments, and have had less influence on public policies to reduce offense rates. They too, however, suggest that there is something about the social-economic environment that influences the behavior of individuals within groups that could account for why rates of offense behavior might vary.

More modern spin-offs of various theories have found expression in a number of explanatory efforts. Most notable is Adler's attempt to use a variant of anomie theory to explain cross-national differences in crime rates (Adler 1983) and her liberation hypotheses (Adler 1975), which sought to account for the increase in offense rates among women and girls near the end of the twentieth century. Hagan, Sampson, and Gillis's (1987) power-control theory attributed the generally low rates of offense behavior among girls to differences in the social/economic situation of girls compared to boys. And Agnew's (1992) strain theory, a new version of social disorganization theory, sought to extend the traditional argument to show how economic disadvantage can cause psychological strain that can lead to crime and delinquency.

Considerable interest still exists among criminologists in assessing and explaining crime and delinquency rates, especially their apparent increases and decreases within specific populations. Yet theoretical efforts to understand variations in rates have largely waned in contemporary criminology. Literature is still being produced that investigates various correlates of offense rates, and there is much debate about why such rates may change over time. New theory or even testable refinements of earlier arguments that specifically address the issue, however, are not to be found in the literature. Instead, criminologists have largely turned to the second explanatory question faced by the discipline—Why do they do it?—the question of etiology. Consequently, criminology still lacks a theory of delinquency rates.

The Wrong Question

In part, empirical support of older theories that focused on rates has been lacking because most of the tests of these theories have treated them as if they were explanations of individual offense behavior (the question of etiology). Unable to successfully link measures of variables proposed to explain why rates of behavior varied (the question of epidemiology) to the occurrence or nonoccurrence of such behavior, this research has concluded that the theory in question was flawed. Consequently, anomie, disorganization, and related theories are largely treated as historical anachronisms in criminology, not serious ideas for thought and further research (although, brief periodic revivals do occur). However, the question of rates still remains. And it continues to be as intellectually and policy relevant as it ever was.

To some extent criminology's failure to provide a sound, empirically supportable explanation of delinquency rates, one that would explain why these rates vary within and across countries, is the result of the failure to address the question properly. Current arguments (strain and power/control theories being possible exceptions) provide little insight as to how social/economic/cultural conditions are linked to behavior. Specific arguments may present a kind of causal chain argument suggesting how certain social conditions (such as poverty) lead to psychological conditions (such as strain), which make people prone to committing delinquent acts. However, a theory of why the psychological condition is a cause of delinquency is normally missing or left vague in the theory, or may be inadequate to explain the behavior.

In the haste to explain differences in rates directly, criminologists have focused on the wrong dependent variables—the rates themselves. According to Sutherland, if there is a theory of why individuals within categories or groups are more or less prone to commit crime, there should also be an explanation of why rates of crime vary across social categories or groups (Cressey 1960; Reinarman and Fagan 1988; Sutherland and Cressey 1955). This argument is correct in that before one can explain cross-category or cross-group differences in rates one needs an explanation of why individuals within categories or groups are more or less prone to commit crimes. The implication that the explanation of why people within categories or groups are more or less prone to commit crimes is somehow also an explanation of why the frequency or prevalence of such behavior would vary across those categories or groups, however, is incorrect. An explanation of the occurrence of behavior cannot be used to explain the relative frequency of that behavior. Instead, what is needed is a theory of why whatever it is that makes people more or less prone to commit crimes varies across categories or groups. Symbolically, all else being equal, if X causes Y and X is a universal and the only cause of Y, then variations in the frequency of Y are to be explained by whatever it is (Z, perhaps) that causes X to vary across categories or groups. Existing theories of epidemiology hint at what that Z causing variations in X might be. The point, of course, is that we need to explain why the forces that produce individual behavior vary across categories and groups in order to explain why the rates of individual behavior vary. However, criminology has yet to formulate a specific theory explaining variations in X to help us understand variations in rates of delinquency (Y).

Social Control and Interpersonal Relationships

From a global perspective, two things stand out among the persistent patterns found in offense rates: (1) although ratios vary, offense rates are higher among males than among females, and (2) reported offense rates tend to be higher in modernized societies (economically developed/Western) than in traditional (economically less-developed/non-Western) societies and increase in societies that are modernizing. These two phenomena are interrelated in that women and girls in modern/modernizing societies, compared with women and girls in more traditional societies, have higher offense rates and more closely resemble males. Both patterns suggest a common dimension—social control and interpersonal relationships.

The two dominant and largely empirically supported contemporary arguments regarding the etiology of delinquent behavior are differential association (social learning) and social control (self-control) theories. Differential association attributes individual proneness to commit delinquent acts to the individual's significant associations and the learning experience these associations provide (Burgess and Akers 1965; Sutherland and Cressey 1955). Control theory argues that people are more or less prone to commit delinquent acts depending on the extent to which they are subject to social controls and/or have developed adequate self-controls to refrain from offending (Gottfredson and Hirschi 1990; Hirschi 1969). The relative merits of the two opposing ideas are hotly contested in criminology and not a matter for the present discussion. But, for purposes of illustration, let's assume that they are both correct, that together they constitute the X that explains Y. Very simply, all individuals who acquire pro-criminal sentiments and skills from their associates, and who lack adequate social and internal self-control not to act on these sentiments and skills, will engage in delinquent acts. Why, then, are the children in modern/modernizing societies engaging in more of these acts than youths in more traditional societies? Why are males more delinquent than females, especially in traditional societies? What is the Z that differs between genders and these two types of societies that might account for associational and/or control differences (X) among individuals that lead more or less of them to commit delinquent acts (Y)?

Criminology is not yet in a position to even begin to answer this question, although the small but growing body of cross-national research being produced may soon allow speculation. To date, however, too little is known about modern versus traditional social/cultural systems or about associational/control differences between genders in various types of societies to draw any definitive conclusions. It will take a marriage of criminological/sociological/anthropological/economic research to fully understand how broader social situations influence associational patterns and social controls and how these, in turn, are reflected in different frequencies of offense behaviors.

Some Examples

As mentioned earlier, relatively poor, traditional-types of societies appear to have low delinquency rates and rich, modern-types of societies tend to have higher rates. India provides an example. By any measure India has very low delinquency rates, especially when compared to the United States and Western European societies. However, India still suffers from all the adverse social-economic conditions traditionally associated with high crime rates (e.g., poverty, illiteracy, blocked access to legitimate opportunities, ethnicism, urbanization, etc.) in spite of the economic advances that have taken place in India. Research by Hartjen and Priyadarsini (1984) and Hartjen and Kethineni (1996) suggest why, in spite of the adverse social-economic conditions, India's rates are still low. Essentially, it appears that features of strong family relationships, caste networks, and the economic interdependence of family/caste members in Indian society impede associational patterns that may be conducive to delinquency while imposing a net of social controls that help to block any delinquency orientations a youth may acquire. As these associational ties and informal controls weaken, and as India modernizes and develops economically, rates of delinquency will increase in this century. Recent information seems to confirm that this may be starting to happen.

Delinquency rates (as with crime generally) also appear to dramatically increase in societies experiencing political change leading to rapid social and economic change. Yet the people in those societies remain the same. So, why the increase? Research by Finckenauer and Kelly (1992) on the impact the breakup of the former Soviet Union had on delinquency in Russia is illustrative. By the 1990s delinquency rates in Russia began to increase substantially. The increase, Finckenauer and Kelly argue, was the result of the emergence of youth subcultures and gangs coinciding with the economic chaos of the transition from a planned to a market economy, along with a decrease in the Komosmols that had traditionally provided Russian youth a form of organization and control. In addition, the extended family, historically a strong force in Russian society, began to break down as the Western nuclear model began to dominate. Many children were left unsupervised or lived in fatherless homes, creating a fertile soil in which delinquency could grow. In short, dramatic shifts in associational relationships and traditional mechanisms of control engendered by political-economic change produced an environment that fostered increased involvement in delinquent behavior; Russian juveniles were no longer subjected to traditional constraints and encountered a host of opportunities to acquire pro-criminal sentiments and skills. As a result, more of them more frequently came to engage in offense behavior.

Finally, the gender gap in delinquency (and adult crime) rates has been a matter for much research and argument. Most of this inquiry has been limited to single society debate, most specifically the United States, with little by way of broad cross-national reflection that could cast some light on the whole argument. The gender-gap is universal, but the extent of the difference between males and females is not. Women and girls in very traditional societies have offense rates close to zero. Offense rates for men in these societies may also be low, but the difference in the (wide) gap between girls and boys in countries like Afghanistan, Yemen, Saudi Arabia, and similar countries, compared to the (narrow) gap for girls and boys in the United States, England, and most European countries, must be striking. Solid data on which to base these comparisons unfortunately is still very limited. Assuming the differences in the size of the gaps to be real, why are girls more like boys in Western countries compared to girls in the Middle East or other non-Western societies? As suggested by power/control theory and the liberation hypotheses, one can speculate that girls in traditional societies are far more subject to social controls and much more restricted in the people they can associate with than are girls in Western countries. Indeed, the practice of teen dating, a very common and expected activity in Western countries is largely unknown and frowned upon in more traditional societies. Girls who are sequestered, chaperoned, married off at puberty, and otherwise kept under close social control within family and clan relationships are less free (in a Westerner's eyes) compared to American or European girls. Consequently, they are less able and probably, because of restricted association/learning experience, less inclined to deviate (e.g., Anderson and Bennett 1996; Bowker 1981; Hartjen 1997; Steffensmeier et al. 1989). Hence, they are likely to have lower rates of offense behavior. What remains the same are the conditions that lead girls of any society to engage in delinquent forms of behavior. What differs is the social situation of girls in the two types of societies that affect those conditions.

Conclusion

In spite of a vast body of information on delinquency rates, close to nothing is known about the extent, distribution, and forms of delinquent activity among much of the world's youth. The data is simply lacking. One might assume that juveniles in the countries about which little or nothing is known resemble youths in similar countries about which some, even if inadequate, information exists. However, this cannot be known for sure until the research is done or records are compiled by authorities and made public.

Using available information, criminologists are able to piece together a plausible, tentative picture of how the world's youth resemble and differ from one another in terms of the types and frequencies with which they commit delinquent acts. Much remains speculative. What is clear from the available evidence is that delinquency is a worldwide phenomenon. In a broad sense, the world's youth look to be very much alike in the seriousness and types of behavior they engage in. In that regard, for young people to engage in delinquent forms of behavior, whether legally prohibited or not, is normal. Indeed, a society where none of its youth misbehave would be truly abnormal.

What varies is the extent to which the youth of different societies commit delinquent acts and/or the relative seriousness of the offenses they commit. Thus, while delinquency of some kind is found among all juveniles of all kinds everywhere in the world, juveniles are by no means equally delinquent, nor do they all engage in the same behaviors with the same frequency. Why these variations exist, and not why delinquent behavior per se exists, is the question for criminological explanation.

The foregoing information sketches some summary features of the similarities and differences in delinquency across the globe. Assuming this picture reflects reality, explanations are needed as to why the differences exist. All the world's youth may be delinquent, but why are they not equally so? Answering that question is a task that criminology has yet to complete successfully. Research may help illuminate the social/cultural/economic conditions that affect the forces that compel or facilitate delinquent conduct. Identification of correlates alone will not reveal why rates vary. To elucidate this question fully we need to first provide a viable explanation of why youths of any kind anywhere commit such acts in the first place. Explaining why rates of delinquency vary across societies, among groups within societies, or among similar groups across societies is one issue. Explaining why juveniles anywhere engage in delinquent acts is quite another issue.

4

Forms of Delinquent Behavior

Research on rates of delinquency and youth crime suggests that the frequency and distribution of such behavior varies across the globe. However, this research also suggests that all youth everywhere seem to engage in forms of behavior normally frowned upon by adults and for which young people could be subject to official sanctioning. In that respect, delinquency and youth crime are universal. But, is such conduct universally the same?

An answer to that important, yet so far largely neglected, question has profound implications. If youth everywhere engage in much the same kinds of behavior in much the same way, even if with differing frequencies, then delinquency and youth crime are natural, normal phenomena—products of human social life. This behavior may still demand explanation, if only to satisfy the desire to understand human behavior of any kind. On the other hand, if this behavior varies in meaningful ways across social, cultural, economic, or other dimensions, then youth crime and delinquency are relative. And it is the relativity of this behavior that becomes a meaningful question for criminological inquiry. Why, for example, are delinquent or youth gangs not consistently the same from place to place or time to time? Is violent behavior by juveniles the same everywhere? If not, why the differences? Drug abuse may be a worldwide problem, but are the types of drugs, the mechanisms for becoming involved with them, and behaviors associated with addiction identical wherever we look? These are just three examples of the kinds of delinquent activities criminologists and others have researched, to greater or lesser extent, in countries around the globe. In a few cases, multinational investigations of behaviors such as drug-use patterns and gang activities have been undertaken. In some instances, results from comparative analyses of two or more countries are available. In the vast majority of research, however, the findings reported are from single societies, usually involving non-national samples, for specific offense behaviors, such as bullying, school violence, and alcohol consumption. The findings from these studies may be combined to arrive at some understanding of the similarities and differences in the character and forms of delinquency to be found throughout the world. However, in doing so we should keep in mind that the different methodologies, samples, data collection devices, and techniques used in these studies may make any conclusions we might draw at best tentative, if not highly misleading.

This chapter explores the universality or relativity of forms of delinquent behavior by looking at research produced in a variety of countries on several types of illegal activities. The information on delinquent forms of behavior across the globe is so limited that any extensive exploration or meaningful conclusions about the universality of delinquent forms of behavior would be quite premature. One can, however, gain some understanding of the nature of youthful offending by comparing how young people resemble and differ from one another in the character of their offense behavior in societies around the world.

Gangs

The lone-wolf offender does exist, but he or she is more an anomaly than a commonality in the world of offending youth (Bursik and Grasmick 2001). Instead, delinquent behavior generally is a group activity. Collective misconduct by juveniles, or some forms of misbehaving youthful collectives, have been of particular concern and official interest since the beginnings of criminological inquiry. Normally referred to as gangs, these kinds of groups and the behavior of their members have been one of the most researched criminological topics in the United States, with an entire scholarly journal devoted to the subject and literally millions of dollars spent on the phenomenon. Indeed, Hazlehurst and Hazlehurst (1998) note that the gang has become a multimillion dollar law-enforcement and research enterprise, particularly in the Untied States.

Perhaps more than any other country, it is in the United States that the delinquent or youth gang has come to epitomize serious delinquent activity. American gangs have been credited, or charged, with a healthy percentage of the violence, drug dealing, and general lawlessness of many communities. From major cities to contemporary rural areas, a considerable amount of concern and resources of law enforcement agencies have been devoted to combating the conduct of gang-affiliated youths. In addition, the media image of the gang delinquent has become embedded in modern American culture (Klein 2001a). But, is the delinquent gang a uniquely American form of delinquency? Are there youth gangs in other societies? If so, are they similar to or different from the prototypical image people have of the gang found in American society? In either case, why or why not? A limited but growing body of research provides some answers to questions such as these.

What Is a Gang?

One of the problems in attempting to gain a global understanding of youth-gangs and the behavior of their members is determining just what constitutes a gang. To the lay reader this may seem like a simple problem, but to gang experts it remains an unresolved issue (cf. Covey 2004; Duffy 2004; Hazlehurst and Hazlehurst 1998; Klein 2001). One reason for this is the observation that gang-like groupings of youthful offenders come in a remarkable variety that defy satisfactory categorization. Few of them even come close to resembling the well-organized, turf-protecting, rumble-loving street gangs of popular media fiction. In structure, cohesion, organization, behavior, and permanence, gangs seem to evolve rapidly, so that the zoot-suiters of the post–World War II era, the ethnic street gangs of the 1950s–60s, and the drive-by-shooting, drug-dealing mobs of the 1980s have little if anything in common to warrant their being similarly classified as delinquent gangs, as far as criminological research is concerned. Even what these groupings are to be called is problematic. The terms "delinquent gang," "street gang," "youth gang," and "juvenile gang" have all been used, sometimes interchangeably, and little agreement exists on just what term is preferable. In keeping with the general terminology of this book, the term "delinquent gang" will be used here.

In an effort to provide a typology of gangs to help order our study and understanding of them, Klein (2001a) identified five common gang types found in a sample of 201 cities throughout the United States. Table 4.1 depicts the distribution of these various types of gangs in countries around the world. "Traditional gangs" are strongly territorial, tend to be large and long lasting, and have distinct subgroups whose members vary widely in age. "Neotraditional gangs" are similar to traditional ones but are smaller in size and have shorter histories. "Compressed gangs" are relatively short-lived, small groupings of youths of similar age with no territorial identity. "Collective gangs" exhibit no territorial identity, tend to exist for about ten to fifteen years, are medium to large in size, have members of various ages, and exhibit no identifiable subgroups. "Specialty gangs" are territorial, tend to exist for under ten years, are small with no subgroups, and their members are usually of similar age.

If gangs differ and evolve within one country, what about the variety of youth collectivities found across the globe? Whether true delinquent gangs are even found in countries outside the United States is a topic that scholars still debate. Most likely, they do exist. As Weitekamp (2001, 309) concludes regarding the existence of gangs in European cities, "One cannot deny any longer that European cities have street gangs or gang-like youth groups. . . . [T]hey are mainly specialty gangs and compressed gangs and not the older, traditional American gangs." As in the United States, a number of forms of nongang group delinquency are also found, most notably "hooligans," "drug posses," "tagger crews," "skinheads," and other youth groups that often have many similar

TABLE 4.1

Gang Types in Various Countries

Country	Traditional	Neotraditional	Compressed	Collective	Specialty
Argentina	x				
Australia		x		x	x
Belgium					x
Brazil			x		x
Cambodia		x			x
Canada		x	x		
China		x	x		x
Columbia					x
Denmark			x		
El Salvador		x			
England		x	x		x
Ethiopia			x		
France		x	x		x
Germany	x		x		x
Guam			x		
Guatemala		x	x		
Hungary					x
India		x			x
Israel			x	x	
Jamaica		x			
Japan			x	x	x
Kenya			x	x	x
Korea					x
Malaysia			x		
Mexico			x		
Northern Ireland			x		
Netherlands	x	x	x		x
New Zealand		x	x		x
Nigeria				x	x

(Continued)

TABLE 4.1

(Continued)

Country	Traditional	Neotraditional	Compressed	Collective	Specialty
Norway			x	x	
Pakistan			x		
Palestine		x			
Papua New Guinea			x		x
Philippines			x		
Puerto Rico		x			
Russia	x	x		x	x
Rwanda			x		
Sierra Leone				x	x
Slovenia		x			
South Africa	x	x	x		x
Sweden			x		x
Taiwan			x		
Trinidad/Tobago		x	x		x
Uganda					x
Zaire	x			X	

Source: Based on Covey 2003, 220–222.

characteristics and engage in behaviors typically associated with delinquent gangs (cf. Covey 2003, 24).

If the diversity of ganglike forms complicates the study of delinquent gang activity, it makes drawing conclusions about gang delinquency on a global scale all that more tenuous. As Duffy (2004, 3) notes: "The homeless children of the streets of Brazil who engage in crime in order to survive are different from the street gangs of Chicago and Los Angeles. Those American street gangs are not the same as the mixed-age-group gangs linked to organized crime and political patronage [of] the Jamaican posses." As difficult as it may be to draw precise definitional boundaries around the phenomenon, based on the research at hand, some tentative observations about ganglike groups and the behavior of their members can be made.

Gangs Universal or the Universal Gang

Perhaps the most fundamental question about gangs from a global perspective is whether gangs are culturally relative or universal. If gangs are found in only some or some types, of societies, or if the gangs found in various societies differ from one another in significant ways, then the existence or nature of gangs is in some way a function of the social-cultural context in which they form. If, however, young people in all, or all types of, societies band together in delinquent groupings of similar characteristics, then the gang and the behavior of its members is a normal feature of adolescent social life.

Given the embryonic nature of global gang research, an authoritative answer to this question is not yet possible. Diverse research does suggest, however, that gangs and gang forms of delinquency are to be found in societies of diverse types throughout the world. While they may be more common in some countries, the gang is not limited to one social-cultural form. On the other hand, gangs are extremely varied, both within specific societies and across different countries. Based on this research, one authority on the subject concluded that, although differing in various ways, delinquent gangs were to be found in all manner of country (Spergel 1990). In addition, reports from around the globe suggest that we may "be witnessing a world where street gangs are becoming a permanent feature of the social landscape" (Covey 2003, 4). Undoubtedly, idiosyncratic features of particular societies, or settings within specific countries, are responsible for producing particular forms of the gang, and these features may be so patterned and systematic that we may one day be able to predict that localities with certain characteristics will likely produce gangs with certain characteristics, and these are different from other gangs in other localities. Our knowledge of gang types and the settings in which they are formed is not, as yet, sufficient to make such predictions. At this point, Covey (2003, 214) perhaps best summarizes our ability to answer the question:

> There are substantial differences among gangs in different countries at varying times, but there is also evidence that the American youth subcultures of the 1950s through the present have made a lasting impression on street gangs throughout the world. In turn, the United States and other countries also have been influenced by British gangs, most notably the skinheads. Likewise, Chinese secret societies and organized crime have partially shaped street gangs in several countries. However, in some areas, street gang phenomena appear to spring from independent cultural influences, as exemplified by the relatively nonviolent Argentine and Puerto Rican gangs of the 1960s and 1970s and the street gangs of Papua New Guinea and Guam that incorporate traditional cultural values into their operations.

In short, while delinquent gangs may be universal, or nearly so, they are not necessarily universally identical, being influenced by a variety of national internal and external forces. Yet, it is becoming increasingly apparent that the problem of the delinquent gang is growing everywhere in the world.

Why Gangs?

Considerable effort has been given by criminologists interested in gangs to explain why they exist at all. In attempting to answer that question, Duffy (2004) notes that a common element of gang membership in diverse societies seems to be marginalization. Young minority males who are economically excluded are likely to be marginalized and among the ranks of gang members.

A number of theories have sought to explain why groups of marginalized young men would band together in gangs or why some societies produce the conditions wherein such banding together is widespread and pervasive. The most globally relevant of these ideas suggest that particular socioeconomic conditions are responsible (Curry and Decker 1998; Decker and Van Winkle 2001; Short 1968).

One argument grounded in a Durkheimian, or Mertonian, concept of anomie suggests that an underlying condition for gang formation is rapid social change, especially that associated with modernization, industrialization, and urbanization. Closely linked to this idea is the notion that gangs are prevalent in societies experiencing extensive immigration, either by population shifts within the society (e.g., rural to city) or from large-scale migration of peoples from other societies into the host country or locality. For the migrants, marginalization is a common experience, especially among young males. It should be no surprise, therefore, that ethnic minorities are commonly found among the ranks of gang members in virtually all societies where gangs exist.

Marxian theorists suggest that "inherent inequalities and social classes present in capitalistic economies create socioeconomic conditions ripe for the formation of street gangs" (Covey 2003, 12). In a sense, the delinquent gang is a kind of social adaptation to the economic inequities produced by capitalism. Similarly, a fourth argument combining the differential opportunity ideas of Cloward and Ohlin with a Marxist economic perspective suggests that "street gangs are simply a mechanism used to take advantage of the absence of legitimate economic opportunity in a climate of surplus wealth" (Covey 2003, 12).

Common to all these ideas are the themes that socioeconomic change and inequality are the underlying foundations for delinquent gang development and probably behavior. While gangs may differ in many ways across the globe, it is undeniable that delinquent gangs everywhere are composed of individuals who are, for whatever reason, excluded from and have little chance of ever becoming part of the mainstream of the societies in which they are found (cf. Duffy 2004; Hérault and Adesanmi 1997; Werdmölder 1997).

Delinquent gangs appear to be most common in urban, rapidly changing, economically disparate societies, particularly localities with significant populations of minorities and/or immigrant groups. But, the globalization of delinquent gangs also seems to be taking place in the shrinking world (Covey 2003; Hagedorn 2001; Hazlehurst and Hazlehurst 1998). Evidence exists that youth in other countries are beginning to emulate the ideal-type American street gang popularized in the mass media. Gangs germinated in American cities such as Los Angeles are apparently being transplanted in other countries, just like organizations from abroad—e.g., Chinese Tang and the Sicilian Mafia—were transported to the Untied States in earlier decades. And, either in fact or because more professionalized law enforcement agencies are noticing and reporting on them, gangs of various types appear to be a growing problem in countries around the world.

Gang Members

Although delinquent gangs and gang-like organizations are quite varied, the individuals that make up the membership of these organizations are very much alike across the globe (Klein 2001a, 2001b). Gang members are mostly males. Female gangs are an anomaly. Where they exist, they often emulate portrayals of male gangs but are relatively small in size and short in duration. In the United States, reports of gang activity in suburban and rural areas have increased in recent decades. Nevertheless, globally delinquent gangs are predominantly an inner-city phenomenon. While the age ranges of gang members are extensive (including preteens to mature adults in some cases), most commonly the youths actively participating in and identifying with delinquent gangs are adolescents of roughly fourteen to nineteen years of age. Significantly, just about everywhere, gang members hail from economically deprived homes and localities and are also overwhelmingly of ethnic minority status. The prototypical gang member to be found anywhere in the world, therefore, is a poor, urban, ethnic male, commonly of recent immigrant origin, who lives in an economically deprived or downwardly mobile area and comes from a family that is disorganized, abusive, and characterized by drug abuse. The parents typically hold negative attitudes toward society and authority, and older siblings are gang members and/or are involved in extensive criminality.

Gang Delinquency

The common image of the delinquent gang is that of a highly organized group of young ethnic thugs dedicated to violence, drugs, and virtually any other form of criminality typically committed as a collective enterprise. That image may fit some gangs or types of gangs, but as gangs vary tremendously in form and structure, so too does the criminality (nature and extent) of their members (cf. Klein 2001a; Miller et al. 2001; Sarnecki 1990, 2001).

It is difficult, but not impossible, to distinguish between what might be called "gang delinquency" versus "gang-member delinquency." Gang delinquency is delinquent or criminal behavior that is undertaken as a function of the gang's existence. This may consist of an economic enterprise such as dealing in controlled substances, stealing cars for profit, or acting as enforcers for political organizations. It could also include turf rumbles or drive-by shootings stemming from gang rivalries or protection of economic or territorial rights. It could also consist of acts of criminality as prerequisites to joining a gang or advancing in gang position (e.g., initiation or promotion rituals involving violence or daring).

Such criminality is quite different from the acts of criminal behavior individual gang members might engage in, although that also may often involve several other gang associates and consist of virtually any form of criminality one might contemplate. This behavior might better be viewed as gang-member delinquency rather than gang delinquency.

In comparison to other youthful offenders, the members of delinquent gangs appear to be significantly more criminally involved than are nongang delinquents, both in terms of the frequency and seriousness of their behavior (Miller et al. 2001). This is especially true regarding drug use and violence. The widespread existence of gangs in some societies undoubtedly increases the magnitude of the crime problem simply by virtue of the existence of these groupings. And, as gangs become more widespread globally the problem of youth crime and delinquency can only increase.

Why do some youths participate in gang delinquency? On the one hand, gang membership is a self-selected phenomenon, in that criminally oriented individuals (youths oriented to violence, drugs, and general disruptive behaviors) are attracted to gangs, and the behavior of the collective simply reflects the criminal predispositions of its members—a kind of "birds of a feather flock together" explanation. On the other hand, the behavior of gang members is a reflection of a group dynamic emanating from the mutual support and stimulus of gang membership itself—a kind of "herd behavior" explanation. Sorting out which, if either, of these two ideas explains the behavior of delinquent gang members across the globe is, as yet, beyond the capacity of criminological research. Undoubtedly to some extent the gang is attractive to delinquency-prone individuals, and participating in gang-life both promotes and provides social-psychological support for engaging in delinquent acts, resulting in extensive, often very violent and widespread acts of criminality. In this regard, the delinquent gang, already a problem in many parts of the world, is likely to pose a serious law enforcement challenge in countries throughout the world as societies modernize, population migrations intensify, and large numbers of youth from societies across the globe feel excluded and marginalized. As Covey notes, "Cultural, economic, ethnic, racial, language and other forms of prejudice and discrimination fuel much of what is observed in the formation and continuation of street gangs. The world is most certainly marginalizing large populations of youth that when faced with overwhelming odds for success or survival may turn to street gangs for remedies. This is occurring in several countries in Africa, South America, and for that matter, most of the remainder of the world" (2003, 222).

Violence

Regardless of how or where it is measured, violent conduct, especially serious aggression, is among the least frequent form of misconduct youths and adults engage in. Comparatively few juveniles admit to such conduct on self-report surveys, and arrest and official processing rates for violent delinquent acts are typically among the lowest in any society's crime rates. Yet violent acts by juveniles—especially extreme or bizarre forms of such behavior—engender considerable public, law enforcement, and particularly media attention almost everywhere. Killings by juveniles, particularly by very young individuals, become major media events that can lead to outcries by politicians and members of the public to crack down on school violence or other concerns. For example, as reported by the BBC (2004), "There has been considerable hand-wringing in Japan over youth crime, ever since a shocking incident in 1997 in which a 14-year-old boy killed an 11-year-old and placed his severed head outside the gates of his school. That prompted the country's parliament to lower the age of criminal responsibility from 16 to 14." In Europe, public perceptions of rapidly increasing juvenile violence have led to more punitive responses by officials and calls for fundamental reforms in juvenile justice across the continent. However, according to an analysis of the situation in Sweden, Estrada (2001) questions whether these public/political concerns are more a reflection of media attention and reporting than actual increases in the levels or seriousness of violence by juveniles. Similarly, a study of the rise in violent crime arrests for girls in the United States concluded that "the rise in girls' arrests for violent crime and the narrowing gender gap have less to do with underlying behavior and more to do, first, with net-widening changes in law and policing toward prosecuting less serious forms of violence . . . and, second, with less biased or more efficient responses to girls' physical or verbal aggression on the part of law enforcement, parents, teachers, and social workers" (Steffensmeier et al. 2005:387, 390).

Although relatively rare, is violence on the part of young people normal? Do youths everywhere engage in violent acts of various kinds and to a similar extent? On the other hand, are violent youths somehow abnormal in any population? A quite different issue concerns the epidemiology of such behavior. That is, are the youth of some societies more prone to violence than others? And, are the underlying causes of violent behavior universal or culturally idiosyncratic?

In contrast to the media and public concern with the violence of young people, questions such as these have received scant criminological attention. Crime rate data may show differences in homicide or other violent crime rates from society to society, or over time, but from a global perspective there is little information on the extent and nature of violent misconduct among young people around the world. For many places there is no information of any kind whatsoever.

Normal Violence

Scientific information and that produced by the media and various organizations regarding violent criminality and its global dimensions is suggestive of certain patterns (cf. Heitmeyer and Hagan 2003; Hérault and Adesanmi 1997). Self-report research, for example, consistently shows that violence of every kind is much more common among boys than girls. This research also shows that relatively mild forms of violence (e.g., hitting, fistfighting, school bullying, and verbal assaults) appear to be fairly common and universal. In this regard, mild violence is probably normal among the world's juvenile populations.

On the other hand, research on youths apprehended for committing very serious acts of violence suggest that this conduct is not only statistically abnormal but also the product of underlying personality or psychobiological abnormalities (Andrews and Bonta 2003). In this regard, abnormal violence everywhere is probably the product of abnormal youths, and such individuals may be found in any social environment.

As with most other forms of delinquent conduct, violent acts, although comparatively rare, are not uncommon among young people, especially males, worldwide. Some youths are apparently more violent or prone to using physical force than others. Research indicates that some categories of youths (typically from economically deprived environments) tend to be more frequently engaged in violence than others, and violence that causes death and personal injury is more common among these youths. Extreme or bizarre acts of violence rarely occur in any society. In short, youthful violence exhibits global similarities and variations. What remains to be systematically explored by criminology is why such similarities and variations exist.

Explaining Violent Behavior

In an effort to gain a better understanding of the relationship between youthful violence and the social and cultural settings in which it takes place, Rashid (2000) suggests that four theoretical approaches have been taken: psychological, sociological, anthropological, and historical. These different approaches may help explain different aspects of youthful violent behavior rather than its etiology.

Psychological theories may help explain why some youths engage in violent acts while others do not. Or, they may be useful in understanding why some youths are more violent or more frequently violent than others. Indeed, a number of studies from diverse societies suggest that chronically violent youths, or youths who engage in extreme and bizarre acts of violence, may suffer from various psychological maladies or exhibit unusual psychological profiles (Osuna et al. 1992a, 1992b; Sutherland and Shepherd 2002).

Epidemiological research on patterns of violent behavior routinely shows that violent acts are not randomly distributed among the juvenile population of any society. Instead, while violence is found among youth of all groups in all societies, frequent and serious violent behavior appears to be more common among economically deprived youths of any society. Studies that link violent behavior to social structural factors, especially economic disadvantage and deprivation or ethnic and racial discrimination, report similar findings from diverse societies. For example, in a study of the unprecedented rise in violent crime, especially among young males, that has taken place in Britain since 1987, Oliver James argues that "there is substantial evidence that the greater the degree of inequality in a society, the more violent it is. Thus [i]nequality is held to be a direct, immediate cause of violent behavior in young men of low income as well as affecting them indirectly through the parenting they receive" (1995, 1). Similarly, a study of delinquency and juvenile violence in Jos, Nigeria, attributes such conduct to social structural conditions centering on poverty, political instability, and the general sense of lawlessness that pervades the environment of an urban center chafing from religious conflicts and border disturbances. As Smah concluded, "The social environment in which children are brought up is visibly violent. This is one explanation for the growing trend in juvenile delinquency and the explosive nature of violence among youths" (1997, 46).

Findings from this kind of inquiry may be more appropriate in explaining the epidemiological distribution, as opposed to the etiology, of violent acts. This research does suggest that, at least as far as its relative occurrence is concerned, violence is not simply a reflection of individual pathology or psychological abnormality. Instead, although universal, like other forms of criminality, violent behavior is universally relative as well.

The concept of "culture of violence" was formulated by Gastil (1971) in an early effort to explain why rates of violent behavior in the U.S. South were comparatively consistently higher than for other regions of that country (also see Inciardi and Pottieger 1978). The idea that a general cultural orientation toward violence may help explain what criminological data and media information suggest: some societies are considerably more violent than others. The United States, for instance, routinely has the highest rates of homicide and other forms of violence among youths and adults than any other country in the Western developed world. South Africa, Russia, Lithuania, Estonia, and Latvia are among the top five.

Regardless of economic situation, are some countries, societies, or people more violence prone than others? Is the use of violence—either as a way to solve problems, express status, or mark life transitions—culturally sanctioned and variable? If so, some acts of violence may be the result of individual pathology or deprived social position in all societies, but an orientation to engage in violence, or certain types of violence, may have more to do with the culture than the individual. Criminological research investigating this possibility on a global scale is practically nonexistent, although some information suggests that more extensive investigation of the cultural underpinnings of violent behavior may be worth exploring (cf. Scheper-Hughes and Bourgois 2004; Schmidt and Schröder 2001).

Another approach to understanding violent behavior and criminality in general that has also been largely ignored by contemporary criminology is the historical context in which such activity takes place. Historical factors may be critical for making sense of both the commission of violent acts, particularly with regard to youthful violence, and the objects toward which such behavior is directed. Little criminological research can be found in this regard, but such inquiry could throw light on interethnic violence in various countries, such as in Northern Ireland, Palestine, and former Yugoslavia. Moreover, historical circumstances may provide the context wherein youths are schooled in weaponry, aggression is held up as a positive virtue, or there is an overall climate of violence, all of which foster expressions of violence, either on an individual pathological base or as a group expression of political will.

Drugs

One of the greatest fears of parents is to discover a cache of marijuana, pills, or some other controlled substance stashed away in their son's or daughter's room. Of all the forms of youthful criminality, the problem of drug abuse appears to have become one of global proportions.

The Youth Drug Problem

Drugs are probably the prototypical international social problem. In part, this is because of the global distribution network for illicit substances. Most substances, especially opium derivatives, are produced in a handful of countries but are distributed illicitly across the globe. In addition, even though prevalence and usage patterns vary, illicit substances are consumed around the world. Few, if any, societies are totally drug free. And, wherever they are distributed and consumed, drugs are associated with criminality, exploitation, and human misery.

How widespread the phenomenon might be is anyone's guess, but concern over drug use by teenagers and other youth remains a constant of the modern world. Self-report and official statistics suggest that, in contrast to the widespread concern over adolescent drug use, the actual prevalence rates for such activity are globally quite low relative to other forms of delinquency, although they do vary from country to country. International research by Killias and Ribeaud (1999), for example, found significant differences in lifetime prevalence rates of hard drug use among fourteen- to twenty-one-year-olds in four countries (N. Ireland = 14 percent; USA = 11 percent; Switzerland = 3 percent; Netherlands = 2 percent). Moreover the average age at which youths first use hard drugs also varies among the four countries (USA = 14.7; N. Ireland = 16.4; Switzerland = 17.3; Netherlands = 18).

The World Drug Report (UNODC 2005) provides estimates of global drug use prevalence rates for persons age fifteen to sixty-four. According to this report, less than 4 percent of the world's population have used cannabis and less than 1 percent have used any other form of controlled substance. Given that young juveniles tend to exhibit much lower usage rates than do older adolescents and young adults, globally the drug problem for juveniles is, comparatively, hardly a problem at all. Table 4.2, for example, depicts the United Nations' estimates of lifetime prevalence rates of substance abuse by youths in countries throughout the world. Since the data on which this table is based were obtained from samples that are not matched, used different methodologies, and were conducted at different times, the prevalence rates presented are meant to be illustrative only and should not be interpreted as statistically comparable. The two most striking features of the numbers reported here are (1) their similarity in pattern, if not absolute magnitude, and (2) the extreme differences in percentages for so-called soft drugs (mainly cannabis) compared to hard drugs (mainly opiates).

The results are similar in official arrest and processing data. A study in Oslo, Norway, for example, found that a disproportionately small number of individuals below age twenty-one were formally charged with drug offenses and that, contrary to common sentiment, even though the overall number of persons charged had increased between the mid-1970s and mid-1980s, for persons below age twenty-one the number remained very stable (Hauge 1987).

TABLE 4.2

Estimated Number of Illicit Drug Users, Globally, 2003–4

	All illicit drugs	Cannabis	Amphet- amines	Ecstasy	Cocaine	Opiates	Heroin
All ages (millions)	200	160.9	26.2	7.9	13.7	15.9	10.6
Age 15–64 (% of global population)	5.0	4.0	0.6	0.2	0.3	0.4	0.3

Source: Based on UNODC 2005, 5.

As indicated in table 4.3, globally the youth drug problem consists primarily of marijuana use with limited involvement in synthetic or hard drug use. Although, as also indicated by the notes presented in this table, involvement with drugs of one kind is by no means uniform among young people across the world's societies.

The potential and actual harm that drug abuse and addiction can cause are legitimate reasons for concern. While some countries exhibit an apparent tolerance for at least some kinds of substance use, criminal penalties for drug possession and sale are among the harshest on the law books of many countries. Against whom and how often such penalties are actually imposed is, of course,

TABLE 4.3
Lifetime Substance Abuse Prevalence Rate by Youths in Various Countries

Country, sample ages, year	Cannabis	Ecstasy	Inhalants	Heroin
Unweighted country average	13.5	2.6	7.7	1.0
Austria, 13–18, 1994	8.7	3.2		
Australia, 12–17, 1996	36.4	3.6	25.5	1.4
Belgium, 15–16, 1996	18.9	6.0	3.6	1.1
Bolivia, 12–24, 1996	3.6		9.9	
Brazil, 10–19, 1997	7.6		13.8	
Canada, 15–24, 1994	33.6		1.4	
Chile, 12–18, 1995	22.7		3.4	0.5
Colombia, 12–24, 1996	4.6		5.9	0.1
Croatia, 15–16, 1995	9.0	2.5	13.5	0.9
Cyprus, 15–16, 1995	5.0	1.5	2.0	
Czech Republic, 15–16, 1995	21.5		7.5	0.6
Denmark, 15–16, 1995	28.0	0.5	7.0	2.0
Dominican Republic, 12–24, 1992	1.8		3.6	
Estonia, 15–16, 1995	7.5		7.5	
Finland, 15–16, 1995	5.2	0.2	4.2	0.1
France, 15–16, 1993	11.6		5.5	0.8
Germany, 18–24, 1995	21.2	5.1	1.7	1.0
Greece, 15–16, 1993			6.3	2.0
Hong Kong, 12–16, 1992	0.7		0.4	0.4

TABLE 4.3

(Continued)

Country, sample ages, year	Cannabis	Ecstasy	Inhalants	Heroin
Hungary, 15–16, 1995	4.8	0.8	5.3	0.5
Iceland, 15–16, 1995	10.0	1.5	8.0	
Ireland, 15–16, 1995	37.0	9.0		2.0
Italy, 15–16, 1995	18.5	4.0	7.5	2.0
Kenya, 12–18, 1993	12.0		19.0	
Lithuania, 15–16, 1995	1.5		16.0	
Luxembourg, 15–16, 1995	6.0	0.9	2.6	
Malta, 15–16, 1995	8.5	1.5	17.8	
Mexico, 12–25, 1993	2.8		0.6	
Netherlands, 10–17, 1990	20.9	5.6	3.2	1.1
New Zealand, 15–24, 1990		1.4	1.8	0.3
Norway, 15–20, 1996	12.3	1.17	6.3	0.6
Panama, 12–24, 1991	2.2		3.2	
Peru, 12–19, 1995	1.7		3.0	
Poland, 15–18, 1995	12.2	0.5	9.6	0.7
Portugal, 15–20, 1995	8.5	0.5	3.3	1.3
Slovakia, 15–29, 1996	15.7	0.3	6.1	1.9
Slovenia, 15–16, 1995	13.0	1.5		
Spain, 14–18, 1996	26.0	5.1	3.3	0.6
Suriname, 12–18, 1995	5.0	0.4		
Swaziland, 15–24, 1997	9.9	0.3	11.8	0.7
Sweden, 15–16, 1997	6.8	0.8	8.7	0.5
Ukraine, 15–16, 1995	14.5		5.5	
United Kingdom, 15–16, 1995	37.0	8.3	20.0	2.0
United States, 13–17, 1996	35.9	3.1	19.0	1.2
Zimbabwe, 12–18, 1994	6.0		12.0	

Source: Based on UNODC 2005, fig. 1, p. 7; fig. 2, p. 10;
fig. 4, p. 13; fig. 5, p. 14.

quite another issue. In the United States, for example, street-level dealers in crack cocaine make up a healthy portion of the offenders incarcerated in federal and state prisons, even though they and the drug they deal in are by no means the only, or necessarily the most significant, segment of the drug problem in that country. Although juveniles most frequently use soft drugs, the potential for serious hard-drug use remains an ever-present concern (Goulden and Sondhi 2001; Hamersley et al. 1999; Harrison et al. 2001; Pape and Rossow 2004).

Becoming a User

No juvenile anywhere wakes up one morning saying to his- or herself, "I'm going to go out and get me some drugs to see what it's like." Or, "Being a junkie looks cool, I think I'll try it." Probably even more than any other form of crime or delinquency, becoming a drug user is a process that involves association with other individuals—and not simply a conniving dealer who cons some innocent into just trying it once in order to get yet another sucker hooked on dope. Study after study indicates that juveniles who experiment with drugs do so in association with peers who are similarly involved. A drug-using youth anywhere may have nonusing friends and associates, but he or she certainly has some who are also users. The same need not necessarily be true about youths who don't use and never have been involved in drugs.

Therefore, if peer-use and individual-use are coincident when it comes to drugs, the fundamental question to answer in understanding this behavior and its differential distribution among youths across the globe is this: Are the peer-relationship processes involved in becoming a drug user universally the same, or are they culturally, structurally, economically variable? If they are the same universally, then criminologists can identify a common etiology to the problem, and strategies to deal with it can be applied across the globe. If varied, the problem (if any) of adolescent drug use would have to be handled on a nation-by-nation basis, with little cross-national enlightenment to be gained from successful programs found in other societies. The first step is to determine the universal or varied processes involved in becoming a drug user.

In spite of the literal mountain of research and speculation on drug abuse, treatment, and addiction patterns, an answer to that question is, at present, impossible to come by. We simply know too little about how young people, much less young people in diverse social-cultural settings, become involved with drugs, including alcohol and tobacco. Users may have had predispositions or various propensities to experiment with drugs and/or become addicted to them. Youthful curiosity and experimentation may also lead some to experiment, with some winding up addicted. Some researchers suggest that some forms of drug use are best understood as expressions of a youth culture identity. For example, in one conference addressing this question, scholars from a number of countries discussed the association between youth cultures and drinking and drug use. The theme of the conference was based on the premise that "as a largely social behavior, drinking together is often an expression of collective solidarity. Drug use is also frequently a collective cultural activity. Beyond this, the fact of alcohol or drug use (or non-use) and the behavior associated with it is often a marker of identity and membership in a social world" (Room and Sato 2002, 6). Most important of the insights gained from the presentations published from this conference is the possibility that there are differences and similarities in the alcohol- and drug-using behavior of youths in societies across the world, and this may be true of other drug use as well. As Room and Sato observe:

> There are some clear differences between youth cultures in one country and another. But there also seem to be some striking similarities—to some extent simply reflecting international diffusion processes of youth-oriented mass media. . . . As a field of forbidden and potentially dangerous behavior, in country after country illicit-drug use takes on a range of important symbolic meanings for youth, so that most young persons, wherever they are in the industrialized world, find themselves at some time in their adolescence or young adulthood defining themselves in terms of which drugs and modes of administration they will experiment with and which they will not. (2001, 9)

In this regard, it should be no surprise that at some point in their adolescence young people will experiment with substances of one or another kind. Whether or not they will go beyond experimentation to become regular or heavy users of such substances, of course, is quite a different issue.

Research from diverse countries suggests that a fairly common profile may fit heavy or regular users. The prime factors seem to be backgrounds of family trouble, school failure, and association with siblings and others peers who are also drug involved. But, the causal direction is unclear. That is, whether these background characteristics cause drug use or are a function of drug involvement itself.

Regardless of locality, study after study of regular users produces similar findings. In Norway, for example, based on a general population study of young people, Pape and Rossow (2004:389) observe that "ecstasy users, cannabis users, and users of 'traditional' hard drugs were all relatively unremarkable with respect to socio-economic characteristics. On the other hand, they all tended to have a less favorable family background than nonusers of drugs, and their rates of past and present legal substance use, mental health problems, and antisocial behavior were also much higher." Similarly, in a study of street youths in Canada, Baron (1999) found that backgrounds conducive to drug use were common to homeless youths and that being on the street exacerbated their risk of drug and alcohol use. A lifestyles survey of vulnerable young people in the United Kingdom (Goulden and Sondhi 2001) found that young people with certain characteristics had higher levels of use of a range of drug types. These characteristics included being school truants or excluded from school, exhibiting prior criminal behavior, being homeless, having runaway from home, and having another drug user in the family.

In societies where alcohol is not readily available and its consumption is culturally frowned upon, young people are both relatively unable to obtain or likely to even think of experimenting with drinking. In societies where liquor is readily available (even if illegal for minors), it would indeed be the deviant youth who refrains from even trying it. Therefore, one might look to the cultural environment in which young people are situated, rather than just the individual juveniles themselves, to understand both the patterns and extent of substance-using behavior, and also why young people are involved in such activity at all (Ruchkin et al. 2002).

To what extent poor school performance, dropping out of school, running away from home, committing crimes, associating with drug-using peers, or other such characteristics cause or are products of drug use remains a matter of debate. As Baron (1999) found, different factors seem to be associated with different types of drug-using behavior. Youths in any society who become heavily involved in substance abuse behavior may suffer from a variety of adverse experiences and background characteristics. The association among these factors and their behavior, however, appears to be quite complex.

Drugs and Other Delinquency

It is generally believed that besides being illegal, drug and alcohol use in most instances directly leads to other criminality (e.g., to sustain a habit) or contributes to criminality (e.g., vehicular homicide, fighting, sexual assault, etc.) due to the physiological effects of the substances used. Research has found that users of drugs and alcohol tend to have higher offense involvement rates, and drug or alcohol use seems to be involved in many reported crimes.

However, in spite of the large volume of research addressing the substance-crime association, the causal relationship between these two has yet to be empirically established. A study by Otero-Lopez et al. (1994) of the drug-delinquency relationship in Spain suggests three possibilities: (1) drug abuse causes delinquency; (2) delinquency causes drug abuse; or (3) other variables influence both drug abuse and delinquent behavior and the apparent association between them.

First, delinquent behavior could result from the need to commit crimes to obtain drugs, and/or being involved in the world of drugs puts users in situations conducive to the commission of other forms of delinquency. Second, it has been argued that drug usage is simply another form of delinquency engaged in by those already involved in or inclined to be offenders. Being associated with delinquents increases the probability that one would also use drugs. Third, as a form of delinquency, drug abuse is caused by the very forces that produce other forms of delinquency, and any apparent causal connection between the two is coincidental.

In an attempt to grapple with the drug problem in the United States, Boyoum (1996, i) notes that "it is not clear how much of the violence surrounding the drug-trade is attributable to the business itself, as opposed to the character of the individuals involved in it, or the economic, political, social, or cultural conditions of their communities." In addition:

> The relationship between heavy drug use and criminality is also complicated. To be sure, some drug users commit crimes to get drug money, and drug use causes some individuals to commit crimes. But there are other possible explanations for the observed link between drug use and crime. Additional factors, like deviance and delinquency, may cause both drug abuse and crime. Or there could be the paycheck effect: just as some heavy drinkers splurge at their local bar on payday, drug-involved offenders may buy drugs because crime gives them the money to do so. In other words, crime may cause drug abuse.

These are more than academic issues. If drugs cause delinquency, combating drug abuse would be a priority in reducing offense behavior generally. If being associated with drug-using delinquent peers leads offenders into drug abuse, fighting drug use would require strategies such as preventing youths from joining gangs and cliques. And the focus of antidrug/crime efforts would be quite different if both offense forms—criminality and drug use—are a product of family, peer, personality, or other factors. In their study, Otero-Lopez et al. (1994, 474) concluded that "drug abuse and delinquency can be included in a single syndrome in which a single set of major causes is responsible for both aspects." They suggest that "institutional action against drug abuse and delinquency should not only be directed at the individual, but also at supra-individual environmental factors."

A similar conclusion regarding delinquent offending generally was reached in a British Home Office study. This report suggests that, as an alternative to law enforcement alone, officials should "identify the strongest influence on offending and reoffending during the transition to adulthood in the context of an individual's personal and social development and develop policies which encourage natural processes of desistance and discourage criminogenic influences" (Graham and Bowling 1995, 83). A more recent British Home Office study of substance abuse by young offenders also concluded the following:

> Even in this selected cohort, that was highly criminal and included extensive users of drugs, two types of risk factors predicted the extent of both substance use and offending. First, low affiliation with school and, second, having had more traumatic life events in the last two years along

with a lack of positive coping mechanism. In other words, young people who are not flourishing at school and who have had stressful things happen to them offend and take drugs more. This implies a need to teach young offenders—as well as other young people—positive coping mechanisms, including mechanisms for dealing with past events and overcoming trauma. (Hamersley et al. 2003, 67)

Cross-national or comparative research may not only help resolve questions regarding the drug-delinquency connection, but also cast light on the possible impact that different approaches to dealing with drug-using youth may have on their criminal activities (e.g., Bruno 1984). One such study was conducted by Killias and Ribeaud (1999) using data on self-reported delinquency and drug use among youths in twelve European countries. As with other research, this cross-sectional data from the self-report surveys does support the view that, regardless of country, drug use has an important impact on property crime and drug trafficking. Very simply, drug users are more involved with property crimes and drug selling than are nonusers, and heavy users are even more involved. In short, just about anywhere the link between drug use and at least some forms of crime is strong.

Importantly, this study also revealed that the strength of the link between drugs and crime was not universally the same. For example, considerable variation exists across countries in the percentage of users of hard drugs who also report trafficking in drugs (e.g., Switzerland = 61 percent versus Spain = 41 percent) or other forms of criminality. The question is "Why the differences?" Killias and Ribeaud (1999, 200) speculate that "countries differ substantially with respect to the extent to which addicts finance their habit through the resale of drugs. There are no obvious factors explaining this, but the price addicts usually have to pay for drugs may be important together with their access to other incomes (including welfare benefits) and alternative illegitimate incomes (such as crime)."

Also significantly, this study reports that there is no correlation between the intensity of police control and the extent of drug use among a country's youth. A comparison of the drug scenes in Amsterdam and Frankfurt also demonstrated considerable similarities despite profound differences in drug policy and control efforts in the two countries (Kemmesies 1995).

On the other hand, approaches other than law enforcement may reduce the drug-caused criminality of users. The results of their study of the heroin prescription project launched in Switzerland led Killias and Ribeaud (1999) to conclude that addiction to hard drugs leads to substantial involvement in property crimes of all kinds. And programs such as the Swiss heroin prescription experiment promise to considerably reduce the program participants' property-crime and drug-trafficking behavior (up to 83 percent). The alternative approach, adapted in the United States and elsewhere, of large-scale incarceration of drug dealers/users may also reduce the criminal involvement of incarcerated addicts, but at tremendous economic, social, and moral costs.

Conclusion

The limited analyses of the three forms of delinquent conduct presented here cannot come close to answering the kinds of questions raised in this chapter. Although criminology cannot yet provide answers, some tentative conclusions can be drawn regarding the global similarities and differences in the delinquent conduct of the world's youth.

The main issue of concern here is whether, or to what extent, the delinquent behavior (as opposed to overall rates) of youths in one country is similar to or different from that of youths in any other. Whether delinquent conduct is universal in its forms and nature or culturally—socially, economically—relative has profound implications for explaining such behavior and for dealing with it as law-enforcement or social-problems issues. As illustrated by research on gangs, violence, and drugs, it appears that both are true. That is, the forms and character of delinquent activities are universal, but they are also culturally varied. Gangs, violence, and drug abuse appear to be common among youth worldwide. Some countries may be more or less free of one or another of these problems, while others may be plagued with serious issues across the board. However, it appears that similar forms of delinquency, with similar behavior and causative characteristics, exist in societies of quite diverse characteristics. There is probably a universal explanation to delinquent behavior, and ways of combating delinquency may, in fact, be based on similar approaches across the globe. What these approaches might be, however, remains a controversial, unresolved question.

Equally important is the observation that, while found universally, youths in different societies vary in the extent and nature of the forms of delinquent behavior they commit. Even if delinquent gangs are universal, they do not appear to be universally identical. Children everywhere engage in some violence, but to what extent, against whom, and in what form are not the same across the globe. The drug scene may become indistinguishable from place to place as the world globalizes, but different substances and different settings for such behavior are still noticeable across societies. Understanding how cultural variations influence differences in the behavior of the world's youth is difficult and little researched by any field of study. Such inquiry can not only enhance our theoretical understanding of delinquent forms of behavior generally, but also help shape public policy in dealing with wayward youth. Much remains to be learned in both respects.

5

Justice for Juveniles

With the creation of the first fully recognized separate system of justice for juveniles in Cook County, Illinois, at the turn of the twentieth century in the United States, what many saw as a revolution took place in how juveniles accused of misconduct were treated (Bartollas 1996; Bensinger 1991; Platt 1969; Sussman 1959). The legislation that established this first juvenile court clearly articulated that the main purpose of juvenile justice was the welfare, not the punishment, of young offenders. To do this it stipulated an entirely separate judicial/correctional system specifically designed to address the needs, as opposed to behavior, of young people. The creation of this court gave substance to the fundamental issue of juvenile justice that has yet to be fully resolved— that is, to what extent can the state exercise judicial authority to protect or punish children who offend or are in danger of doing so.

The ideals reflected in the Illinois legislation spread throughout jurisdictions within the United States and were soon emulated by countries across Western Europe and elsewhere (Doob and Tonry 2004; Hendrick 2006). However, in spite of the laudatory goals of this new "best interests of the child" approach to dealing with young offenders, the informal, welfare model of juvenile justice created at that time soon came under attack from virtually all sides. In the United States, by the mid-1950s for example, significant changes began to emerge in how juvenile justice was to be practiced so that contemporary American juvenile courts and correctional practices now often have little resemblance to the ideals envisioned by its founders. Other countries have similarly modified or radically changed their juvenile justice systems.

However, the central issue remains: What is the best way to pursue justice and corrections for juvenile offenders or those likely to become offenders? That problem has by no means been confined to North America. Over the past quarter of a century, countries around the globe have attempted to grapple with the problem. So far, no universally satisfactory specific model has been found. As a result, as with laws and patterns of offense behavior, there is a multiplicity of approaches to juvenile justice around the world.

General Approaches

Some countries appear to have no identifiable system specifically devoted to handling children or young people who break the law. For these countries, no provisions exist in law or procedure to distinguish juveniles from adults, and no identifiable differences in penal sanction based on age exist for those found to be guilty of crimes. Although children and young people may be treated somewhat differently from adults, there exists no legal compulsion for authorities to do so. Given the absence of any kind of research on the handling of children accused of crimes in most of these societies, there is no basis on which to assume children and youths are in any way differentiated from adults in legal proceedings or penalties. These societies tend to be in the same regions (e.g., Middle Eastern, Sub-Saharan Africa, and many Asian countries) about which criminologists know the least regarding anything related to crime and justice.

In many other countries no separate judicial correctional system exists in law or practice for the processing and correction of juvenile offenders. However, in these societies provisions may be made in law for the separate judicial processing and correctional treatment of young offenders within the general judicial system. In these countries, cases that involve juveniles may be heard in the same building and by the same judges who hear adult cases, but the juvenile proceedings may be modified or physically separated or distanced from the adult proceedings. Under law, the penalties for adult and juvenile offenders may be the same, but the severity of these penalties may be lessened in the case of a young person convicted of a crime. In addition, youths may be housed in the same confinement as adults, although separately. These countries may take into consideration the age and vulnerability of young people accused of crimes, but not officially.

Other countries—particularly North America, Western Europe, and nations influenced by them—have created distinctly separate judicial and correctional machinery to deal with young people. This machinery may be totally separate, such that juvenile courts have their own judiciary, proceedings take place in facilities apart from other courts, and the places and people who deal with young offenders are distinct from those designated for adults. In other places, juvenile justice and corrections may be subsumed under a larger authority responsible also for adults, but for all intents and purposes the two are distinctly separate.

Whether the juvenile justice system is subsumed under or distinctly separated from adult jurisdiction, the significant idea is that young people are to be treated as a special class of people. The issue these societies still face, however, is "How different?" This question has produced a number of distinct models of juvenile justice around the world.

Models of Juvenile Justice

Researchers have defined six juvenile justice models in countries with an identifiable distinction between the judicial/correctional treatment of adults and juveniles (see Corrado 1992; Muncie 1999; Reichel 2005a; Winterdyk 1997a). Few countries adhere to the precise characteristics of a particular model, although its dominant features may best describe how juveniles are treated within it. In some countries, such as the United States, Canada, and Australia, local authorities may depart markedly from a model used to characterize the country as a whole.

Although specific countries, or jurisdictions within countries, may follow practices that are unique, the six models depicted in table 5.1 can be distinguished from one another in terms of the emphasis they place on protecting versus punishing young offenders, informality versus formality in procedures, and the extent to which adversarial versus cooperative relationships among participants in the proceedings are emphasized. Keeping in mind these variations, one can identify three distinct orientations toward juvenile justice: welfare, legalistic, and corporate.

At one extreme, informal proceedings are carried out by educators and community members geared to the reeducation of young offenders perceived to be basically good but wayward. At the other extreme are systems that assume offenders are responsible individuals who can be held accountable, deserve punishment for their misdeeds, and should be accorded all the rights and procedures of due process available to adults. In between, a corporate, or administrative, model of justice has emerged in a number of countries that views young offenders as unsocialized individuals who need intervention. Following an administrative decision-making process, the offending conduct is to be corrected through the cooperation of legal, welfare, and various specialists.

Juvenile Justice as Welfare

In its pure form the welfare approach to juvenile justice rests on four fundamental principles: the concept of *doli incapax,* determinism, informality of proceedings, and, most important, a concern for the best interests of the child (Muncie 1999).

Doli incapax is the common-law principle that presumes a child below a designated age is incapable of forming mens rea and therefore cannot be held culpable of a crime. Although this age can vary from society to society and can change over time, the underlying principle remains the same: children and adolescents lack the ability to reason as adults and therefore cannot be subjected to the full weight of criminal processing and punishment.

In addition, a welfare approach, rather than seeing punishment as the goal of judicial action, pursues the rehabilitation of the offender based on the principles of deterministic or scientific criminology. Criminal and status offense behavior, as well as dependency and neglect, are viewed as symptomatic of some deeper malady or situation that is out of the juvenile's control. Moreover, the underlying disorder or child's needs can be identified and rectified through purposive activities oriented to intervening in the best interests of the child.

Formal judicial proceedings followed in adult criminal courts not only impede identifying and delivering needed interventions, but also cause further trauma and damage to the youth. Informal extrajudicial proceedings—but proceedings that carry the force of law to compel compliance with intervention activities—are deemed necessary. Wide discretion is also essential. Since proceedings are not considered to be criminal proceedings, due process rights and other trappings of formal criminal justice are dispensed with.

Although due consideration is given to protecting the public and the rights of parents, the overriding concern is always the best interests of the child. The central concern is not what the child has done but what that child needs to lead a crime-free, productive adult life.

In practice, no jurisdiction strictly adheres to these four principles, at least not in all cases. To some extent, societies practicing forms of juvenile justice at odds with a welfare approach goal of the best interests of the child take age, and therefore the assumed lessened capabilities of young people, into consideration in deciding how the child is treated and how his or her case is disposed. Some countries are clearly exemplifiers of a welfare model as a foundation for dealing with wayward youth in law and/or in practice.

One such country is Germany. Although now probably more closely reflecting a justice model country, at least since the end of the nineteenth century, the prevailing idea behind justice for juveniles in Germany has been that "both punishment and education should be reconciled within the framework of juvenile justice" (Albrecht 1997, 2004; Wolfe 1996). While the youth court law is a subsystem within the larger criminal justice system, German juvenile justice has been characterized by the resocialization of youth through welfare intervention. Indeed, even youths age eighteen to twenty who are considered legally responsible adults can be treated as juveniles and sentenced under the youth court law if it is deemed to be in their best interests.

In Australia, children's courts are separate from adult criminal courts, but they have traditionally departed minimally from their adult counterparts. However, even today, with a general move toward a legalistic approach to juvenile offenders, Australia remains an exemplar of welfarism in the way it treats young offenders. Especially in some Australian states, a variety of diversion strategies

TABLE 5.1.

Models of Juvenile Justice

	Participatory	Welfare	Corporatism	Modified justice	Justice	Crime control
General Features	Informality Minimal formal intervention Resocialization	Informality Generic referrals Individualized sentencing Indeterminate sentencing	Administrative decision making Offending Diversion	Due process Informality Criminal offences Bifurcation	Due process Criminal offenses Least restrictive Alternative Determinate sentencing	Due process/discretion Offending/status offenses Punishment Determinate sentencing
Key personnel	Educators	Childcare experts	Juvenile justice specialists	Lawyers Childcare experts	Lawyers	Lawyers Criminal justice actors
Key agency	Community agency School Citizens	Social work	Intragency structure	Law Social work	Law	Law
Tasks	Help and education team	Diagnosis	System intervention	Diagnosis Punishment	Punishment	Incarceration Punishment

	People basically good	Pathology Environmentally determined	Unsocialized	Diminished individual responsibility	Individual responsibility	Responsibility Accountability
Understanding of client behavior						
Purpose of intervention	Reeducation	Provide treatment (*parens patriae*)	Retrain	Sanction behavior Provide treatment	Sanction behavior	Protection of society Retribution deterrence
Objectives	Intervention through education	Respond to individual needs Rehabilitation	Implementation of policy	Respect individual rights Respond to special needs	Respect individual rights Punish	Order maintenance
Implemented	Japan	Australia New Zealand	England/Wales Hong Kong	Canada	Italy The Netherlands Russia	United States Hungary

Source: Winterdyk 1997a, xi–xii.

Note: Specific countries may have modified their systems since this table was originally constructed.

and community programs have been implemented to keep offending youths from judicial processing and punitive disposition. Most notable of these are juvenile aid, suspended action, and community justice panels. In addition, innovations such as family group conferencing, police cautions, and juvenile justice teams have been put into place to soften the punitiveness of, or offer alternatives to, formal judicial processing (Reichel 2005a).

In bypassing formal judicial procedures, New Zealand has gone even further. According to Reichel (2005a), New Zealand's orientation toward juvenile justice stresses the well-being of children and the empowerment of families and young people. An important aspect of this approach is the use of restorative justice principles. New Zealand's system appears to be more concerned with restoring the community balance that was upset by the offender's actions, as opposed to treating the needs of the offender that led to the offense in the first place. This, in some ways, departs from a traditional rehabilitative approach that has characterized welfare juvenile justice throughout the Western world. However, it is the informal, conflict-resolution approach using victim-offender mediation techniques aimed at achieving the best interests of all that renders New Zealand an example of a welfare model of justice.

On the surface, casual observation of the proceeding in a French juvenile court would lead one to assume that juvenile justice in France is highly inquisitorial and harsh, and not appropriate for treating young offenders. Hackler's (1991a) observations (and those of this author) of how the French treat wayward youths clearly suggest it is an open secret welfare approach (see Blatier 1999). When youths have actually made it to the juvenile court in France, having somehow bypassed the myriad social service agencies at their disposal, the machinery of juvenile justice is, indeed, official and formal. Cases are brought to the attention of a *procureur,* who, like a prosecutor in the United States, represents the interests of the state. Young offenders are likely to appear before a *juge des enfants,* the French equivalent of a juvenile or children's court judge, and in complicated cases brought before a *juge d' instruction,* all of whom are magistrates under French law. The formal proceedings are indeed inquisitorial in character, at least to the eyes of anyone versed in adversarial law. But, outside the courtroom, where the real proceedings of importance take place, all the legal officials involved in the case clearly take on the role of social worker. The vast majority of cases never appear in court. They are handled in the office of the *juge des enfants* in an informal manner typically oriented to dealing with the needs and best interests of the child. Indeed, by even deciding to hear the case outside of court, the judge gives up his or her punitive power. "Instead of handing down a decision, the judge works out options, tries to persuade, and arranges for a variety of services" (Hackler 1991a). It is perhaps the orientation of French juvenile authorities, rather than the official mechanisms for processing young offenders, that epitomizes the essence of a welfare approach in juvenile justice.

Differing in organization and specifics, Germany, Australia, New Zealand, and even France reflect an orientation to dealing with young offenders that is neutering rather than punitive in purpose. However, some form of punitive sanction may be one result of official action. Avoiding that action and using it for corrective purposes, as opposed to social protection, is the overriding purpose of all.

Legalism and Due Process for Juveniles

In the United States and other countries, the founders of traditional welfare-oriented juvenile justice were adamant about decriminalizing young offenders while creating an authoritative mechanism to ensure that they, and other potentially delinquent children, would get the services they needed—whether they wanted them or not. Their ideals were encapsulated in a court that provided a model of an organization with the authority of law, but without the trappings of formality that characterized existing courts. The organization created was the juvenile court. As juvenile offenders were deemed not to be criminal offenders, and since the new court was not to be seen as a criminal court, although it was to have the courtlike enforcement powers necessary to implement its benevolent decisions, the due process rights enjoyed by adults facing trial in an adult criminal court were deemed irrelevant and inapplicable in the juvenile court. It was the needs, best interests, and rehabilitation of the juvenile that was of concern, not punishment for misdeeds. Legal truth, the nature of the offense, indeed even the harm it may have caused, were, if anything, secondary considerations.

Heralded as "one of the great social inventions of the nineteenth century" by the legal scholar Roscoe Pound (Hartjen 1977, 220), this organization came under attack almost from its very inception (Krisberg 2006; Muncie 1999). Some people oppose welfare and rehabilitative approaches because they view them as not being punitive enough. They believe that offenders, regardless of age, are responsible and therefore deserve to be punished for their misconduct. Anything short of that is unacceptable to them. On the other hand, some people have criticized welfare as being overly restrictive, widening the net of judicial control, and disguising control with the rhetoric of benevolent help. A third group of critics see the informality of a welfare model as running roughshod over the rights of children, and they feel that all offenders have a right to due process and legal protections.

Beginning in the 1950s the movement to "save the children" became the movement to "save children from their saviors." In the United States a series of Supreme Court decisions led to dramatic changes in and brought due process procedures to the juvenile court (Weinstein and Mendoza 1979). Later, England and Canada passed legislation designed to fundamentally alter the welfare approach they had been practicing for decades. Although few made the radical transformation in juvenile justice that the United States experienced in the last decades of the twentieth century, other countries also made changes in, or at least seriously considered, abandoning the "best interest of the child" approaches they had been practicing (Muncie and Goldson 2006).

As depicted in table 5.1, three legalistic approaches to juvenile justice characterize practices in several countries: modified justice, justice, and crime control. These are distinguishable largely in terms of their degree of punitiveness and concern with the unique circumstances of the individual offender.

Perhaps the most punitive approach and one that most closely adheres in formal proceeding to an adult model of judicial proceeding is the crime control model found in the United States—the very country that gave legal birth to a welfare model of juvenile justice nearly a century earlier (Bartollas 1996; Corrado and Turnbull 1992; Craig and Stafford 1997; Kratcoski and Kratcoski 1991). It is inappropriate to talk about an American system of juvenile justice, since each state has its own system and the federal government has recently begun to be involved with youthful offenders. However, the overall tone of juvenile justice in the United States currently leans toward an extreme crime control approach. Adhering to the procedural requirements mandated by Supreme Court decisions, in stark contrast to a welfare model, in legalistic systems proceedings involving juveniles accused of crimes, closely resemble adult criminal trials with an adversarial format, prosecuting attorney, defense representation, and trappings of judicial formality. Increasingly, judicial waiver of juveniles to adult criminal courts has been either mandated by law for certain offenses and/or offenders of specific ages or made easier by procedural modifications, as well as changes in judicial attitudes regarding the purpose of juvenile justice. In effect, in contemporary America a system of justice for juveniles that is procedurally and philosophically parallel to and intertwined with the adult criminal justice system has emerged. Juveniles who would have ordinarily been handled by the welfare court of bygone eras may still appear in the new juvenile court, although in many jurisdictions some kind of alternative is often available to deal with them (e.g., family court, diversion programs) so that the main work of the new U.S. juvenile court can concentrate on young criminals. To this end, some speculate about the possible demise of juvenile justice in the present century as a separate and distinct entity within the judicial system (Bazemore 1991; Bensinger 1991).

According to Herczog and Irk (1997), Hungary has vacillated since at least the mid-nineteenth century between a welfare and crime control approach in its treatment of juvenile offenders. In its quest to become a member of the Council of Europe and a full member of the European Union, Hungary has sought to move away from its crime control approach to juvenile justice. In its place it has sought to develop a system that is closer to a welfare model and thereby embraces the United Nations Beijing Rules that advocate such an approach as a universal model for countries to follow. However, just as a seeming increase in juvenile (especially violent) crime helped fuel the transformation of juvenile justice in the United States, increased delinquency in Hungary is among the reasons little actual change has taken place in that country. Indeed, it has led some to advocate lowering the age of responsibility from fourteen to twelve years to help combat the growing problem of juvenile delinquency.

Thus, Hungary still does not have a separate system of law for juvenile offenders. Instead, within the penal code special provisions that apply to juveniles of various ages are specified, largely relating to the severity of sanctions they may receive. The law defines a juvenile as someone between ages fourteen and eighteen. Such an individual, if found guilty of a crime, could be subjected to punishment or other legal measures, with the primary intent being the correction of the offender. For juveniles, a number of restrictions on the severity and nature of these punishments are mandated in the criminal code. For example, a juvenile's sentence must be served in a juvenile penitentiary; for juveniles who offend past age sixteen, the longest terms of confinement are fifteen or ten years, depending on the respective adult maximum sentence; and for those who offend before age sixteen the longest term possible is ten years, for crimes that would bring a life term for adults. Other modifications apply to various measures (e.g., probation) a convicted juvenile may receive. While a broad social safety net legally exists for young offenders in Hungary, and a corporatist network of agencies may be found to provide for juveniles, in practice the legal rights or needs of young offenders are rarely pursued by Hungarian juvenile justice (Herczog and Irk 1997).

In the United States, each state can enact its own laws and establish its own system of juvenile justice, subject to constitutional interpretation by the Supreme Court. Unlike the United States, in Canada the House of Commons can pass national legislation that applies throughout the country. This occurred in 1982 with passage of the Young Offenders Act (YOA) (see Corrado et al. 1992; Doob and Sprott 2004; Winterdyk 1997b). But, as with the United States, each of the Canadian provinces is free to interpret and apply that law pretty much as it sees fit. And research suggests that individual provinces do just that. Thus, in Canada the justice a juvenile receives from the juvenile justice system depends on the province in which the youth lives or in which an alleged offense took place. Referred to by Corrado (1992, 10) as a "Modified Justice Model," the YOA embodies four principles: responsibility, protection of society, mitigated accountability, and special needs of young offenders. The legislation seeks to secure the best of both worlds by embracing the welfare and legalistic approaches: "Less severe sanctions, for example, limit the punitiveness of the juvenile justice system compared to the adult system. The greater use of medical and psychological assessments of young offenders, and the extensive monitoring and review of dispositions, not only by judges but also by the young offender, parents and Crown counsel, are seen as promoting the individual needs of young offenders" (Corrado 1992a, 10–11). Among other provisions of the law the legal rights of both parents and children are guaranteed, age and jurisdiction restrictions apply, and treatment-oriented programs are specified.

The example of Canada shows how legislative ideas, especially those that try to encompass inherently contradictory objectives, can produce controversy, confusion, and disparate justice (Corrado et al. 1992a). For example, the separation of status and criminal offenders under the YOA along with modifications in age requirements for responsibility have led to many jurisdictional disputes over just who has jurisdiction of what juveniles and for what behaviors. Additionally, law enforcement authorities complain that the change to a legalistic, due process, approach for youths accused of criminal offenses has actually impeded their investigatory ability in many cases. The numbers of and the criteria used to transfer cases to adult authorities in different provinces has also been an issue of contention. And, most significantly, the mixing of sentencing criteria based on the welfare model as well as a crime control model has led to confusion and considerable disparity in sentences among the provinces. The attempt to have the best of both worlds may have led to a system that achieves neither (see Leschied 1991).

Differing considerably in operation and legal structures, the United States, Hungary, and Canada share a common philosophical orientation. All see the care, protection, and correction of juvenile offenders as desirable but not necessarily the essential business of juvenile justice. Instead, individual responsibility, due process, and, above all, the protection of society have become the overriding concerns in how these three societies respond to troubled and troublesome youths.

Coordinated Processing

Few societies have one all-inclusive authority with responsibility for, and the authority to handle, all matters concerning offending and needy children. The ideal welfare model envisions the juvenile court as a kind of superparent that oversees, and has the authority to coordinate, the activities of diverse agencies— all working in concert to secure the best interest of the child. A strict crime control model sees the court as the authoritative referee ensuring that procedural safeguards are adhered to in the criminal processing and disposition of juvenile offenders. Regardless of philosophy, in most cases the real work of juvenile justice is typically carried out by disparate agencies that are, at best, ill-coordinated, often at odds with one another, and just as motivated by considerations of turf, budget, and professional interest as by the child's needs and social protection. The juvenile is often lost in the shuffle.

Corporatism, a model of juvenile justice that attempts to better coordinate the efforts of the concerned agencies, is practiced in Hong Kong and England/Wales.

Juvenile justice in Hong Kong has changed little since the first laws establishing the present system were enacted in 1932, although changes are likely to occur as the colony becomes increasingly transformed under the direct rule of China (Gaylord 1996; Traver 1997). Reflecting a "welfare-under-judicial-authority" approach to juvenile justice, Hong Kong can be termed a cooperative model largely because most of the activities that involve juveniles operate under the umbrella of the social welfare department, and a unified philosophy guides the work in the system. As quoted by Gaylord (1996, 163), the following guideline on how to treat juveniles is mandated by law: "Before deciding how to deal with the child or young person, the court shall obtain such information as may be readily available as to his general conduct, home surroundings, school records, and medical history, in order to enable it to deal with the case in the best interest of the child or young person."

Magistrates have formal authority over juvenile cases. In actuality, which juveniles are dealt with by them and how they are treated is at the discretion of the social welfare department. This is because judges still tend to articulate a welfare orientation toward delinquent and needy young people. Gaylord (1996, 165) notes: "Hong Kong's juvenile court judges continue to believe that most youthful offenders are redeemable; therefore, when discussing sentencing alternatives, judges as well as social welfare personnel often use such terms as 'training,' 'treatment,' and 'care.'" In addition, judicial decisions regarding cases are based on the information that comes largely from probation officers, who, although being officers of the court, provide their services as part of the Youth and Rehabilitation Branch of the Social Welfare Department. It is also the Social Welfare Department that largely provides "residential care" for persons under age sixteen. But the Correctional Services Department, which provides custody for offenders above that age, works in close collaboration with the Social Welfare Department.

In this regard, Hong Kong's present juvenile justice system is a coordinated-welfare approach that has arisen more by fiat than design, reflecting the Chinese cultural values and respect of law that dominate Hong Kong society. Concern with raising offense rates among young people and the potential changes Hong Kong faces as it becomes subsumed by China may strain and ultimately lead to changes in this approach.

John Pratt (1989) argues that, while ostensibly the justice model assumed ideological dominance in England after the 1970s, in actual policies and practices Anglo-Welsh juvenile justice more closely corresponds to a corporatism model. As with the YOA in Canada, a series of legislative changes in England, especially the Crime and Disorder Act of 1998, appear also to be seeking the best of both worlds by providing for the needs of, while dishing out justice to, juvenile miscreants. But what is distinctive about this approach is its apparent emphasis on efficiency in processing youths—whether needy or delinquent—in a coordinated way relying on the expertise of juvenile justice specialists, who, according to Pratt (1998, 250), "are at the hub of the juvenile justice system itself . . . the socio-technical experts of corporatism."

The key ingredient in the corporatism system that has emerged in England and Wales is the Youth Offender Team (YOT). Seeking a more efficient and effective way of handling the seemingly ever-growing number of needy and offending young people, England-Wales sought to retain the justice ideology of holding youths responsible for their conduct while employing welfarism to help them avoid engaging in offense behavior (Reichel 2005a).

To help young people recognize and take responsibility, YOTs were designed to play a crucial role. Under a justice or welfare model, teams drawing their members from diverse agencies would likely be antagonists rather than partners in dealing with young people. Each team is made up of at least a social worker, probation officer, police officer, education officer, and a health official. In addition, local teams are coordinated at the national level. Other than direct involvement in trial proceedings or institutional care, the YOTs have broad authority and discretion, including court services, supervision of all manner of community sanction, and prevention measures.

Besides a team approach to dealing with delinquents and potential delinquents, a host of semi-informal sanctions called "orders" have been added to the repertoire of ways authorities can handle young people and divert them from more severe treatment. As Pratt (1989, 245) notes, this approach to juvenile justice reflects a historical movement in advanced welfare societies toward "the centralization of policy, increased government intervention, and the co-operation of various professional and interest groups in a collective whole with homogeneous aims and objectives."

It remains to be seen whether the bureaucratization of juvenile justice in the hands of coordinated specialists in juvenile justice will advance or hinder either the best interests of the child or the achievement of justice (Bottoms and Dignan 2004; Wakefield and Hirschel 1996). The approach holds promise for better, less chaotic, less disparate, more focused, effective, and just ways of dealing with young people in societies where family and clan have become of little or no relevance to either their care or future. It increases the risk of arbitrary, agency-oriented, net-widening governmental intrusion into the lives of young people. Reichel (2005a, 350) has observed that "as administrative discretion grows, so too do the extralegal sanctions available to these agencies. Minor breaches by juveniles in community programs can be handled by the program staff without requiring appearance before the juvenile court. Social workers and other treatment personnel who already had been co-opted into the welfare approach's adjudication and decision-making process are now involved in constructing and devising the penalty itself." The judge, in effect, could become the executioner. However, the question of who is to save the children from their saviors remains.

Conclusion

Models offer representations of reality that in practice are rarely observed. Juvenile justice in the world's societies often defies classification, except in terms of broad philosophical orientation. Law in practice typically draws on diverse and often contradictory orientations, so that a description of formal criminal court proceedings, for example, is more a rough guide of what may transpire than an accurate description of what one might observe in any criminal case. So it is with the world's treatment of its young people.

The models briefly outlined here can serve as guides for understanding and contrasting any society's approach to juvenile justice, even if in practice no society actually follows a strictly crime control or welfare approach. More important, the discussion of these models reveals the underlying tension inherent in juvenile justice no matter where or how it is practiced. No society perceives its young miscreants as fully responsible malefactors deserving punishment. Nor does any society completely hold a view that young offenders are somehow misled innocents wanting only care, protection, and guidance to lead crime-free lives. How any country treats its children is ultimately a consequence of its cultural history and prevailing political orientation. Juvenile justice is a balance of care and punishment—an attempt to achieve the apparently irreconcilable goals of the best interests of the child and the protection of society. In the twenty-first century, juvenile justice will continue to reflect how people of different cultural histories and political persuasion elect to deal with that problem.

6

Processing the Offender

Some societies have created distinct laws and bureaucracies for dealing with juveniles. Others make legal distinctions between juveniles and adults but lack designated actors or apparatus for processing youths. In yet other societies, juveniles are legally, at least in formal practice, the equivalent of adults. Furthermore, for a large number of countries there is no information whatsoever on their legal/processing systems, many of which probably have no distinctive juvenile justice system.

Information on countries that have recognizable systems for dealing with needy and delinquent youths indicates that how they are processed varies across the globe. These countries share the common problem of how to handle individuals who are not thought to be fully competent and culpable individuals. Furthermore, they must deal with the conflict between informal versus formal proceedings, as well as the punitive versus rehabilitative treatment of needy and delinquent youths.

Processing Systems

In any society, the detection, apprehension, and ultimate disposition of juvenile offenders is carried out by individuals working in sometimes complementary and sometimes contradictory capacities. Typically, the personnel involved in juvenile justice agencies have their own interests and concerns in dealing with young offenders. A smoothly operating, interconnected system for processing youths is rarely found in any society. Nevertheless, one can investigate the similarities and variations in how youths across the globe are handled by the societies in which they live by identifying the actors in formal processing agencies and the interconnections among them in various societies. The examples presented below help reveal the varieties of processing approaches that have been created in countries around the world.

Japan

The guiding principle of the Japanese juvenile justice system is the sound upbringing of juveniles to be achieved by protection and education. Thus, exemplifying the participatory model of juvenile justice, the formal machinery for dealing with Japanese young people is a blend of formalized informality that is hinged on the crucial decision-making authority of the family court. However, it involves a diversity of actors, including police, judges, welfare workers, probation officers, and public prosecutors.

As outlined by Tanioka and Goto (1996), Japan distinguishes among three categories of juveniles based on age and behavior. Youths above and below age fourteen who are accused of a crime are deemed "juvenile offenders" and "child offenders," respectively, and "pre-delinquent juveniles" are youths above and below age fourteen who have committed a statuslike offense or exhibit a situation of need. Although the police are the main agency for bringing both delinquent and predelinquent youths to the attention of the system, virtually anyone or any agency can initiate procedures where appropriate. In delinquency cases, for trivial offenses or predelinquent cases, the police normally refer the case to the family court. In more serious cases, the referral may be to the public prosecutor, who is required to pass it to the family court in any case. Thus, the family court has the crucial discretionary power of deciding whether or not the youth is charged with an offense and what proceedings thereafter will be followed.

Predelinquent cases involving Japanese youths below age fourteen are to be referred to the child guidance center or child welfare station. These authorities could, in turn, refer the case to the family court, which then takes responsibility for the matter. If not, the disposition decision of the guidance center or welfare station is final.

Should any case appear before a family court, the probation office undertakes a full social investigation of the juvenile's history and life situation, with possible further psychiatric testing also being possible. Following an inquisitorial system, full due process is not guaranteed in Japan's family courts. Thus, the social investigation provided by the probation department becomes the primary instrument for family court judgments. The judge can decide to commence a formal hearing or the youth can be referred to the child guidance center. Should a hearing take place, the judge can either dismiss the case after hearing or impose a protective disposition in the form of probation supervision or institutional treatment in rare cases. In some situations, where the juvenile is sixteen or older, the judge can refer the case to the public prosecutor for criminal procedures; similar to the waiver decision in U.S. juvenile justice. Any penalties that may be imposed following the criminal procedure would necessarily be of lesser severity than an adult would receive.

A distinctive feature of the Japanese juvenile justice system is the central role that judges in the family court play in the authoritative decision-making

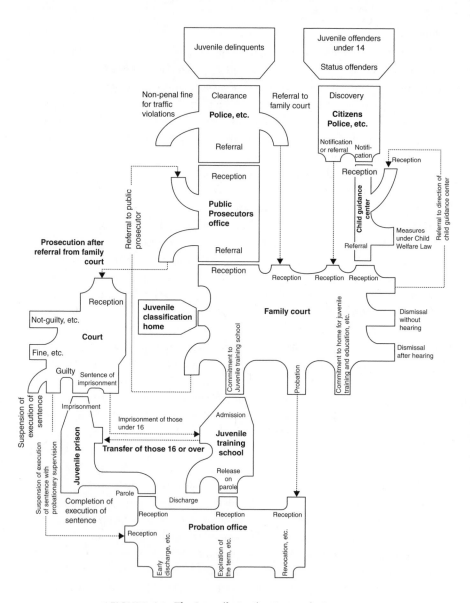

FIGURE 6.1. The Juvenile Justice System in Japan.

Source: Research and Training Institute, Ministry of Japan 2004, 237.

process while incorporating a large variety of citizen, government, and welfare agencies to protect and educate, as opposed to punish, offending and potentially-offending youths.

New Zealand

Following legislation enacted in 1989 creating the Family Group Conference (FGC) as the central element of its juvenile justice system, New Zealand created what is perhaps the most innovative formal system for dealing with young people in the world. As noted by Reichel (2005a, 340–341), this system "stresses the well-being of children and the empowerment of families and young people. An important aspect of this approach is the use of restorative-justice principles."

Morris and Maxell (1991, 97–103) describe the formal practice. As in other societies, the police in New Zealand are likely to be the primary agency for bringing action against juvenile offenders. However, the 1989 law mandates that in New Zealand juveniles cannot be arrested unless certain very specific restrictions are met. Primarily, police are prohibited from arresting a youth simply because the police believe he or she was involved in an offense. Instead, a juvenile can only be arrested if it is deemed "necessary to ensure the juvenile's appearance in court, to prevent the commission of further offenses, or to prevent the loss or destruction of evidence or interference with witnesses" (Morris and Maxwell 1991, 97–98). First offenders and those suspected of minor offenses are to be diverted with a "street warning" or be referred to the "Youth Aid Section," a specialized police unit that deals with juveniles, which can impose warnings and various sanctions, such as community work and the like.

Although New Zealand is best classified as a welfare model approach, as with justice model countries, youths suspected of criminal activity and not referred to the youth justice coordinator (YJC) encounter a procedure much like that of any Western adult criminal trial, with various restrictions. These include confidentiality of proceedings and the appointment of a youth advocate if needed and a lay advocate to ensure awareness of cultural matters. As in other countries, the case can be transferred to the adult district court and treated as an adult criminal case if the offender is at least fifteen years of age and a variety of conditions are also met.

What is unique about the New Zealand system is that prior to disposition of the case, all cases go before a family group conference (FGC) proceeding, and the court must take the FGC's plan and recommendation into consideration in handing down a disposition. Even more significantly, status and minor delinquency cases referred to the YGC typically result in an FGC. Although most are not trained in social work, youth justice coordinators are officers within the department of social welfare and primarily play the role of negotiators in determining how cases are to be handled and the dispositions ultimately agreed upon.

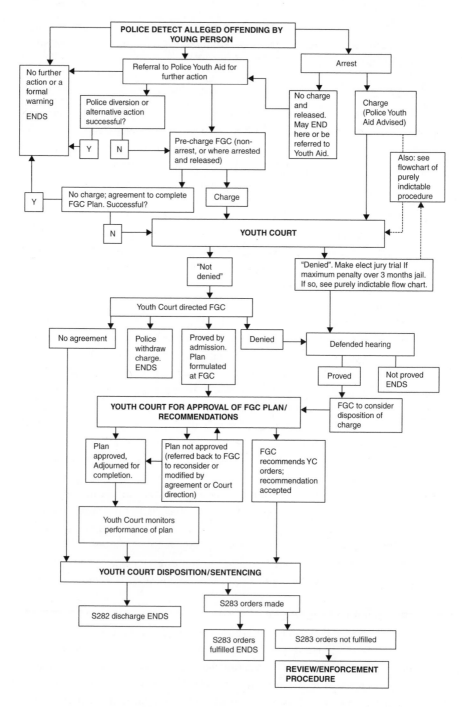

FIGURE 6.2. The Juvenile Justice System in New Zealand.
Source: Becroft 2003, 18.

The FCG is composed of the youth, the advocate for the accused, his or her family members, the victim or victims and support people, the police, a social worker, and the YJC. Such conferences can be held wherever the family wishes. Except cases where guilt is denied, which are therefore heard before the youth court, the FGC is primarily responsible for the disposition of the case. The decisions of these groups, while not binding on police or judge, are generally accepted. Once accepted, the plan is binding and failure to fulfill its mandate could result in prosecution.

The key features of the New Zealand approach is diversion from prosecution, the use of least restrictive sanctions, and community empowerment and involvement in the pursuit of justice. In part, born out of the clash of cultures and the sense of injustice that the imposition of European criminal justice traditions engendered among the diverse populations that occupy the country, particularly the Maori people, the New Zealand system represents a blend of justice and restorative principles rarely found in other countries across the globe.

United States

It is, of course, incorrect to speak of a U.S. system of juvenile justice, since no single body of law or procedure applies nationwide. Instead, fifty-one separate systems of juvenile justice (the fifty states and the federal system) exist across the country. While they may be similar in many respects and covered by due process rulings handed down by the U.S. Supreme Court, considerable diversity in philosophy, procedure, and structure is found among the separate systems. It is best to keep this reality in mind when trying to describe and make generalizations about juvenile justice in the United States.

Perhaps more than any other country, the United States' jurisdictions have moved away from the ideal, welfare-based, best-interests-of-the-child model created in Cook County, Illinois, at the beginning of the twentieth century and have embraced a strict crime-control approach. In part, this transformation was dictated by the due-process requirements imposed in the mid-1960s on American juvenile justice by a series of rulings handed down by the U.S. Supreme Court (Weinstein and Mendoza 1979). In an effort to protect the legal rights of young people accused of crimes, and subject to incarceration as a result, these rulings largely undermined the informal procedures deemed essential to a welfare model of juvenile justice as envisioned by its creators. In addition, the fear of crime, and the politically conservative get-tough approach that gripped the country in the 1980s, did much to transform the best-interests-oriented juvenile court, dominated by probation officers and welfare-oriented judges, into a "lock-'em-up" junior criminal court dominated by prosecutors and a society-protection oriented judiciary (Empey 1979b).

Figure 6.3 presents a version of juvenile processing commonly found in U.S. jurisdictions today. As with the other countries discussed here, the system is much more complicated than that depicted.

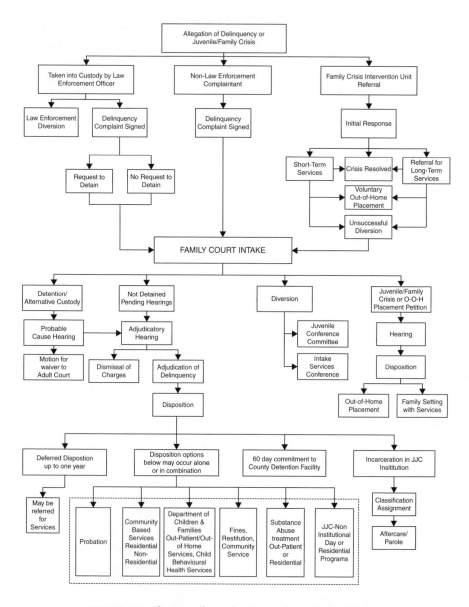

FIGURE 6.3. The Juvenile Justice System in the United States.

Source: Courtesy of Juvenile Justice Commission, State of New Jersey, New Jersey, Department of Law and Public Safety.

As elsewhere, the police are the likely agency to initiate delinquency proceedings in the United States, although individuals, school officials, welfare
agencies, probation officers, and others may also be responsible for initiating
action. Often when the situation involves minor or status offenses, or in cases of
need or neglect, the police in America will handle the matter informally and
unofficially or refer the case to some other agency, such as a department of
youth and family services or the probation department. Otherwise, as in criminal
matters, the police can formally arrest and detain a juvenile and hand the case
over to the juvenile court intake screening personnel. Many youths are effectively diverted from further formal processing at this stage, although it is likely
that some kind of intervention activity will be mandated.

The distinctive feature of contemporary U.S. juvenile justice is the central
role county prosecutors play in the proceedings. If a criminal matter, the case is
likely to be presented to the prosecutor, who can either decline to prosecute or
bring a formal accusation against the juvenile in the form of a petition. In many
jurisdictions, proceedings to transfer (waive) the case to the adult criminal justice
can be initiated at this point. This can be done either by means of statutory
exclusion, whereby the law mandates that youths of specific ages accused of certain crimes be automatically transferred to the adult system, or by prosecutorial
discretion, whereby the prosecuting attorney decides to initiate the action
(Coalition for Juvenile Justice 1994).

If a delinquency petition is filed, the accused appears before a judge in the
juvenile court. At this stage a transfer decision can be made to take the case out
of the juvenile system and put it into the adult system. Should a waiver not
occur, proceedings in the juvenile court are much like those in any American
adult criminal court. Two hearings are held. The first of these, an adjudication
hearing, is concerned with the guilt or innocence of the youth. This hearing is
similar to a criminal trial before a judge in an adult criminal court with the
accused youth enjoying most, but not all, the due process rights of an adult.

If the petition is not sustained, the case is dismissed. If the youth is adjudicated a delinquent, a second hearing, a disposition hearing, is typically held.
In such hearings a social investigation report, usually compiled by the probation department, is available to the judge; victim statements may be presented;
and virtually any other testimony or information the court may allow can be
taken into consideration in deciding what to do with the youth. Much like an
elaborate sentencing hearing in adult criminal courts, the purpose of the disposition hearing is to decide punishment and/or treatment.

Probation department representatives, social welfare agencies, and various
interested parties may be involved in these proceedings at various stages.
Unless the case is diverted or dismissed early in the process, the primary actors
in the contemporary U.S. juvenile justice system are the prosecuting attorney
and the judge, both of whom have wide discretionary and dispositional power

in determining the course and outcome of the proceedings. Except for Supreme Court–mandated due process requirements, the guiding principle for those not screened out or diverted early in the proceedings has largely become societal protection through the control of juvenile crime—something to be achieved by punitive sanction rather than the protection and education of wayward youth.

Key Players in the Game of Juvenile Justice

Regardless of its guiding philosophy, organizational make up, or locus of decision-making power, the official juvenile justice system in any society comprises individuals employed by diverse agencies responsible for making decisions about youths that affect their lives and the lives of numerous other people. Criminological research in the United States and several other countries offers an extensive literature delving into the behavior, thinking, and forces that impact the actions of these actors. The power of these actors is likely to vary across justice systems. Based on research in the United States, and other countries, regardless of where the decision-making power is located, actors in the system typically cooperate, if not necessarily agree, with one another in processing cases.

For all the research that has been devoted to understanding the behavior of delinquents, only a smattering of studies reveal anything about agencies worldwide that are given authority to determine who are offenders or in need, and what is to be done with them. Given the profoundly intrusive role these agents can play in the lives of individuals, and their impact on the very integrity of civil society, one can only wonder why this knowledge is so limited.

Various actors, such as police or welfare workers, may influence what transpires in juvenile justice proceedings, depending upon the particular justice model involved. However, primary decision-making power normally lies with probation officers, prosecutors or procurators, and (juvenile court) judges.

Probation Officers

In many countries, probation officers play a critical role in determining the course of post-apprehension proceedings. They are often very influential in determining who is diverted from further processing at the initial intake stages. The influence of these officials, however, can vary greatly depending upon the system. For example, in Japan probation officers appear to play a critical role in determining what is done with youths brought to the attention of the system (Tanioka and Goto 1996, 200; Yokoyama 1986, 104). Since passage of the Young Offender Act in Canada, on the other hand, the advocacy role of probation officers in juvenile proceedings has been largely undermined, and they have assumed a more neutral advisory/supervisory role (Corrado and Markwart 1996, 44–45). In the United States, the central position probation officers once held in the juvenile court has been usurped by prosecutors, and they have increasingly become correctional, as opposed to child-advocate, players in juvenile justice.

Still they have considerable, if unofficial, influence to sway decisions with their social investigation reports and recommendations.

Prosecutors

Since delinquency accusations were not considered criminal matters, prosecutors in the United States had little, if any, say in whether or not youths were charged with violations. As the country has become increasingly legalistic in approach, and crime-control in orientation, prosecutors increasingly have become central authorities in initiating and directing proceedings against juveniles and presenting cases in juvenile courts. In effect, prosecutors have come to occupy a pivotal position in the entire procedure, with the additional authority to initiate or recommend the waiver of a juvenile to adult jurisdiction (Cox and Conrad 1996; Laub and MacMurray 1987; Shine and Price 1992; Thomas and Bilchik 1985).

Prosecutors enjoy similar power in other countries. In the Netherlands, they are key to deciding if a case is prosecuted or not. However, unlike American prosecutors, Dutch prosecutors have some dispositional power. They can impose an alternative sanction of up to forty hours of confinement or community work, order a conditional dismissal, order a fine or payment of damages, or require that a youth accept probation supervision for up to six months (Junger-Tas 1997). In Russia, according to Finckenauer (1996, 275), the procurator is a kind of "superprosecutor" with diverse powers unthinkable in a country such as the United States.

In most countries, especially those based on inquisitorial principles and/or where judges are central in the accusatorial process, the prosecuting official—normally called a procurator—has less pivotal authority than prosecutors in the United States. Instead, the judge has primary power. In Japan, unlike the United States, prosecutors do not have discretion in screening cases and must refer all cases to the family court. They are even prohibited from attending family court proceedings or stating their opinion (Tanioka and Goto 1996; Yokoyama 1997). Although in minor cases procurators in France may dismiss youth with no action, depending upon the seriousness and complexity of the offense, the central issue for the prosecutor is determining which of several alternative courts the case will be presented to. Once presented to the court, the principle investigation becomes the responsibility of judicial authorities (Ottenhof and Renucci 1996). In Finland, if the offense is of moderate severity, a prosecutor can choose not to charge a youth under age eighteen. In more serious matters involving a potential sentence of three months or more, charges must be brought against a Finnish juvenile (Nylund 1991).

Judges

In some countries juvenile court judges are a separate and distinct branch of the country's judicial structure. In many of these countries, juvenile court judges undergo special training and occupy a unique position in dealing with juvenile matters. Elsewhere, regular trial court judges may be assigned to hear juvenile cases, usually on a temporary and rotating basis. Or cases involving juvenile offenders may on occasion be placed on the docket of a judge normally responsible for trying adult criminal matters. Generally these judges have little, if any, special training or experience in dealing with young people.

Regardless of the system, judges who routinely deal with juveniles are typically accorded less prestige than adult-court judges, and, compared to cases tried in adult courts, juvenile cases are normally considered less compelling. Nevertheless, as far as the ultimate fates of juveniles accused of offenses are concerned, the authority and decision-making power of the judge is often crucial in virtually all juvenile proceedings.

Depending on the system—whether purely juvenile or not—the judge can play a central role in the entire procedure or act as a referee and ultimate arbitrator in an adversarial contest. In most instances judicial authorities have veto power over probation officers or prosecutors. Sometimes they themselves make the decision, while other agencies provide input and/or are delegated the responsibility of carrying out the judge's decision. In inquisitorial (or inquisitorial-like) judicial systems such as France (Ottenhof and Renucci 1996), Greece (Petoussi and Stavrou 1996), Japan (Yokoyama 1997), and Italy (Gatti and Verde 1997), judges may encompass the functions of both prosecutor and judge by deciding whether or not to charge the youth as well as rendering adjudication and making dispositional decisions. They may also serve as the central arbitrator of proceedings by coordinating the activities and interaction of all parties. In accusatorial systems, such as the United States (Bartollas 1996), Canada (Corrado and Markwart 1996), and England (Wakefield and Hirschel 1996), the decision to charge is left to other officials, although the judge may still reverse that decision before trial proceedings commence. In all societies it appears that once the decision to charge a youth with an offense has been made, the judge (or judicial tribunal) has the critical power to stop the proceedings and summarily dismiss the case, assess the legitimacy of the charges logged against the youth, and determine the punitive or educational fate the youth will face.

Lawyers, Juries, and Others

Regardless of the specific makeup or organization of the system involved, intake screening officials, changing authorities, and judging officials are common to all formal juvenile judicial systems. In most societies some form of representation (usually a defense attorney) for accused juveniles is allowed and/or provided. In some countries, such as the United States, these individuals may sometimes serve as strong advocates for the accused. Most often, however, they probably play a protective role in ensuring that accusers at least play by the rules and do not run roughshod over the rights or welfare of young defendants (Sanborn and Salerno 2005; Milne et al. 1992). The U.S. trial jury is not used in most justice systems around the globe. Since they are not legally mandated in U.S. juvenile courts, the jury is virtually absent in juvenile cases (except for individuals tried as adults in U.S. jurisdictions). With few exceptions, therefore, juvenile proceedings are heard before a judge alone or a form of tribunal (professional and/or lay judges).

Although juvenile justice just about everywhere is dominated by professional justice actions, many societies have attempted to bring elements of the larger society into the proceedings at various points or in various ways. The clearest example of this is the family group conference approach practiced in New Zealand. A similar approach has been taken in various countries where mediation programs have become official or extralegal parts of their juvenile justice systems. Finland and some U.S. jurisdictions, for instance, have adapted similar mediation programs based on restorative justice principles (Nylund 1991). In other countries, extrajudicial organizations of diverse types are involved with the prevention, processing, or treatment of young offenders. For example, the Danish SSP-system of crime prevention is a network of local crime prevention projects targeting children and juveniles. Combining institutions from education, leisure, social and health services, as well as the police, this program, launched in 1971, seeks to engage agencies in a host of non–law-enforcement activities aimed at preventing delinquency (Wita 2000). In China, despite recent efforts to Westernize its formal juvenile justice system, various community organizations still play a very active role in how that country deals with its offending youths. These organizations serve as *bang-jao* (help and education) groups, mediation committees, and *gongdu* (work-study) schools and play other informal roles under the ideal that the proper behavior of Chinese children is a collective responsibility (Ren 1996).

In countries where the community has a meaningful role in how juveniles are treated, such inclusion may stem from a sincere realization that justice is essentially a societal matter, something of relevance to everyone.

Critical Processing Stages

Regardless of the particular system individual societies exhibit, three critical stages in the processing of delinquent or needy juveniles can be identified: initiation, charging, adjudication. The body of information about the formal machinery of juvenile justice across the globe that is now available helps to identify the key players and the roles they may carry out. Though not thorough, a survey of this information can help broaden awareness of who these actors may be and the processing roles they may play in their respective societies.

Initiation

In virtually all societies it is apparent that essentially anyone, or at least anyone of repute, can initiate procedures resulting in offending (or needy) youths being processed by juvenile officials. Parents or guardians, victims, welfare workers, clergy, probation officers, and health workers commonly bring young people to the attention of authorities. In some instances specific agencies are entrusted with the responsibility of looking out for the welfare of young people. For example, in New Zealand, if the police feel action is warranted in dealing with a youth, the case is referred to the Youth Aid Section, a specialized unit that deals exclusively with young people. In turn, if these officers feel further action is needed, the case is referred to a YJC, an intake screening officer who negotiates with police to divert juveniles from court (Morris and Maxwell 1991). In Finland:

> If the crime is committed by a young offender, child welfare social work-
> ers must decide whether or not the juvenile needs support and assis-
> tance during this process. Social workers have a right to be present at the
> police examination, if the young offender is under 18 years of age. More-
> over, social workers must be present at the juvenile court and give their
> opinion about the sanctions being considered. (Nylund 1991, 260)

Probably in all countries welfare workers, health workers, and parents are the ones most likely to notify juvenile authorities of a juvenile offense or situation of need. In most instances, the police are most directly involved in initiating action that could lead to further processing. Given their broad discretionary authority, the police are the gatekeepers to the juvenile justice systems in all societies.

Early research on police-juvenile encounters in the United States reveals that even in cases where relatively serious offense behavior was suspected, police frequently chose not to initiate formal proceedings. Instead, they decided to treat the matter informally (Black 1970; Piliavin and Briar 1964; Reiss 1986). Although the research is limited, informal treatment of juvenile matters appears to be prevalent throughout the world.

In some societies the informal actions of the police in dealing with youthful offenders are actually unofficial and extralegal. In other countries, however, these informal practices have been institutionalized in law. In England, for example, a formal police cautioning process has been instituted. After compiling information about the offense, the offender's background, and other matters, a semiformal procedure involves the juvenile, the juvenile's parents, and possibly the victim. If the juvenile admits the offense and all parties are willing, the chief inspector may issue a formal caution to the juvenile in the company of his or her guardian (Lee 1998; Wakefield and Hirschel 1996). A similar, if somewhat more elaborate, approach has been implemented as a pilot program in Belfast, Ireland (O'Mahony et al. 2002). This program employs a restorative strategy for juveniles under age seventeen who are accused of an offense but are diverted from prosecution. Informal cautioning undoubtedly also continues to exist in England, as virtually everywhere.

Given the guiding philosophy of the "best interests of the child" underlying juvenile law, the police in New Zealand are prohibited from taking action unless certain conditions are met (Morris and Maxwell 1991). All effort is directed to resolving the matter extrajudicially to avoid formal processing and adjudication. In the Netherlands, Junger-Tas (1997) reports that about 30 percent of juvenile offenders are sent home with a warning. In accordance with specific guidelines, other cases are diverted to a program called HALT *(Het Alternatief)*, meaning "stop" in Dutch. Only serious cases, or juveniles who do not satisfactorily follow the diversion program, are referred to the prosecutor for charges.

In some countries the police may still exercise considerable discretion in not initiating formal action. However, in these societies the arrest and official charging of even mild offenders may be much more likely than in countries such as France or New Zealand, where police are encouraged to take a more welfare-oriented approach to misbehaving youth, or in England and Wales, where official-informal alternatives are mandated by law. In the United States, the net of official control and processing appears to have widened substantially in recent decades (Blomberg 1984; Fuller and Norton 1993; Hinshaw 1993; Polk 1984).

Reflecting U.S. concern with societal protection, other countries have cracked down on juvenile offenders. This reaction has been partly a response to public concern with youth crime and violence and partly the result of changing political fortunes. Surveys conducted in several English-speaking countries reveal that public fear of youth crime, and especially violent crime, has been a driving force behind calls to facilitate the transfer of juveniles to adult courts or to toughen penalties for youths sentenced in juvenile court (Roberts 2004). Ironically, Kyvsgaard (2004) reports that throughout Europe, as well as the United States, rates of juvenile crime appear to have actually declined during the late 1980s. Nevertheless, get-tough legislation and policies proliferated in the 1990s. Atkinson (1997), for instance, notes that the state of Western Australia in Australia passed a law in 1992 called the Crime (Serious and Repeat Offenders) Sentencing Act. This legislation was designed specifically for young recidivist car thieves whose activities and apprehension by police led to much public unrest. The law "mandated a fixed minimum term in detention, to be followed by an indeterminate period of detention at the governor's pleasure for those fitting the criteria of serious, repeat offender" (Atkinson 1997, 46). Following reunification, Germany experienced a heightened crime and delinquency problem. There were numerous proposals and some action taken to fundamentally change the welfare-oriented system that has dominated German juvenile justice in the postwar period (Albrecht 2004). Similarly, in Hong Kong official and public concern over a serious, and potentially more troublesome, delinquency problem resulted in policy decisions that extended police supervision of juvenile offenders. While intended as a tactic to divert youths to a treatment program, the new policy actually resulted in a net-widening effect. Due to the increased number of youths appearing in official statistics, this heightened concerns. Whether any actual juvenile crime wave took place is unknown (Traver 1997).

Young people of interest to juvenile authorities in most societies are likely first encountered by general police officers responding to victims, witnesses, or concerned others. Oftentimes these police officers are not trained or skilled in handling cases involving young people. Consequently, they either use life experience to deal with the problem or they treat the situation as a law-enforcement matter. In some countries specialized juvenile police initiatives have been established. In Japan, for example, a host of police initiatives involving volunteers, schools, and various organizations specifically targeting juveniles and delinquency prevention have been implemented (Yokoyama 1997). Similarly, Norway has recently taken purposive action to curb juvenile crime through enhanced community policing policies specifically targeting young people (Hareide 2000).

Typically, juvenile-oriented policing activities are found in jurisdictions that reflect a welfare-oriented juvenile justice system or in communities that have a large enough juvenile population or delinquency problem to warrant such attention. To what extent these programs or initiatives actually reduce delinquency or protect the best interests of juveniles is a subject for debate. However, prevention and diversion from formal processing are central aspects of these programs. In contrast to the largely preventive orientation of community policing policy, especially in the United States and increasingly in some European countries, concern with widespread delinquent gang activities has prompted the formation of specialized police units oriented to juveniles.

Charging

Regardless of how individuals are brought to the attention of legal authorities, perhaps the most crucial stage in delinquency proceedings is the charging decision—what is typically referred to as intake screening. Someone may complain that a youth is being abused or in need of care and protection, but in terms of remedying the situation that means little unless some official takes action to respond to the problem.

When charging a youth with an offense, a choice is made to either dismiss, divert, waive, or charge the suspect. As one would expect, a youth's chances of dismissal become increasingly reduced the farther along the process his or her case is brought. For example, Bottoms and Dignan (2004) report that in Scotland, even when a potentially chargeable offense is brought to the attention of the police, in most instances no further action is taken. If an official police referral is involved, about three-quarters are forwarded to a court intake officer, known as a reporter. Of the cases that come to the court reporter's attention, more than 60 percent receive no action, while only about 25 percent appear before the court for a hearing. Similarly, in the Netherlands about 48 percent of the juveniles interrogated by the police are diverted to some program. Of the

47,900 juveniles interrogated by the police in 1999, only 8,000 were ultimately convicted of offenses (Junger-Tas 2004). By contrast, of the juveniles taken into police custody in the United States, formal processing statistics reflect the concern officials have with due process laws and crime control. About 25 percent of the cases that are taken into custody (the number that do not reach this stage can only be estimated) are handled within the police department and released. Thus, three out of four arrested juveniles are referred to juvenile court intake. Almost one-half (although the percentage is declining) of the cases processed at intake are handled informally, usually involving some kind of voluntary sanction such as voluntary probation or restitution (Snyder and Sickmund 1999). Thus, regardless of the system, in virtually all societies numerous outlets are built into the processing so that guilty youths can be spared further processing and its potentially negative consequences. What varies is exactly which officials in the proceedings have the authority to exercise this discretion and at what point in the procedure this takes place.

Thus, in most judicial systems, especially in welfare-oriented countries, mechanisms for diverting juveniles from formal adjudication proceedings exist. In keeping with the original ideals of juvenile justice, diversion procedures are ideally geared to preventing court hearings and the official label of delinquent. Instead, efforts are made to direct the offender to some kind of program designed to provide the care and education deemed necessary for the juvenile. Often the diversion is informal, with the case being dismissed providing the youth agrees to participate in a program. In many places, however, diversion is an official step in dealing with wayward youths. This could be either instead of or as a consequence of judicial processing. Israel, for example, diverts cases as a normal stage of the proceedings before they reach juvenile court. This is true in cases where the offense in question was circumstantial and/or where the court experience itself is likely to harm the juvenile (Sebba 1986). A similar policy exists in the Netherlands. Junger-Tas (1997, 69–70) explains that the Dutch juvenile justice system is a "well-articulated and flexible system." She notes that interventions are possible at any level of the system. The objective of these interventions is to stop further proceedings and to deal with the juvenile in an informal way whenever possible. Dutch police send about 30 percent of juveniles home with a warning. Almost 70 percent of all remaining cases submitted to the prosecutor are dismissed, either with a written note or an official reprimand.

In some countries, such as Hungary and Denmark, juveniles are subjected to processing by the officials who deal with adults, and their processing is not officially distinct from that received by adult criminal offenders. The juvenile appears before the same judge who handles adult criminal cases and in the same courtroom following the same due process procedures. The only concession in such systems may be the legal stipulation of less severe punishments. Undoubtedly, unofficial consideration is taken of the competency (and thus culpability) of the accused due to his or her age. Similarly, in Germany definitions of crimes apply equally to adults and juveniles, and the same standards in establishing criminal responsibility are followed in juvenile cases as in adult criminal cases, although penalties for juveniles differ from those that may apply to adults. Significantly, German law does not allow transfer of juvenile cases to adult criminal courts (Albrecht 2004).

In jurisdictions that do not differentiate between juvenile and adult systems of justice, the question of waiver or transfer from the juvenile to the adult system is a mute issue. However, in those societies where a clear distinction exists between the juvenile and adult justice systems, the question of waiver is a crucial, and in some places a growing, issue. Most societies that separate juvenile from adult jurisdiction (or proceedings) have some kind of waiver option. In some instances, unless mandated by law, the waiver decision is a prosecutorial decision. In others it is a judicial decision, or one that requires judicial approval. In rare instances, cases brought before the criminal court may be transferred to juvenile authorities, although it is the reverse that is the most likely procedure.

Jurisdictions also vary in the procedures and grounds for transferring cases involving a juvenile offender to adult criminal court jurisdiction. In Scotland, under very limited circumstances, children under age sixteen can only be referred to the adult court for prosecution. However, the vast majority of offenders aged sixteen and seventeen are prosecuted in the adult criminal court. In England, by contrast, juveniles can be dealt with in the crown court instead of the youth court under the following conditions: they are charged with homicide, are jointly charged for committing an offense with someone eighteen years of age or older, or are charged with a crime for which an adult would receive a sentence of fourteen years or longer. Special circumstances can also lead to transfer when a case involves other offenses or the penalties are deemed to be inappropriate for the case (Bottoms and Dignan 2004).

A comparison between the United States and Canada illustrates how the use of this alternative can vary even between countries that are very similar in their overall approach to juvenile justice. As reported by Doob and Tonry (2004) in the United States approximately 200,000 juveniles under age eighteen are tried in adult criminal courts. In comparison, fewer than 100 are so treated in Canada. This difference exists even though the use of juvenile courts in both countries is comparable and both have adopted similar due process legislation regarding the treatment of juvenile suspects.

How extensively the transfer option is used in different countries is unknown. Given the diverse mechanisms by which transfer is pursued even within some countries, it is particularly difficult to accurately assess its use, much less draw cross-national comparisons. However, in countries that exhibit legalistic juvenile justice models, especially those dominated by a crime-control mentality and/or exhibit extensive concern with youth crime as a serious problem, waiver procedures are extensively used (Fagan and Zimring 2000). Also, to what extent treating young offenders as adult criminals, with the usually harsher potential penalties this foretells, as an effective way of combating juvenile crime remains a matter of debate and controversy (Fagan and Zimring 2000; Feld 1987, 1991). The issue of waiver does, however, clearly reflect the underlying tension between treatment versus punishment and the ambiguity inherent in using age as a basic criterion in drawing a line for criminal responsibility.

Adjudication

Whether a delinquency case is heard or tried in a specifically designated juvenile court or juvenile proceeding or before a judge in an adult criminal court, two decisions affect the future of the youth that are normally the sole responsibility of the judge (or judicial tribunal): the finding of guilt or need and the disposition. The power of judicial officials to render these decisions varies somewhat across the globe. Although typically restricted and guided by the dictates of law, judges normally have the ultimate say in such matters. It is likely, however, that they do so with the advice and influence of other interested parties. Indeed, in some societies it is mandated that judges be guided by the advice of others. A case in point is the family group conference system of New Zealand, Fiji, and Australia. Even if not officially mandated, the information provided by probation officers in Japan, Canada, The Netherlands, Sweden, and many other countries influences judicial decisions, especially when it comes to dispositions.

In the United States, the founders of the juvenile justice system envisioned that a juvenile offender would receive an adjudication rather than a conviction. Instead of a sentence a youth would receive a disposition. And rather than punishment, an adjudicated offender would be given the care and treatment needed to prevent future offending. In a few welfare-oriented countries this ideal still dominates. In France, for instance, *juges des enfants* are clearly oriented to this ideal (Blatier 1999; Hackler 1991a). Even where guilt is established, usually by means of a confession in an in-chambers hearing, judges are reluctant to impose penal sanction on the offender and take pains to find alternative ways of dealing with the matter. Similarly, in other countries, notably Germany, Sweden, Fiji, New Zealand, and Japan, all parties go to great lengths to avoid the formal labeling of youths as offenders or to invoke punitive sanctions.

Universally, comparatively few delinquency cases actually survive the screening procedures of intake, charging, and hearing, and still fewer wind up being disposed as official offenders. Limited juvenile court data from several countries reveal a common pattern. Only a handful of youths that could be officially labeled delinquent actually are so designated in any country. For example, of the charges dealt with by the children's courts in New South Wales, Australia, 54 percent were resolved without penalty (Atkinson 1997). From 1984 to 1991, the ratio of minors convicted to those tried in Italian juvenile courts averaged around 18 percent (Gatti and Verde 1997). In New Zealand in 1990 about 30 percent of cases charged were "not proven/withdrawn," while another 20 percent were "proved but discharged" (Statistics New Zealand 1991). The percentage of youths processed and found to be delinquent in American juvenile courts is somewhat higher (58 percent) than in many other countries (Snyder and Sickmund 1999). Given the large number of cases usually involving serious offenses that are waived to adult courts in the United States, the actual conviction rate is probably somewhat higher.

At least in law, virtually all countries have dispositional alternatives to punitive sanction and the incarceration of juveniles from which judges may select. However, it is unknown to what extent different countries employ these alternative sanctions. Where data is available, it is clear that even in the most punitive of societies, the imprisonment of juveniles is a comparatively rare event. In the United States, departing from the practices of many other countries, the availability and use of nonpunitive alternatives vary widely across jurisdictions. Generally, however, incarceration in ever more punitive and secure correctional facilities has become the preferred alternative in many U.S. jurisdictions (Snyder and Sickmund 1999).

Conclusion

The sayings "all roads lead to Rome" may, in many ways, be descriptive of how societies everywhere have come to deal with their needy and delinquent children. Given the limited research available, an authoritative picture cannot yet be drawn of how offending youths across the globe go from detection to disposition and what forces influence the decision making of various authorities along the way. Thus, it is not possible to predict what might happen to youths engaged in identical conduct in various societies or to explain what differences may occur in how they are handled. It may very well be that it really does not matter what ideological approach a country takes or who is vested with decision-making authority in processing youthful offenders—just about the same outcome is likely to occur. On the other hand, it could matter a great deal to the individual juvenile, and the society, generally, as to just how a country elects to handle offending youths. In that case, it behooves criminologists to seriously investigate the different processing approaches found in societies across the globe, both to better delineate the options of policy makers in their own countries and to help understand the forces that influence justice for juveniles wherever and however it is pursued.

7

Correcting Juveniles

The most perplexing question facing any system of juvenile justice is what to do with young people who have been adjudicated offenders or found to be in some kind of pre-offending situation. In most societies considerable effort is expended in diverting youths who could be labeled delinquents from being so adjudicated. Often this involves requiring the youth to participate in a program or to submit to a life-changing adjustment (e.g., foster care) or face the prospect of further processing. More often this diversion activity simply consists of the juvenile being initially contacted by authorities (police questioning, intake office screening, etc.), followed by a stern warning to the youth and/or the youth's guardians and release from the system.

Those who make it to the final stages of judicial proceedings are, in most cases, a relatively select group. Throughout the process, the central concern is what should be done with youths warranting action, which is decided by judicial officials. Carrying out the decision of these officials is the responsibility of correctional authorities. As the philosophies that guide, and the structure of the systems created to dispense, justice for juveniles differ yet share many commonalities among the world's societies, the ways in which different countries choose to correct young offenders are diverse, yet quite similar, across the globe.

Dispositions

The terminology used to delineate the action judicial officials might order in dealing with a young offender varies depending on the model being followed and the court in which the case is heard. If handled in a criminal court, the "convicted" offender would likely receive a "sentence." If processed in a traditional juvenile court, the "adjudicated" youth would normally receive a "disposition." Compared to typical dispositions, the sentences juveniles usually receive are likely to be harsher, in that the length of time one is under correctional control may be longer with a greater probability of confinement in a secure facility. However, even in countries oriented to a crime-control approach the use of long-term, punitive confinement in prisons or prisonlike institutions is a relative rarity. Indeed, wherever a recognizable distinction between juveniles and adults is found, regardless of the guiding philosophy behind the system of juvenile justice, the range and types of dispositions delinquent youths experience appear to be similar across the globe.

Table 7.1 provides an illustration of the possible dispositions youths can receive if found to be delinquent in the juvenile courts of various countries—countries with divergent judicial systems and philosophies. Scrutiny of the dispositions reveals that one would be hard pressed to deduce the judicial philosophy (welfare, justice, crime control, etc.) guiding judicial processing in specific countries. Although the terminology may vary among the countries in table 7.1, in any of them what could happen to a juvenile found to be delinquent (or criminal) appears to be similar. In all, offenders could receive a disposition or sentence ranging from commitment to an institution to outright release, even if found to have been engaged in the offense in question. It is evident that intermediate sanctions, typically involving some kind of community supervision and/or compensation, are likewise similar.

If the list of countries and their respective dispositions were expanded from those represented in table 7.1, it is conceivable that the dispositional lists would not change much. In short, what could happen to young people considered serious offenders is likely to be similar regardless of the country or juvenile justice system involved. However, what actually does happen to young offenders can vary considerably from society to society. The existence of similar disposition possibilities in two societies does not mean that similar offenders are treated the same. In other words, the laundry list of possible dispositions may be alike for countries across the globe; however, the relative numbers of offenders experiencing particular dispositions or the nature of how they are treated when they are similarly disposed may be quite different. To document and explain these differences one would need detailed, comparable data on how young offenders are actually treated in countries around the world. Currently, such data is lacking. One cannot say, therefore, that delinquent children in welfare societies are treated differently from criminals in crime-control countries. Nor is it possible to know if societies that require their young offenders to undergo therapy in juvenile rehabilitation facilities have a materially different impact on the lives and future behavior of youths in other societies who are sentenced to juvenile boot camps or labor colonies.

In the broadest sense, the various dispositional alternatives countries employ in dealing with delinquent youths can be categorized into two general measures: punitive versus therapeutic/educational. The distinction between

TABLE 7.1

Dispositional Alternatives for Juvenile Offenders in Selected Countries

Greece	India	New Zealand	Russia	Canada
Correctional institution placement, indefinite	Committed to special home, varies by gender	Supervision with residence	Imprisonment up to 10 years	Custody up to 5 years
Therapeutic measures	Probation supervision up to 3 years	Supervision with activity	Placement in correctional institution	Treatment up to 3 years
Reform school placement up to age 21	Fined	Community work	Community service without imprisonment	Probation up to 2 years
Placement under supervision, unspecified duration	Released on probation on good conduct to "fit institution"	Supervision	Fine	Fine up to $1,000
Placement under supervision of parent or guardian	Released on probation on good conduct to "fit person"	Fine, reparation, restitution, or forfeiture	Victim reconciliation	Up to 240 hours community service work
Reprimand	Sent home with admonition	Come up if called within 12 months	Confiscation of property	Restitution or compensation
		Admonition	Depravation of rank	Absolute discharge
		Discharge from proceedings	Absolute discharge	
		Police withdrawal of the information		
		Disqualification of a driver		

Sources: Greece: Petoussi and Stavrou 1996, 150–151; India: Hartjen and Kethineni 1996, 38; New Zealand: Morris and Maxwell 1991, 102; Russia: Shestakov and Shestakova 1997, 227–228; Canada: Winterdyk 1997b, 164.

these is unclear and arbitrary. All societies rely on a variety of approaches in dealing with offenders. Often a mixture of measures may be applied to specific offenders. What differs is the preference of one approach over another (e.g., incarceration versus counseling). Choosing, for example, between secure versus open confinement, psychotherapy versus job-skill training, or a punitive versus helping orientation of correctional officials.

Systematic research on how young offenders are treated in diverse societies is not available. However, some worldwide data on specific correctional approaches may be found in United Nations and other surveys. In addition, some understanding of the alternative approaches one might take in dealing with young offenders can be gleaned from the limited research conducted by criminologists and others throughout the world.

Punishing Children

Regardless of the system or judicial philosophy, the legally possible and actual punishment of young offenders is universal. All societies do it. But they differ in the nature, severity, and extent to which such dispositions are used. Some societies submit substantial segments of adjudicated youths to adult or adult-type punishments, primarily confinement in penal facilities. Others do so only rarely, and normally only after all other options have been exhausted or when the circumstances of the offense/offender are quite unusual.

There appears to be no direct relationship between the seriousness of a society's delinquency problem and how punitively a society reacts to young offenders. Nor is there any clear evidence that a punitive response to youth crime has anything to do with reducing either the frequency or seriousness of delinquent behavior. Instead, how severely or frequently a country punishes its young people appears to be related more to its cultural history and the prevailing political climate. Indeed, a number of criminologists have observed that changes in judicial/correctional policies reflect changing political orientations more than any specific changes in youthful behavior—much less any guidance criminological research may provide policy makers (Greenwood 1986; Jacobs 1990; Schwartz 1992).

Killing the Kids

The most severe punishment juvenile or adult offenders can receive is the death penalty. In the early decades of the twenty-first century almost all countries in the world had abolished the death penalty altogether or had legally prohibited the execution of juveniles. According to Amnesty International (2006), the execution of child offenders—persons under age eighteen at the time of the offense—is prohibited by international law. Since 1990 Amnesty International, however, reports that forty-eight known instances took place in eight countries—China, the Democratic Republic of Congo, Iran, Nigeria, Pakistan, Saudi Arabia, the United States of America, and Yemen. Nineteen of these executions occurred in the United States. Since then, the minimum age for application of the death penalty has been raised to age eighteen in Yemen, Zimbabwe, China, and Pakistan. Due to administrative problems in implementing these laws, some juveniles were apparently still executed in China and Pakistan after the laws were changed. The United States halted the execution of juveniles by the landmark Supreme Court decision *Roper v. Simmons* in 2005. When that decision was rendered, seventy-three juveniles were awaiting executions in various American prisons.

It appears that throughout the world law and public sentiment generally prohibit executing juvenile offenders as punishment for crimes. Occasional reports still appear suggesting that the extralegal killing of troublesome youths occurs in some countries. In spite of official denials, squads of police in Brazil are believed to assassinate street urchins in an unofficial attempt to reduce the ranks of a troublesome element Brazilian authorities are unwilling or unable to deal with otherwise (Scheper-Hughes and Hoffman 1994). Similar practices are reported for the Philippines (Conde 2005), Guatemala (Kline 1998), and elsewhere (Wernham 2001). Although operating outside the law as vigilantes, these death squads normally comprise police officials or unofficially sanctioned groups. Reports of extralegal executions often detail the general physical brutality that is also unofficially directly inflicted on youths caught up in the web of officialdom in many countries.

Imprisonment

Virtually all societies allow the incarceration of juveniles. What differs is the extent to which adjudicated youth may be subjected to this penalty—the incarceration rate; whether or not young offenders may be imprisoned as adults; the conditions under which juveniles are confined—for example, prisonlike versus school-like facilities; the length of time youths may be held in such facilities; and whether confinement itself may be perceived as a punitive disposition in and of itself or considered to be a necessary condition for therapeutic or educational purposes.

Incarceration as a way of dealing with suspected or adjudicated juvenile offenders is a relative rarity in any society (as with adult sentencing). Research by Walgrave (1987) on the dispositions boys and girls in Belgium received for various offenses is illustrative. According to this study, boys and girls accused of similar behavior are likely to experience different consequences. Moreover, incarceration was not necessarily directly related to the seriousness of the offense. Indeed, both boys and girls were more likely to be placed in some (presumably nonpunitive) facility for status offenses (misconduct, being in danger, running away from home) than they were for crimes against the person. Since these dispositions were to private institutions as opposed to state institutions, it is likely that the youths were being incarcerated more for their welfare than for any punitive response to their behavior. For criminal activity, rather than being incarcerated, youths in Belgium at this time were more likely to receive a simple reprimand or to be kept under noncustodial control.

Although the disposition proportions are likely to vary considerably from country to country, incarceration of juvenile suspects or adjudicated offenders universally appears to be an exceptional, as opposed to preferred, way of dealing with juveniles who come into contact with the law. Some societies, however, seem to be much more prone to incarcerating youths in juvenile and/or adult facilities. The United States, for example, is characterized by its punitive approach to youth crime and delinquency. Table 7.2 suggests that substantial numbers of young people are incarcerated or detained in juvenile institutions. In addition, it is estimated that 7,600 youths under age eighteen were held in adult jails in 2000, and 5,600 were committed to state adult prisons during that year (Sickmund 2004). Add to this the number housed in juvenile facilities, more than 150,000 juveniles are under some kind of incarceration in the United States at any given time. The bulk of these youths are confined for delinquency, often involving personal violence, while about 4 percent are confined for status offenses. A substantial number (19 percent) are not charged with any offense but are referred for such things as abuse, neglect, emotional disturbance, or

TABLE 7.2

U.S. Youths in Juvenile Correctional Facilities, 1999

All residents	134,011
Offenders	108,931
Delinquency	104,237
Person	38,995
Violent	27,221
Status	4,694
Incorrigibility	1,843
Runaway	1,083
Truancy	913
Other residents (older, detained, etc.)	25,080

Source: Sickmund 2004, 3.

retardation. This disparity in the use of confinement suggests that the incarceration of juveniles in the United States is primarily a punitive response to offense behavior, as opposed to a protective measure for children in need or danger.

One might assume that the apparently extensive use of incarceration in the United States is directly related to the emphasis on crime control that has characterized American adult and juvenile justice since the 1980s and the substantially higher rates of delinquency reflected in official arrest and processing statistics. But, the extent to which a society may use incarceration as a way of dealing with offenders could have more to do with policy than the actual extent or seriousness of offense behavior. Legal change in Canada provides one such example. An analysis by Markwart (1992) of custodial sanctions in Canada after passage of the Young Offender Act in 1982 revealed progressive and substantial increase in the use of all manner of institutionalization. These increases can only be attributed to the impact of the law itself. Similarly, in summarizing some of the changes that were taking place in European countries during the 1980s, Junger-Tas (1991) notes that the use of lighter and more diverse sanctions for younger offenders was becoming more common, but, at the same time, deprivation of liberty for older juveniles was also increasing. Paradoxically, these changes were taking place while delinquency rates had either stabilized or declined in much of Europe.

Currently, it is virtually impossible to provide a reasonably accurate cross-national count of the numbers (rates) of juveniles incarcerated—either as detainees awaiting disposition or as adjudicated offenders. Comparable data from most countries simply does not exist, and efforts to conduct international surveys have failed to cast statistical light on the question. For example, one study conducted for Defense for Children International (Tomasevski 1986) to determine the extent to which children across the globe were imprisoned in adult facilities could provide only summaries of the individual reports compiled by researchers in each country because of the grossly divergent methodologies used by researchers to gather information. However, noncomparable data from individual countries does suggest that the use of incarceration of any kind as a way of dealing with young people varies considerably.

For example, Huizinga et al. (2004) conducted a cross-national comparison of Bremen, Germany, and Denver, Colorado, regarding the effects juvenile justice-system processing had on the subsequent delinquent behavior of youths subjected to arrest, adjudication, and sentencing. They observed that the two cities disposed of adolescent, young adult, and adult offenders in quite different ways. In Bremen, for offenders up to age twenty the preferred strategy was diversion, while fines were most common for adult offenders. In Denver, juveniles and adults were treated much the same. The majority of offenders in Denver, regardless of age, received intermediate sanctions with about 10 to 20 percent sentenced to incarceration. In contrast, in Bremen the most frequent use of incarceration was for fifteen-year-old males, with fewer than 4 percent receiving this disposition.

A report on juvenile crime and justice in Australia suggests that the incarceration of juveniles in correctional institutions was rare and had even declined in the last quarter of the twentieth century. In 1981 only 1,352 juveniles were incarcerated—a rate of 65.04 out of every 100,000 youths aged 10–17. By 1996 the number of incarcerated youths had declined to 716, at a rate of 34.70 per 100,000 youths (Mukherjee et al. 1997). Similarly, Japan reported declining numbers of juvenile incarcerations during this period. In 1985 Japan held an average daily population of 6,029 youths in juvenile training schools, 66 percent of which were considered to be long-term incarcerates. By 1993 that number had dropped to 3,183, even though the proportion being held long term had increased to almost 80 percent (Correction Bureau 1995). In Italy, admissions to juvenile prisons between 1984 and 1994 fluctuated but also decreased from 6,474 in 1984 to 2,240 in 1994 (Gatti & Verde 1997). In contrast, in the United States over 50 percent more juveniles were committed to residential placement between 1991 and 1999. The number sentenced to adult state prisons rose by 65 percent, even though this figure represents a slight drop in prison admissions between 1995 and 1999 (Sickmund 2004).

Comparing raw numbers across jurisdictions, of course, is potentially very misleading. Besides questions of accuracy, methodology, and comparability, one society may have relatively high incarceration rates for youths adjudicated by juvenile and/or adult courts, while another society may have very low rates. One possible reason for the disparity could be that the low-rate country diverts large numbers of youths to residential programs for educational or therapeutic purposes, with few juveniles ever actually being adjudicated and placed in a correctional institution (training school or prison). Thus, both countries may have about equal incarceration rates. In Russia, for example, juveniles eleven years or older who commit socially dangerous acts—basically status offenses—can be administratively placed in various special schools administered by the Ministry of Education. As Finckenauer (1996, 280) notes, "This 'administrative' handling, in contrast to judicial handling, is, in many ways, a distinction without a difference, when viewed from the perspective of the child." Further, Finckenauer points to the reality of relying on official statistics to arrive at conclusions about a country's delinquency problem or its response to it. He notes that, for Russia, placing status offenders in special schools as opposed to correctional institutions has "the political attractiveness to the state of keeping the juvenile delinquency statistics relatively low, since cases that are handled administratively do not count as juveniles registered for crimes."

It is highly speculative to assert that society X is or is not more or less punitive than society Y based on differences in the numbers of institutionalized youths each reports without detailed data on contact, processing, and placement to compare one jurisdiction with another. That caveat notwithstanding, the wide disparities in the numbers of juveniles, both in terms of relative rates and proportions processed by authorities, that different societies incarcerate in secure facilities suggest that some fundamental differences exist in how societies choose to deal with their troublesome youth. These differences have not as yet to been explored in any systematic way by criminology.

Like relative and absolute numbers incarcerated, the world's societies tend to be similar but often quite different from one another concerning the nature and conditions under which incarcerated youths are housed in various facilities. Where distinctions by age are made in their criminal codes, virtually all societies stipulate that juveniles (varying by age) are not to be housed with adults in correctional or detention facilities. Most jurisdictions have entirely separate facilities for juveniles awaiting processing, placement, or correction. Some of these societies have elaborate systems of graded facilities that include short-term, jail-like detention facilities; home-like cottages; and prisonlike, long-term training schools. Other countries have few, if any, separate facilities exclusively for juveniles. Instead, the typically few youths detained or incarcerated in these countries are housed in facilities built for adults, although they are kept separated from the adults. Policies vary in countries where juveniles can be processed and sentenced as adult criminals. In some, such offenders are incarcerated as if they were adults. In others, young offenders are separated from adults until they reach the age of majority, primarily for their own protection. At that time, if still incarcerated, they may be transferred to the regular prison population.

In spite of the lack of strong empirical data, it is clear that many countries do little, if anything, to ensure the separation of juveniles from adults, or to even meet minimal standards of welfare for young incarcerates. In a 1994 report for the United Nations, Kibuka (1995) described the situation of juveniles in most African countries. Although many of these countries had ratified the Convention on the Rights of the Child, few actually complied with the provisions of the United Nations Standards. Often facilities to house juveniles in these countries are overcrowded, unhygienic, and materially ill-equipped. Children frequently lack minimal provision of food and other necessities of life. In some countries no separate institutions exist to house detainees apart from youths on remand or serving sentences. Children are frequently incarcerated with adults in jails and prisons with little, if any, protection for their welfare. It is unknown to what extent children in countries outside Africa face a similar situation, but one may assume that even minimal United Nations Standards are honored more in the breach than in practice in many places. Tomasevski (1986) analyzed the legislation regarding policies for separating incarcerated juveniles from adults of twenty-seven countries in diverse parts of the world. All but three had some legal requirement on the separation of children from adults. The three countries not requiring such separation—Denmark, Finland, and the

Netherlands—were surprising since these three countries typify a therapeutic, nonpunitive philosophy in dealing with adult and juvenile offenders. Legislation requiring separation of adults and juveniles was probably not deemed necessary in these countries given their very infrequent use of incarceration in any case and its practical nonuse when it comes to juveniles. More significant, Tomasevski observed that the law at this time allowed no exception to the separation requirement in only three countries—Costa Rica, Spain, and the United Kingdom. In the remaining twenty-one countries that had laws requiring separation, the law itself allowed exceptions to the rule.

In the penal codes of countries without established separate legal systems for juveniles, cases are tried in the same courts, following the same procedures as adults. However, reduced penalties for young offenders are a common stipulation in law. Most often these stipulations prohibit the death penalty for persons under age eighteen. Shorter sentences and prohibition of other penalties are also common. In countries with juvenile justice systems considerable diversity is found across the globe in the length of time a juvenile can face incarceration and the nature of the correctional or detention facility in which their confinement may take place. In Germany, for example, the minimum sentence of incarceration for juveniles is six months, while the maximum is five years. If the adult penalty for the same offense would be more than ten years, a juvenile could be held for up to ten years (Wolfe 1996). In Greece, on the other hand, a judge can sentence a juvenile to an institution for an unspecified time. Minimum and maximum sentences are generally somewhere between six months and ten years. But, a juvenile who commits an offense that would receive more than ten years if committed by an adult can be institutionalized from five to twenty years (Petoussi and Stavrou 1996).

In some countries, confinement of any kind is a last resort and is to be used for as short a time as necessary for youths. The law in Denmark, for instance, allows the imprisonment of offenders under age eighteen at the time of the crime with a maximum term of up to eight years. Actual imprisonment of juvenile offenders, however, is seldom used in Denmark. When it is imposed, authorities must first consider alternative ways to serve the sentence. Typically this involves placement in some nonprison facility such as a hospital (Kyvsgaard 2004). In other countries, detention and incarceration are almost a matter of course. Finckenauer (1996) estimates that from 60 to 70 percent of court-convicted juveniles in Russia are sentenced to terms in juvenile labor colonies. These institutions are of two types: general and reinforced regimes. General regimes are used for all females and for males serving their first sentence. Reinforced regimes are reserved for repeaters and those convicted of especially serious crimes. Sentences in general regime institutions are up to three years and in reinforced from three to ten years. In Russia, youths sentenced to incarceration are not merely housed in institutions; they are also condemned to work in labor colonies reminiscent of the old Soviet *gulag* (prison camp) system that flourished under communist rule. According to Finckenauer (1996, 282), "Even the minimum security facilities have double fences, barbed wire, electric wire, guard towers, and dogs. There is no treatment (such as behavior modification, group or individual counseling, and so on), educational and recreational resources are very limited, and there is a great emphasis upon work—up to eight hours a day for six days a week."

Reports from countries around the world suggest that the terms of confinement and the conditions under which institutionalization may be used are varied across the globe. This is true also in those countries where states or districts enjoy considerable legal autonomy. For example, according to Seymour (1996, 12), "in most [Australian] states and territories the maximum is two years, but in South Australia it is three years, and in Victoria a juvenile over the age of 15 may be committed to an institution for up to three years. In practice, the procedures employed are flexible, and release dates are determined by parole boards or equivalent bodies." In Canada, Corrado and Markwart (1996:48) report that "custodial institutions vary substantially across the provinces for several reasons. Most important, there is no common operational definition for open and secure facilities. . . . . As well, the availability of service and treatment programs and resources differs. Typically, the primary program focus in youth custody centers is the provision of security, health, education, and recreational services, whereas treatment services are usually available on an ad hoc demand basis, provided either by private contractors or by arrangement with noncorrectional government agencies."

The confinement of juveniles in any kind of facility is justifiably pursued by any society for two purposes: the care and protection and/or the correction and rehabilitation of needy and offending youth. The emphasis placed on these two purposes tends to vary among the countries of the world. Regardless of emphasis, action stemming from both purposes may, in fact, be necessary for the protection of others as well as the future well-being of the juvenile. The use of incarceration for any purpose, however, is also fraught with potential abuse and unintended consequence (International Prison Watch 1998). Evidence of net widening, for example, is not uncommon in countries that instituted policies intended to divert children to care and protection and away from more punitive consequences. On the other hand, societies that instituted get-tough policies resulting in long-term confinement in penal facilities discovered that youths subjected to these experiences did not necessarily refrain from future criminality. It is also questionable if rates of delinquency in these countries were lowered. Governments contemplating changes in how they deal with delinquents or potential offenders may want to first explore what has happened in countries that have instituted similar policies.

Other Punishments

Alternative sanctions for juvenile offenders appear to be common among the world's societies. In some instances these alternatives are part of diversion programs, where youth must undertake some action or participate in some program to avoid more severe treatment. In other cases, the alternative is a sanction imposed by the court or similar authority. It is not clear to what extent these sanctions are designed to inflict pain and suffering, ways of controlling young offenders or potential offenders short of confinement, or as necessary adjuncts to therapeutic or educational efforts. What a particular disposition might or could be is a matter of how society perceives the measure than any of its intrinsic qualities. A requirement to engage in so many hours of community service, for instance, could be perceived as a just punishment for misconduct, a way of keeping watch over someone outside of school hours, a way of teaching the youth a lesson, or all three. Whatever the case, it appears that virtually all societies have available a host of noncustodial dispositions that are used in either the pre- or post-adjudication treatment of offending youth. The court dispositions received in Sweden during 2002 for offenders aged 15–17 illustrate the use of these alternatives (see table 7.3).

In Japan, 72.8 percent of the 133,046 non-traffic cases that appeared before the family court were dismissed without a hearing, while almost 16 percent received the same fate after a hearing (Yokoyama 1997). In Germany, almost 30 percent of the cases adjudicated by the Hamburg juvenile justice system received community service or fines (Albrecht 1997). In New South Wales, Australia, between 1992 and 1993 fewer than 7 percent of cases received some kind of confinement, while about 16 percent received probation or fines, and almost 45 percent were released on recognizance or otherwise dismissed (Cunneen and White 1995). Some countries, however, may depart from this general pattern. For example, Ebbe (2006) reports that of the 802 cases in 1999 reaching the juvenile court in Nigeria, over 40 percent were incarcerated in an approved school and more than 33 percent received corporal punishment. Fewer than 8 percent were placed on probation, 5.6 percent were fined, and 3.8 percent were dismissed. As Ebbe explains, these differences reflect features of Nigerian juvenile justice (e.g., lack of status offenses) that depart from those characteristics of most other societies.

Often the line between what is an alternative-disposition versus a diversion-prevention measure is not clear. But, creative, largely noncustodial ways of responding to delinquent and predelinquent youth are found throughout the world. Prominent examples include victim-offender mediation or compensation programs. Resembling negotiation sessions in civil court proceedings, these programs typically involve out-of-court arbitration proceedings in which the victim and offender, guided by an impartial arbitrator, attempt to redress the damage through a negotiated settlement (Bazemore and Schiff 2005, 2000; Nylund 1991). Based on restorative justice ideals, these programs seek to hold the offender accountable, restore relations, and comfort the victim.

TABLE 7.3

Court Dispositions of Offenders Age 15–17 in Sweden, 2006

Number of defendants	13,491
Imprisonment	9
Closed juvenile care	71
Psychiatric treatment	6
Of which with special release inquiry	5
Probation	121
Of which combined with imprisonment	2
Combined with an order on undertaking treatment	0
Combined with an order on community service	10
Suspended Sentence	85
Of which in combination with community service	5
Treatment under the social services act	2,775
Of which youth service	585
Fines	2,134
Order that the earlier sanction imposed shall also apply in current sentencing	31
Of which closed juvenile care	3
Probation	28
Suspended sentence	0
Free from sanction	0
Exemption from sanction	4
Fine issued by the prosecutor	4,216
Of which with suspended sentence	1
Waiver of prosecution	4,039

Source: Adapted from National Council for Crime Prevention 2007.

In some instances, the entire focus of a country's approach to young offenders is to prevent their becoming entangled in judicial processing of any kind. The Dutch HALT program is an example (Junger-Tas 2004; Kruissink 1991; Van Hees 1991). Consisting of a host of intervention strategies by police and local support offices, the HALT program seeks to keep offending youths out of

d to redress matters directly. For instance, a youth may be required
lfered goods and to work in exchange for not being reported to a
Similar strategies have been initiated across the globe (Storgaard
2000; Wolfgangerler and Schäfer 2000).

Treating, Educating, and Training the Delinquent

The juvenile justice systems created in Western nations shortly after the turn of
the twentieth century were based on the common-law principle of *doli incapax*
(Nicol 1995), which views juveniles as incompetent, unable to form legal intent,
and therefore not to be held responsible for their actions. Defined as delinquents rather than criminals, offending youth were to be rehabilitated and salvaged from a life of crime. Based on this idea, children and young offenders were
to be given the care and protection necessary to safeguard them from involvement in further criminality. Juveniles were to be treated rather than punished.

Although not responsible for their misconduct, juveniles were still to be
held accountable and subjected to salvaging intervention, by force if necessary.
To achieve this goal, juvenile authorities were invested with a range of powers
and latitude of actions unimaginable in adult criminal cases. In addition, intervention options were available to authorities to deal with the needs, not behavior, of youngsters in order to secure their best interests and deflect them from
a life of crime (see Empey 1979; Weijers 1999). In practice, the reality rarely came
close to the ideal, and by the end of the twentieth century many countries had
moved away from the rehabilitative ideal, instead emphasizing legalistic principles and crime-control objectives (Hawkins and Zimring 1986).

Throughout the world, salvaging young offenders, or would-be offenders,
from a life of crime by attending to their needs is still a dominant theme in dealing with delinquent youth. Treatment and educational (or vocational) training
are practiced by countries across the globe as alternatives to, or in conjunction
with, punitive responses. Some countries emphasize one approach over another,
while others provide both. Therapeutic, educational, or vocational intervention
alternatives to incarceration or other punishments are frequently part of diversion programs. Commonly, one or more intervention program is also proscribed
for juvenile offenders who are incarcerated or are required to submit to probation supervision, community service, fines, or other punishments. All modern
societies exhibit a blend of punitive/treatment/educational programs in their
arsenal of strategies to respond to delinquent and predelinquent youths. However, little research on the operation and or effectiveness of these programs can
be found for most of the world's societies. Thus, one can do little more than out-
line the essential ideas behind these corrective approaches and illustrate some
isolated examples.

Therapeutic Interventions

The original child-saving movement of the early twentieth century focused on reforming the wayward child. Its key ingredients were education, discipline, and vocational training. Juvenile correctional institutions were called industrial schools or reform schools. Training mostly immigrant children to be useful employees in the booming factories of America and Europe were the primary objectives.

With the development of psychology and psychiatry during the early twentieth century, the emphasis shifted from the reform to the rehabilitation of young offenders. Therapeutic interventions based on a medical model of diagnoses, treatment, and rehabilitation became the guiding principles in juvenile corrections. This ideology viewed delinquent conduct as symptomatic of underlying psychological, emotional, or possibly biological defects. Delinquents were seen as acting out. Those exhibiting antisocial or asocial personality characteristics were thought to be emotionally disturbed or troubled. Once the problem was diagnosed and treated, it was thought that the abnormal behavior would be eliminated. Delinquency, in effect, was viewed as a medical condition to be treated like any other disease.

By the end of the twentieth century, the development of sociological theories emphasizing the social, economic, and interpersonal correlates of offense behavior had undermined the perspective of individual pathology that was integral to the medical model of juvenile corrections. Research suggested that few, if any, of the therapeutic interventions then being practiced did little, if anything, to curb offense behavior. A public concern with increasing rates of crime and violence led most countries to largely abandon a strictly rehabilitative approach in how they responded to delinquent youth or sought to prevent offense behavior (see Greenwood 1986).

Yet, throughout much of the world the rehabilitative idea remains a very pervasive theme in juvenile corrections. And, in some countries, treatment of some kind, primarily counseling or the use of various cognitive or behavioral modification strategies, is very much a part of their response to delinquent and predelinquent juveniles. Hong Kong's program is typical of what one might find in just about any country that has specific programs for juvenile offenders (see Lee 2005). According to Kwan (1988), so-called training centers designed for the short-term detention of juvenile offenders have psychological services that carry out therapeutic assessments of inmates and provide counseling for the early identification and treatment of adjustment problems. Youths who have problems adapting to the center, or who exhibit deep-seated personality difficulties, are given in-depth follow-up counseling by the resident clinical psychologist. In addition, "psychological treatment to combat dependence on drugs given in the form of therapeutic counseling, both in groups and individually, is conducted on a regular basis throughout the period of treatment by operational staff and members of both the Aftercare Section and Psychological Unit" (Kwan 1988, 46).

Most countries appear to offer various kinds of rehabilitative services for predelinquents and delinquent youths, as part of community and institutional corrections. For some, rehabilitation and social welfare intervention appears to be the central theme around which all other correctional and juvenile justice activities are organized. The Philippines is one such country. According to Caalim (1988), in the Philippines the department of welfare is actively involved in all aspects of delinquency prevention and the processing and correcting of juvenile offenders based on the belief that delinquency is primarily a community phenomenon to be solved through rehabilitation. As preventive measures, a host of services, both community and residential, are administered through the Department of Social Welfare and Development (DSWD) for predelinquents and services to young offenders. A delinquent youth on probation, for instance, comes under the supervisory authority of the DSWD, and it is the recommendation of the social worker that the court relies upon when deciding to terminate the case. Youths in residential placement may receive psychological and psychiatric services that could involve "court-directed psychiatric evaluation, group dynamic sessions with residents and their families, psychological evaluation and consultation when indicated to understand [the delinquent's] personality structure pertinent to guidance and counseling and . . . treatment and rehabilitation, as a whole" (Caalim 1988, 139).

While the Philippines places social welfare authorities as central figures in the entire system of juvenile justice and corrections, France centralizes that authority in the judiciary (Blatier 1999; Hackler 1991; Humphris 1991). The author's personal observations of delinquency proceedings, and interviews with French juvenile justice officials in the fall of 2000, suggest that the guiding philosophy and procedures, as various observers have noted as characterizing that country's approach to delinquent and needy youth, have not changed much since the present system was adapted in 1912. According to Strasburg (1977, 24), in France, "law-breaking by juveniles is not thought to demand condemnation and punishment; it is taken as a signal that measures of 'protection, assistance, supervision or education' are required." As such, whatever action authorities take must be tailored to the individual delinquent's needs and unique personality. To achieve this goal a thorough background investigation of the social, medical, and psychological state of an accused youth is an obligatory step in arriving at a judgment and final disposition of a case. While aided by a staff of social workers, psychologists, and doctors in assessing the needs and personality of those youths brought to their attention, the key official who determines virtually all matters relating to these youths is the juvenile court judge *(juge des enfants)*. Besides the normal degree in law, these judges have an additional three years of specialized training in law and human sciences. Emulating the ideal version of the juvenile court judge envisioned by its founders, the French juvenile "judge assumes the roles of investigator, psychologist, family counselor and decision maker all at once and attempts to determine the underlying causes of the child's behavior and the appropriate response to it" (Strasburg 1977, 24). With rare exceptions, acting alone in chambers with only the juvenile and/or his or her parents in attendance, the judge has extraordinary discretionary authority to deal with the child, short of punishment or confinement, in virtually any way he or she deems appropriate and to which the child and his or her parent's consent. However, regardless of the offense in question, that authority is guided and restricted both by a prevailing social philosophy and legal mandate to ensure the best interests of the child. As Strasburg (1977, 28) notes, "The law unabashedly embraces what we might call the treatment model of corrections, directing courts to 'pronounce . . . the measures of protection, assistance, supervision and education that seem appropriate' in each case, no matter how serious the offense charged. Only in exceptional cases does the law permit punishment of juveniles, and then only for those older than thirteen and only 'when the circumstances and personality' of the delinquent seem to demand it."

Judges in other societies, of course, may have similar power, and a commitment to a welfare-type, nonpunitive approach in dealing with young offenders is by no means limited to the few examples presented above. Some societies still exhibit a residual medical-model orientation and treat delinquency as an expression of individual pathology as opposed to wanton misbehavior. More characteristically, countries such as Canada, the United States, and the United Kingdom exhibit a kind of schizoid tension between the desires to punish the bad but at the same time help the wayward child—a tension that in practice frequently ensures that neither goal is satisfactorily achieved.

That does not mean that even in those environments most oriented to crime control that therapeutic interventions may not be found in abundance or that such therapeutic treatments may not have some positive impact on delinquents and their behavior. In 1994 the United States Office of Juvenile Justice and Delinquency Prevention, for example, published a program report assessing a host of promising rehabilitative and habilitative programs that are actively being pursued in that country to combat delinquency and reduce recidivism. Prominently listed were therapeutic interventions of various kinds. The programs listed as promising included behavior management, counseling, milieu management, reality therapy, sex offender and substance abuse treatment, and therapeutic milieu. Also contained in this report were examples of promising educational and vocational programs (Montgomery et al. 1994).

Educational Programs

Juvenile justice was founded in Europe and North America when the idea of mass public education was becoming a reality and compulsory expectation for children of all ranks. Thus, it would be no surprise that academic and/or vocational educational programs and some kind of school attendance requirement would be central themes in juvenile corrections throughout most, if not all, the world. Many of the early laws establishing juvenile justice systems in Europe and elsewhere particularly emphasized the importance of education in the reform of delinquent youth. Laws today specifically require children to attend school up to some specific age, often sixteen. Hence, diversion, community correction, and institutional programs for juvenile offenders and predelinquents throughout most of the world normally also have the requirement that youths below the legal attendance age engage in educational activities. In most instances, as a condition of their being diverted from further processing or remaining under community supervision, youth are required to attend school. Correctional institutions almost invariably provide minimal academic instruction for residents. And, in most countries, failure to attend school is itself an offense for which further, more severe, legal action could be initiated.

An underlying belief in all this is that becoming educated is a necessary prerequisite for an individual to not, or at least not be required out of necessity, to lead a life of crime. Thus, educating young people is not only desirable for their own good but also a way of preventing crime. In addition, keeping young people occupied for much of the day under close supervision is a sure way of keeping them out of trouble. The saying "Idle hands are the Devil's workshop" was not unknown to the founders of the juvenile court. And, of course, a trained and disciplined workforce is essential for economic growth.

Various countries appear to have developed a host of ways to ensure that the educational expectations for delinquent and predelinquent youths are fulfilled. Little research is to be found in the literature of criminology on these educational programs or their impact on youths. In most instances, it is likely that juveniles are told that they must attend school as a condition for suspending treatment. This requirement is ideally monitored by social welfare, probation, or community organizations that have responsibility for the juvenile.

Since many of the youths who come to the attention of juvenile authorities are not equipped to participate in normal school environments, some societies have gone to considerable lengths to establish alternative educational avenues, including alternative schools, vocational/academic educational programs, and special-needs programs designed to help developmentally disabled juveniles and other children achieve academically.

Although practically any country is likely to attempt to have some kind of educational expectation for youths caught up in its correctional machinery, only a few explicitly articulate education as the central theme of juvenile corrections. Germany appears to be one of those exceptions.

> Youth criminal law under the [German] Youth Court Law targets education and rehabilitation of the young offender. Although a juvenile is held legally responsible for a crime (*mens rea* must be proven), the primary goals are education and rehabilitation. The emphasis is not on the offense or its seriousness but on the offender and his or her needs. Rather than punishments, juveniles accused of offenses are to receive "education" measures. The law requires that such measures be "proportional" to the offense but, at the same time, guided by the overriding goal of education. What constitutes an "education" measure, however, can be a matter of interpretation. Under section 10 of the Youth Court Law, a juvenile offender in Germany could be sentenced to community service, participation in a social training course or victim-offender mediation, or he or she could be required to attend traffic education or vocational training. And a child could be placed in a home or foster family to enforce "educational" measures. (Albrecht 2004, 472)

As a guiding principle, China also emphasizes the education of delinquent youths. Xiaoming (2000) notes that educating and correcting juvenile delinquents in China generally follows sequential steps. Younger offenders receive early social-educational intervention. If a youth continues offending, a local social-educational team may be established. If the efforts of this local control team fail, the youth may be sent to work study. A youth's serious misbehavior could result in placement in a juvenile reformatory, particularly if the juvenile's behavior involves violations of the criminal code.

As noted earlier, correctional institutionalization of juvenile offenders remains the disposition of last resort in countries across the globe, regardless of the underlying philosophy guiding their juvenile justice system. Providing meaningful educational experience to young people in such prisonlike environments is a global problem—one that for many countries has been an unattainable goal. This problem is particularly accentuated for the few girls found incarcerated in most countries. A study in the United Kingdom illustrates the issue (Great Britain Office of Standards in Education 2004). Based on a survey of girls under age eighteen placed in institutions under detention or on training orders throughout the country, the inspectors concluded that these establishments failed to provide sufficient quantity and quality of training and education and that the girls received inadequate education that was ill-suited to their needs. However inadequate, it was contended that the education and training provided was still better than what the girls had received before custody or, in fact, would be likely to receive upon returning to the community. A similar observation was made by Hartjen and Priyadarsini (1984) in their study of correctional facilities for boys in Tamil Nadu, India, in the late 1970s. Although custodial, the facilities provided the boys' only hope for academic education and vocational training.

Conclusion

Societal reaction to young offenders emanates from the universal, fundamental tension inherent in the opposing desires to punish those who have harmed or offended versus helping those who are in need or whose behavior is beyond understanding and control. On the one hand, there is the impulse to punish the child who is naughty, bad, or offensive or to protect ourselves from those who seem to threaten us. On the other hand, there is an apparent universal feeling that children are not like adults. Instead, young people are thought to not yet have acquired the self-control attributed to and assumed of adults. They are not fully aware of the potential and consequences of their behavior. They need to be nurtured and guided.

Given these basic assumptions, essentially all approaches to dealing with delinquent youths are efforts to resolve these conflicting desires and the tension they create. How societies around the world pursue this resolution is reflected in the diverse yet similar ways in which young people are responded to.

The essential ideas behind special systems of juvenile justice/corrections has always been to spare young people from the harsh, punitive punishments demanded by the penal codes of all societies and to protect the young from exposure to greater evil and temptation by separating them from adult offenders. To achieve these goals, countries around the world have developed four strategies to deal with offending and potentially endangered young people: reduce adult penalties in the case of juveniles; legislate special penalties for juveniles; where incarceration is called for, house juveniles in facilities separate or different from those holding adults; and substitute rehabilitative or educational measures for punitive ones. Besides separating incarcerated juveniles from adults, most countries emphasize one of these approaches. Many mix them in a complex of dispositional alternatives.

Simply reducing adult penalties when a juvenile is found guilty of some crime is a fairly common and historically grounded practice. Doing so seems to satisfy the desire to be somewhat forgiving of youthful immaturity while holding offenders accountable for their misconduct and securing a sense of justice. In many societies efforts to crack down on youth crime and delinquency have led to legislative moves to up the ante, either through waiving more cases to adult jurisdiction or through making dispositions for juveniles more punitive by subjecting more juveniles to harsher adultlike punishments. Short of abolishing any pretense to juvenile justice as distinct from that applied to adults, increasing the punitive treatment of young offenders means moderating the assumptions of *mens rea*, in which the idea of a distinct system of justice for juveniles was embodied. Moreover, regardless of age, unless the same penalties are to be stipulated for all offenders, establishing just how much less punitive the penalties for juveniles should be is a vexing matter subject to disagreement and controversy, as in the case of the death penalty for young murderers. This approach discards any concern for the reform or redemption of young who are believed to warrant condemnation. Nevertheless, in the last decades of the twentieth century many countries opted for some version of a get-tough approach or experienced calls to do so.

Globally, a host of special programs for juveniles exist, usually combining some punishment/rehabilitative approach. Such programs as outward bound, boot camps, guided group interaction, and the like combine treatment goals with punitive elements thought to instill discipline and increase youths' awareness of the wrongfulness of their behavior. In many countries delinquency laws mandate that juveniles are to be subjected to educational rather than punitive measures and, if incarcerated, housed in facilities that are less secure and less punitive, for shorter periods of time, than those reserved for adults. Even where justice for juveniles is not merged or combined with that of adults, or where young people are not subjected to adult sentences, the predominant approach has been to subject young offenders to correctional programs different from those adults experience and to do so in distinctly different kinds of correctional facilities.

The two central questions regarding any response to juvenile, as well as adult, offenders are (1) "Is it just?" and (2) "Does it work?" The question of "justice" is an evaluative, not a scientific, matter. Subjecting offenders to therapeutic interventions, or doing virtually anything else to, or with, them in response to misconduct are matters for opinion and personal morality. On the other hand, the second question, the issue of prevention or deterrence—determining whether or not doing, or not doing, specific things to or with juvenile offenders, or pre-offenders, does anything to reduce their offending behavior—is something criminology can measure and assess scientifically. Examples of evaluation studies assessing various correctional or diversion strategies or specific programs abound.

A common way to evaluate some program's effectiveness is to measure reductions in crime rates and/or recidivism rates among populations experiencing a program compared to a group not receiving the program. For some countries, primarily the United States, Canada, and several Western European countries, there exists a considerable literature on the question of "What works?" (Burnett and Roberts 2004; Cullen 2005; Lab and Whitehead 1998; Palmer 1991; Sherman et al. 1998; Smith 2005). Unfortunately, as with the availability of programs themselves, research is virtually nonexistent for most of the rest of the world. Thus, even if some strategy does hold promise for reducing delinquency or curbing recidivism in country X, there is no way to tell if this approach would work or if it could even be implemented elsewhere. Based on available research, as with virtually all other aspects of delinquency and juvenile justice explored throughout this volume, one can with some confidence speculate that what does not work in one country is not likely to work elsewhere either. The U.S.-initiated scared-straight (or juvenile awareness) program is one such example. Reviews of the effectiveness of a number of these programs not only cast considerable doubt on their potential to reduce delinquency, but also suggest that such an approach is more harmful to juveniles than doing nothing at all (Petrosino et al. 2003). Similarly, there is reason to believe that incarceration in secure facilities, for example, does little to intimidate young people into obedience or to curb post-release delinquency anywhere in the world. In addition, the handful of comparable evaluations of alternative correctional approaches in the literature suggest that noninstitutional interventions of various kinds may produce similar results regardless of where they are tried. Currently, as it is questionable to say that some specific program or even type of reaction strategy works to reduce delinquency with any degree of assurance, it is close to impossible to assert that any such program or strategy would work universally. One might speculate that whether or not any specific intervention strategy—imprisonment, vocational training, or community service orders—has any impact at all in preventing or reducing delinquency, the effect is probably much the same universally. What is certain, however, is the realization that before embarking on any agenda, governments around the world would do well to look at what has been tried, or is being tried, elsewhere to ensure that well-intended treatments not only do what they are intended to do, but also do not have consequences different from those desired.

8

Children as Victims

As with crime and delinquency generally, the victimization of young people in many of the world's societies remains little investigated by criminologists. Victimization is an exceedingly difficult subject to study scientifically or to even investigate in any systematic way. Nevertheless, scholars from a number of other disciplines have done considerable work in this area, and scientific journals exist that are explicitly dedicated to the subject. The information that has been gathered suggests that all manner of child victimization is both prevalent and universal among the world's societies. Moreover, victimization surveys and other data reveal that young people are the victims of all the crimes that adults experience—murder, rape, various forms of theft, fraud, and the like. In addition, simply because of their age, children and young people are especially vulnerable to all manner of victimizing acts and circumstances. Being dependent on others for their well-being, children around the world are frequently placed in situations where they are subjected to certain kinds of attacks and exploitation from which they are unable to escape—such as bullying at school, physical attack in confinement, and sexual assault in the home. As powerless individuals, children in some societies are forced into behaviors—such as serving as soldiers in combat or working as virtual slave laborers—that are themselves victimizing. Or, they are cast into situations over which they have no control and about which they had no role or say in making—such as being born with HIV/AIDS infection, being orphaned due to war or poverty, or themselves being brutally killed in acts of terrorism.

Most societies have laws on the books designed to combat these victimizing behaviors. The United Nations has taken major initiatives in recognizing and attempting to combat all manner of victimizations involving young people (United Nations Expert Group Meeting 1995). Other international organizations also issue periodic proclamations condemning such activity. In addition, various organizations within and across societies are devoted to combating child abuse and neglect. Occasional media attention centers on such matters as the international trade in children as sex slaves, the use of children as armed combatants in some country's civil war, or the selling of children as indentured servants. Yet children around the world seem to remain vulnerable to adult greed, caprice, incompetence, and exploitation.

Defining Victimization

One of the things that complicate the study of delinquent and criminal behavior is the wide diversity of, and extreme differences in, the kinds of behaviors one might list under these labels. This is equally true of the range of things included under the label victimization. Thus, to even catalog the variety of activities that constitute child victimization is a daunting task subject to disagreement (Crosson-Tower 1999). Explaining and understanding such disparate activities as extorting lunch money from a classmate, extreme corporal punishment, failing to provide adequate medical care, selling one's child into sex slavery, or the murder on one's own infant present a seemingly unsolvable scientific challenge. Doing anything concrete to stop or prevent much of this activity is even more daunting.

Several efforts to categorize the varied forms of child victimization are found in the literature. In the United States, federal laws define child abuse and neglect as "any recent act or failure to act on the part of a parent or caretaker which results in death, serious physical or emotional harm, sexual abuse or exploitation; or any act or failure to act which presents an imminent risk of serious harm" (National Clearinghouse on Child Abuse and Neglect Information 2006). Under these laws each state in the United States is required to provide its own definitions of child abuse and neglect. Most states list four types of maltreatment—neglect, physical abuse, sexual abuse, and emotional abuse—with specific definitions elaborating each of the various types.

Based on how victimization behaviors might relate to the justice area, a broader conceptualization of victimizations involving young people is offered by Finkelhor and Hashima (2001) in a threefold typology. These categories include conventional crimes, such as rape, robbery, and assault; child maltreatment, consisting of acts that violate child welfare statutes, such as abuse, neglect, and child labor; and noncrimes, or acts that would be crimes if committed by an adult against another adult, including fights among siblings, socially accepted spanking, or other disciplinary acts of parents or caretakers. A fourth form of victimization not normally found in abuse/neglect categories identified by Finkelhor and Hashima (2001) are indirect victimizations of young people in which the juvenile is closely affected by the victimization—murder, impoverishment, and incarceration—of a family member or friend.

Referring to the numerous ways in which children can be victimized, Dorne (1989) constructed a threefold categorization using the encompassing term "maltreatment" to refer to the various victimizations covered by civil and/or criminal laws in the United States and elsewhere: abuse and neglect, molestation and incest, and institutional abuse. Although distinct categories, considerable overlap in actual behaviors may occur in specific cases, and any instance of child maltreatment may actually fall under all three categories.

Abuse involves acts that physically or emotionally harm the victim. Neglect, on the other hand, consists of the failure to act in appropriate ways to ensure the well-being of a dependent child or juvenile. The various behaviors that Dorne categorizes as the sexual victimization of children include molestation and incest. Institutional abuse involves young people victimized by an agency or one of its employees. Such victimization could take the form of any of the other kinds of victimization—physical, sexual, neglect, exploitation, etc.

Other ways to categorize the diverse forms of victimizing activities around the globe are to be found in the literature. For a global inquiry, there are four broad types: abuse, neglect, sexual victimization, and institutional victimization. Some forms of these victimizations may be universal. Children in all societies, for example, may be beaten by their parents, even though the extent of corporal punishment may vary considerably from society to society. Other forms of victimization are likely to be common to some situations or countries while unlikely in others. For example, using children in brothels, factories, and mines or denying certain children a chance to attend school. Incest, bullying, and beatings are likely to be universal, if varying in frequency, across societies. Ultimately, it is the task of criminology not only to document and explain the occurrence of victimizing behavior itself, but also to account for variations and universalities in its occurrence.

Abuse

When people think of victimization they typically think of assault or predatory forms of behavior directed against individuals. Although physical attacks of some kind typify such victimization, people can also be abused emotionally and in terms of their life chances or situation.

Physical Abuse

Definitions of abuse range from narrow clinical assessment of physical injury to broad encompassing statements with long lists of acts that constitute abuse, such as "beating, squeezing, lacerating, binding, burning, suffocating, poisoning, and exposure to heat and cold" (Dorne 1989, 7). Determining if some act (e.g., spanking or locking in a room or closet) constitutes an instance of abuse can be a scientific, as well as legal, challenge in any society. This is even more so from a global perspective, since norms and expectations as to how children might be treated vary considerably from culture to culture. In the United States, for example, it is legal for school officials to use limited corporal punishment to discipline children, although individual states may ban its use (Hyman and Wise 1979). In some Scandinavian countries it is altogether against the law, even for parents, to spank and use other forms of corporal punishment (Durrant and Olsen 1997). In other parts of the world, striking a child is a normal, routine activity (Shumba 2001, 2003).

Even if various groups are not uniformly intolerant of such behavior, extreme forms of such practices are probably clearly recognized as abusive by the members of all societies. In most cases, informal social controls are normally used to curb parents or others who go too far in disciplining their children. Undoubtedly, a small fraction of those that could be actually so dealt with come to the attention of authorities, and legal action is taken against abusers. These are likely extreme or bazaar cases of abuse.

Estimating the global extent of physical assaults on young people is impossible at this point. Data on which to base any estimate is simply nonexistent. Figures cited by agencies concerned with combating various forms of abuse may be more self-serving than empirically sound. Where data, even if inadequate, exists, it appears that young people are significantly more prone to violent victimization than adults. For example, the National Crime Victimization Survey conducted each year in the United States suggests that rates of physical victimization of the young are about three times higher than adults (Bureau of Justice Statistics 2003). Research in Canada also suggests that young people are frequent victims of all manner of physical attack (Gabor and Mata 2004; Paetsch and Bertrand 1999; Trocmé et al. 2003). Surveys in Finland (Kivivuori and Savolainen 2003) and Scotland (Scottish Office Home Department Central Research Unit 1998) indicate similar results.

However, a comparison of the United States, Canada, and Australia suggests that the rates of physical as well as other forms of victimization may vary considerably even among countries with similar cultural histories. According to Trocmé et al. (2003), in 1998 the United States registered 12.9 sustained maltreatment investigations per 1,000 children who alleged some form of child abuse and/or neglect. In Canada the rate was 9.7 per 1,000. In Australia, depending on the state in question, the sustained investigation rates ranged from 5.1 to 1.1 per 1,000 children. It is unknown whether these numbers reflect real differences in the physical or other victimization of young people or are the result of differences in processing and recording activities by authorities.

The vast majority of attacks upon young people around the globe are never reported to, or acted upon by, authorities. In some parts of the world, the direct and indirect experience of physical assault, mutilation, and even killing of the young and infants is an ever present threat. The victims go uncounted and unrecognized.

Emotional Abuse

In addition to physical abuse, emotional abuse victimizes young people around the world. This kind of abuse most obviously includes persistent verbal attacks and ridicule by parents, siblings, classmates, or others. Less obvious is Munchausen's syndrome by proxy, a disorder in which someone causes illness in another person, usually a child under the perpetrator's care, in order to gain attention for rescuing or caring for the victim (Moffatt 2003).

How extensive emotional victimization might be is unknowable. In some countries, medical personnel, school counselors, and other officials may be trained to look out for signs of such abuse, although they are more likely to be oriented to detecting physical or sexual abuse. Unless symptoms or activities are extreme or obvious, most cases of emotional abuse are probably undetected and little is done to halt or prevent the problem. In addition, there is no data to judge the extent of and damage done by the emotional trauma that children throughout the world may suffer from seeing family members slaughtered in warfare, being an indentured servant to pay family debts, or being subjected to beatings and deprivation by authorities. It is not surprising that the children raised in an environment of violence turn out to be violent themselves.

Child Labor

The use of children for labor dates from the beginning of human history, and until the twentieth century in Western societies it was an accepted fact of life (Hindman 2002). Indeed, it was not until well into the twentieth century that efforts to regulate and ban the employment of children, at least for the majority of young people in Western industrialized nations, were successful. However, throughout much of the rest of the world today the employment and often abusive use of children and juveniles as, typically, underpaid, often indentured, or virtual slave labor persists. The International Labor Office (2006) predicts that the end of child labor is foreseeable. Still, literally millions of juveniles, often of very tender age, are to be found working in dangerous conditions. Countries in sub-Saharan Africa, Asia, and South America are especially notorious in this regard (see Loyn 2005).

In and of itself, child labor is not necessarily a victimizing activity. Besides earning income, working young people can learn skills, discipline, and status as breadwinners. The use of child labor becomes victimizing when there is exploitative use of such labor; the denial of educational opportunities; and the physical, sexual, and emotional abuse of young workers by their employers, supervisors, or coworkers. Numerous accounts by international organizations such as Human Rights Watch, UNESCO, and ISPCAN present graphic accounts of the mistreatment of children working as domestic servants, employed in mines or factories, or virtually bonded to their employers to work off debts owed by their parents. Many of these underage laborers toil for long hours in conditions that are demeaning, physically dangerous, or pose a risk of long-term health damage. Most such children are denied opportunities to attend school, either because of the hours devoted to work or the inability to pay school fees due to the inadequate wages received. For example, Human Rights Watch (2006a) issued a report on child domestic workers in Central America, Indonesia/Malaysia, and West and Central Africa. The authors of the report note the following:

> Child domestic workers are nearly invisible among child laborers. They work alone in individual households, hidden from public scrutiny, their lives controlled by their employers. Child domestics, nearly all girls, work long hours for little or no pay. Many have no opportunity to go to school, or are forced to drop out because of the demands of their job. They are subject to verbal and physical abuse, and particularly vulnerable to sexual abuse. They may be fired for small infractions, losing not only their jobs, but their place of residence as well. (Human Rights Watch 2006a, 1)

Media reports of child workers—highlighting sari weavers in India; carpet weavers in Pakistan; brick chippers in Bangladesh; slave laborers on cocoa, coffee, and other farms in Mali; and boys enslaved to be camel jockeys in Arab nations—highlight the pervasiveness of the problem.

Under international law, child labor is not prohibited. However, international treaties do address the circumstances under which children may work and minimum ages for workers. Most countries have laws that ban child labor and/or regulate hours and conditions of work. Criminal penalties are often prescribed for violating these laws. However, where child labor is chronic such laws are rarely enforced or the penalties are inadequate to deter the practice.

Obviously, the pervasive employment of children and juveniles as laborers is primarily linked to widespread poverty. Rich nations have little need to exploit children as a cheap labor pool—and rich people have little need to force their children to work. Child labor is thus a clear instance of the victimization of the poor, but poverty only explains the need to work. It does not explain the exploitation and abuse of the children and young people forced into that situation. Beyond poverty, corporate greed, social indifference, and government failure are the culprits behind the exploitation of child labor.

Child Soldiers

In some parts of the world civil war seems to be endemic, almost a normal way of life. In some of these countries boys and girls, many of whom are six to ten years old, are pressed into service by combating forces (Human Rights Watch 2006b; Singer 2005/2006). Sometimes no bigger than the gun they are forced to carry, these children are frequently required to commit horrific acts of brutality, or to witness such acts, and may themselves be subjected to physical injury or death. Particularly notable in this regard is the country of Liberia, as reported by Human Rights Watch (2006c, 1):

> Both of the opposition groups, the Liberians United for Reconciliation and Democracy (LURD) and the Movement for Democracy in Liberia (MODEL), as well as government forces which include militias and paramilitary groups widely used children when civil war resumed in 2000. In some cases, the majority of military units were made up primarily of boys and girls under the age of eighteen. Their use and abuse was a deliberate policy on the part of the highest levels of leadership in all three groups. No precise figures exist as to how many children were used in the last four years of warfare; however United Nations (U.N.) agencies estimate that approximately 15,000 children were involved in fighting.

Similarly, the Liberation Tigers of Tamil Elaam (LTTE) in Sri Lanka systematically use child soldiers in its civil war against government forces. In this battle, Human Rights Watch (2006d) notes that over half of the LTTE soldiers killed in battle were under age eighteen and that children were also used as suicide bombers. Typically fourteen or fifteen years of age, although some as young as eleven, Tamil Elaam child soldiers are over 40 percent female.

Perhaps the most blatantly abusive country in this regard is Burma. According to Becker (2004, 1): "Burma has more child soldiers than any other country in the world. They account for approximately one-fourth of the 300,000 children currently believed to be participating in armed conflicts around the globe. Forced recruitment of children by government forces is so widespread that the United Nations secretary-general placed Burma on an international list of violators that flout international laws prohibiting the recruitment and use of children as soldiers."

Denied education and the nurturing of normal childhood, child soldiers are raised in a world of violence and exploitation. How many children have been abused in this manner is unknown. How many of them suffer physical injury and death as a consequence is unknown. How many, as a result of their servitude, are permanently psychologically and emotionally crippled is unknown. How much future criminality occurs on the part of children in societies where such abuse takes place is unknown.

In the offending countries the United Nations and other organizations have sought to pressure groups involved in this activity to halt the practice. Largely because warfare between contending parties has ceased or moderated and the need for large military forces has dissipated, some have complied. In others, rebel and/or government leaders known or suspected of using child soldiers simply deny the practice or resist pressure. In some instances, leaders of groups accused of this activity are subjected to international criminal prosecution. Few, if any of these individuals have so far been subjected to punishment (Hughes 2000; Human Rights Watch 2006e; Price 2005; Wessells 2000).

Neglect

Neglect involves not providing a child or young person under one's care with life's basic necessities or the degree of adequate care needed for a young person's normal physical and mental maturation (Dorne 1989). Failure to ensure that the youth receives adequate shelter, clothing, food, water, medical care, education, hygiene, and supervision are included in this category. In the United States more than one-half (almost 480,000) of the known cases of maltreated children included some form of neglect during 2003 (Administration on Children, Youth, and Families 2005).

Obviously, what constitutes adequate care is by no means universal and varies on the basis of cultural expectation and economic ability. In North America and Western Europe, for example, consistently not sending one's twelve-year-old to school would clearly be seen as neglectful and could subject the parent to legal action. In many parts of Africa, Asia, and South America, however, economic circumstances necessitate that a large number of young people never even have a chance to attend school. Are impoverished parents guilty of neglect under such circumstances? Even in Western, or economically developed, societies where caretakers might be subjected to legal action for failure to adequately care for those in their charge, notions of "parental autonomy" and the vagueness of what actually constitutes "neglect" often make it problematic to take action against them. In commenting on why cases of abuse and neglect are rarely prosecuted as crimes in the United States, Finkelhor and Hashima (2001, 71–72) suggest several reasons that are probably applicable worldwide: "The noncriminalization or nonprosecution of child maltreatment seems to be related in part to sanctity of parental and family relationships, a widely held distaste for government intruding on family matters, a belief that priority should be given to the preservation of the family unit, and the presumption that criminal justice intervention will do more harm than good."

An annual international survey of child maltreatment in countries across the globe revealed that in spite of official policies against abusive and neglectful activities considerable variation exists, largely based on a country's development status, in the availability of services to combat such practices. In addition, respondents suggest that barriers to providing or invoking preventive services include limited resources, declining family support, and a strong sense of family privacy (International Society for Prevention of Child Abuse and Neglect 2004).

Neglect can take a number of forms. One form is the "failure to thrive syndrome," which involves actions thought to cause an infant to be stunted in physical development. Another form, "dependency," occurs when a dependent young person is in need of public charity or government care because the persons responsible for their care are either unable or unwilling to provide it. An extreme form of such neglect is "abandonment," where dependent youths are simply left to their own resources. As with the emotional abuse young people may suffer, the emotional rejection or coldness parents or others may display toward their children can also be included as forms of "emotional neglect."

Street Children

In many parts of the world hordes of abandoned children are to be found haunting alleys, parks, and other public places. Due to the death of their caretakers or the inability of family members to care for them, or simple dearth of duty by family and other relatives, unknown numbers of children across the globe are abandoned and struggle to survive (LeRoux and Smith 1998). Powerless and vulnerable, such children are frequently the recipients of all manner of victimization—by peers, abusive and exploitative adults, and authorities. In many parts of the world such children are

> subjected to physical abuse by police or have been murdered outright, as governments treat them as a blight to be eradicated—rather than as children to be nurtured and protected. They are frequently detained arbitrarily by police simply because they are homeless, or criminally charged with vague offenses such as loitering, vagrancy, or petty theft. They are tortured or beaten by police and often held for long periods in poor conditions. Girls are sometimes sexually abused, coerced into sexual acts, or raped by police. Street children also make up a large proportion of the children who enter criminal justice systems and are committed finally to correctional institutions (prisons) that are euphemistically called schools, often without due process. Few advocates speak up for these children, and few street children have family members or concerned individuals willing and able to intervene on their behalf. (Human Rights Watch 2006f)

International organizations indicate that the plight of abandoned youth found across the globe is especially severe in Brazil, Bulgaria, Colombia, Guatemala, India, Kenya, and Sudan. These organizations have documented the widespread and apparently sanctioned human rights abuses of children. Victimized by those who would, or should, care for them, abandoned children become victimized again by the simple circumstances of their lives.

Street children in Haiti are a case in point. According to Kovats-Bernat (2000), in a supposed effort to deal with the street violence endemic to Haiti, antigang units were formed as a quasi component of the national police force. A particular target of these units is street children, in large part because these children are easy and readily available targets for street-sweeping exercises or simply as a way of filling idle time. Control efforts are often brutal and arbitrary—"not doing anything" being considered a legitimate reason for picking youths up who just happen to be on the streets of city slums (also see UNICEF 2006a).

In a special report on the plight of street children in the Democratic Republic of Congo, Human Rights Watch (2006g) presents a graphic picture of the situation such children face. According to this report, street children in Congo live in fear of the very people charged with protecting them. They are regularly arrested, whether they actually were involved or not, for crimes that take place in areas known to be frequented by street children. In addition, these children are commonly exploited by people who employ them. Both boys and girls are subjected to rape and sexual assault, which the police fail to investigate or prevent.

Even in nations with large numbers of street children, local and national laws concerning the neglect and abandonment of children in one's care as well as criminal statutes abound. If one were to add the pervasive maltreatment of street children to the criminal statistics of these countries, their crime rates would balloon. In addition, essentially all countries that have numerous street children, and documented widespread abuse of them, are signatories of international treaties protecting the fundamental rights of children. Pressure by international organizations is periodically brought to bear on countries that blatantly violate these standards, generally with little effect. Numerous charitable organizations (e.g., Street Kids International, Street Kids for Christ, Oaxaca Streetchildren Grassroots) seek to provide assistance of one kind or another to street children. As dedicated as many of the efforts by these international and charitable organizations might be, the worldwide persistence of abandoned children and their abuse by virtually everyone seems to be unabated.

Denial of Education

To be uneducated dooms one to poverty, marginality, exploitation, and dependency. Throughout history vast numbers of people (the poor, slaves, females) have been denied the opportunity to be educated. Today, both United Nations resolutions and the laws of most countries demand and guarantee the right and access to, at least, elementary education for all children. In many parts of the world, that right and access is still not provided or is blocked for large numbers of young people (UNICEF 2006b).

In some places the prohibition and failure of access to education and literacy stems from religious and cultural values. Under Taliban rule in Afghanistan, for example, girls were actively prohibited from attending school. In spite of laws mandating universal education in these countries, in South Asia educating girls was, and in some parts of India and Pakistan still is, thought to be unnecessary and a waste of resources. A common sentiment expressed to the author while conducting research in India was the idea that girls will be married off and become homemakers. Why waste the money to send them to school? Indeed, one of the clearest indicators of gender discrimination is girls' exclusion from education, especially in South Asia, sub-Saharan Africa, the Middle East, and North Africa (UNICEF 2006c).

In many other parts of the world, such as Africa and East Asia, attending school is beyond the financial means of many impoverished families. Elsewhere, schools may simply be nonexistent. UNICEF (2006c) reports that, in impoverished countries, of the children who even survive to reach primary school age, 40 percent of boys and 45 percent of girls will not attend school at all. Moreover, in these countries over 80 percent of children of secondary school age will not attend secondary school.

Whatever the cause or explanation, denying children access to education is as harmful as physical brutality, emotional neglect, inadequate diet, or denial of care. Through intervention work in isolated localities, various organizations across the globe have sought to remedy the situation by building schools or providing school materials. Following the United Nations' Millennium Declaration (United Nations 2000), UNICEF launched a major worldwide campaign to ensure that children everywhere had access to at least primary education. Ultimately, however, the source of the problem is a result of one or all three causes: cultural bigotry, poverty, and the failure of government.

In some parts of the world the sole impediment to women's education are cultural norms that devalue the status of women. Keeping girls and women illiterate or semiliterate is a sure way of enforcing their dependency on men and sustaining the power of males over them. The governments dominated by males in these societies have little incentive to change the situation.

A common characteristic of those unable to attend school is poverty. Children of the rich in any society manage to become educated and credentialed. Those of the poor often go without, because the facilities to educate them do not exist, they are too distant to be accessible, or families are unable to pay the necessary fees to attend school. Similarly, even when children are available to attend, poverty often necessitates that they work instead.

In the end, the denial of education to any and all of a country's citizens is fundamentally a failure of government. Governments that support, or do not challenge, cultural bigotry regarding the equality and rights of all citizens are guilty of criminal neglect. Governments that fail to allocate resources to provide educational facilities, no matter how humble, or free children from the need to work instead of attend school, are guilty of the crime of failure to support their children. In this regard, denial of education is, in the end, a form of government-inflicted victimization.

Sexual Victimization

Historians inform us that the involvement of the young, even children in some cases, in sexual activities was a common and accepted practice in the Western world from ancient times (Aries 1962). By the nineteenth century sexual acts with or involving children and juveniles increasingly became perceived as perverse and, ultimately, criminal throughout much of the world. However, as the young came to be seen as in need of protection and nurturance, efforts to protect them from sexual involvement and exploitation intensified. In the modern world few crimes generate more moral repugnance, and fear, than pedophilia and incest.

Occasionally, extreme cases involving individuals who sexually victimize young people receive media and legal attention. In recent years media reports of international efforts to combat sex tourism in various countries have sensationalized the arrests of individuals soliciting sex with minors caught in sting operations. Large-scale crackdowns on the international distribution of child pornography and the solicitation of young people for sexual encounters through the Internet have become major news items. As attention catching as these reports might be, they are probably but a miniscule fraction of the sexual attack and exploitation children and young people experience.

As defined by experts in victimization research, molestation involves numerous acts, including forcible sexual assault, rape, sexual exhibition, voyeurism, sex murder, prostitution, pandering, pimping, pedophilia, pornography, and trading in children for sexual purposes. Incest consisting of sexual interaction between blood relatives is a special instance of the wider category of molestation. Although the definition of "blood relative" may vary somewhat across the globe, concern with this victimizing activity usually focuses on sexually exploitative father-daughter relations.

As troubling as all forms of child-sexual victimization might be, from a global perspective three specific forms of such victimization have raised considerable concern and received attention from international organizations and criminal justice agencies across the globe: the trafficking of women and children for sexual and other purposes, the use of children in prostitution, and the spread, particularly by Internet, of child pornography.

Trafficking

In a major report for the Protection Project, Lederer (2001, 1) notes that "today trafficking in women and children is a big business involving extensive international networks of organized criminals, modern mafias, and unscrupulous and corrupt government officials." Although primarily involving the sale and sexual enslavement of young women, a significant part of the sexual-trafficking business involves juveniles and even children sold for use in brothels and pornography, or as child brides or personalized sex slaves (Kane 1998). Nobody knows how many juveniles, worldwide or even in individual countries, are abducted, coerced, sold, or lured into the sex trade, or how many are sexually abused by those to whom they are essentially indentured as exploited labor. Some estimates suggest that the number of sexually exploited juveniles exceeds 100 million worldwide. How accurate that, or any figure, might be cannot be evaluated (UNICEF 2006c).

What is significant, however, is that the activity is not limited to one country or region, or necessarily to conditions such as a country's economic development. In fact, the movement of juveniles and children for sexual activity is a global phenomenon. At the same time, as with many other forms of child victimization, poverty appears to be a major contributor in that the victims are largely drawn from impoverished countries, and the people victimized are among the most desperate of those countries. Host countries, on the other hand, are largely economically developed societies. However, recent research suggests that, even within countries such as the United States and Canada, significant numbers of resident youths are trafficked for sexual purposes (Estes and Weiner 2001; also see Kelly et al. 1995). As Muntarbhorn (1994, 54) notes:

> While poverty is a root cause of child exploitation, it relates to the supply side and does not explain sufficiently the global demand with, in many instances, customers from rich countries circumventing their national laws to exploit children in other countries. The problem is compounded by the criminal networks which benefit from the trade in children, and by collusion and corruption in many national settings. It is thus poverty plus other factors, such as the role of customers and criminality, rather than poverty alone, which leads to child exploitation.

Whether it is children brought to customers or customers traveling as sex tourists to their victims, or whether it is perversion or misguided beliefs that having sex with a virgin will either prevent or cure AIDS, the underlying pillars on which the sexual trafficking of children is sustained are poverty, greed, and indifference.

Of particular concern has been the apparent rise in the use of trafficked juveniles and children in the sex-tour industry. "While much of the initial international attention on child-sex tourism focused on Thailand and other countries of Southeast Asia, there is no hemisphere, continent, or region unaffected by the child-sex trade. As countries develop their economies and tourism industries, child-sex tourism seems to surface. Economic difficulties, civil unrest, poverty, and displacement of refugees all contribute to the growth of the child-sex industry" (Klain 1999, 32). Some countries are notorious for providing sexual liaisons for the sex-tourism trade. Of special note are Thailand, Brazil, Cambodia, and Indonesia. But the enterprise is by no means limited to these countries (Beddoe et al. 2001).

Women and girls in Eastern European countries are frequently solicited into the international sex trade. Many become virtual slaves, unable to buy their way out of their victimization. Most become subjected to abuse, disease, and psychological trauma. The grim situation in Bosnia and Herzegovina, both during and following the conflict in that region, illustrates the problem (Human Rights Watch 2002). As many as two thousand women and girls, mostly transported from Moldavia, Romania, and Ukraine, are enslaved in Bosnian brothels. These "women and girls are held in debt bondage, forced to provide sexual services to clients, falsely imprisoned, and beaten when they do not comply with demands of brothel owners who have purchased them and deprived them of their passports" (Human Rights Watch 2002, 4).

In spite of well-publicized crackdowns on the international trafficking trade, little is really known about this form of criminality, and criminological research on the behavior is scanty. With little by way of governmental effort to prosecute or severely punish offenders, the combination of poverty, perversion, and greed seem to be the primary forces fostering such activity. Concerned with the negative publicity this activity has received, hotel and tourist organizations in some countries have taken creative steps to combat the enterprise. Some countries have enacted or begun to enforce laws against their citizens who travel to other countries for sexual encounters with minors. The success of such measures is impossible to estimate at this time (Klain 1999).

Prostitution

Most of the women and children trafficked across the globe are transported, knowingly or not, for use in the commercial sex industry. The criminal sexual victimization of children and juveniles by individuals, whether the offenders are strangers, acquaintances, or relatives, is universal and much more prevalent than any official statistics might imply. UNICEF (2006d) reports the following:

> An estimated 2 million children, the majority of them girls, are sexually exploited in the multi-billion dollar commercial sex industry.

- At the end of 2000, as many as 325,000 children were at risk of commercial sexual exploitation in the United States alone.
- An estimated 16,000 children in Mexico are exploited in prostitution, with tourist destinations being among those areas with the highest number.
- In Cambodia, a third of those in prostitution are children under 18 years of age.
- In Lithuania, 20 percent to 50 per cent of those in prostitution are believed to be minors. Children as young as 11 can be found in brothels and children between 10 and 12 years of age have been used to make pornographic films.
- An estimated 30 percent of trafficking victims from Moldavia are adolescent girls trafficked for commercial sexual exploitation.

Other estimates of the involvement of juveniles and children in prostitution activities suggest significantly higher numbers. Of course, no one knows just how prevalent such activity is, in large part because it is nearly impossible to count. This is confounded by the wide varieties of prostitution activities to be counted. The occasional exchange of sexual favors for drugs by a runaway compared to the long-term, daily sexual encounters of a child bonded to a brothel by an organized sex-tourism enterprise are quite different forms of victimizing activities.

> The range of child prostitution varies from individual cases to mass victims of organized crime. This may encompass a selection of children: some runaways from home or from State institutions, some sold by their parents, some forced or tricked into prostitution, some street children, some involved part-time, some full-time, some amateurs and some professionals. Although one tends to think first and foremost of young girls in the trade, there has been an increase in the number of young boys engaged in prostitution. (Muntarbhorn 1996, 7)

Whatever the actual numbers might be, one can assume that the involvement of juveniles and children in commercial prostitution is extensive and global.

The International Tribunal for Children's Rights (2006) suggests that as much as child sexual exploitation, largely involving the prostitution of juveniles, is an international problem, it also has national dimensions that would likely call for different strategies to combat the problem. For example, the Tribunal notes that while sex tourism, sometimes involving minors and foreign adults, exists in Brazil, as it does in many countries, child sexual exploitation in Brazil is more "of a 'traditional' kind, in that most cases are of simple prostitution, with or without the services of an intermediary" (International Tribunal for Children's Rights 2006, 22). Nor does the sex-tourism industry in Brazil have the characteristics of an organized, lucrative, commercial enterprise normally found in other countries such as Thailand and Cambodia.

In accordance with the Convention on the Rights of the Child, the age of consent should be universally set at eighteen. But many countries set the age of consent for sexual intercourse between thirteen and seventeen. Thus, international efforts to combat child prostitution become complicated, not only because of the corruption and incompetence of authorities in many countries, but also because of variations in law, custom, and tolerance regarding sexual activity across the globe (Ghosh 2002). In the Philippines, for example, a foreign pedophile accused in the death of a girl was acquitted on appeal, in part because the court ruled that pedophilia was not a crime according to the country's laws (Muntarbhorn 1996).

International and national awareness of the increase and spread of the child sex trade, along with pressure from international organizations and numerous groups concerned with this activity, has led to extensive efforts to crack down on the child-sex trade in various countries. Virtually all countries now have laws on the books that can be used to prosecute exploiters of children for prostitution. Many countries appear to be paying serious attention to the enforcement of these laws. It remains to be seen how long they will continue to do so. In addition, countries in Africa, Asia, and South America that have not, as yet, implemented provisions of international agreements have begun to do so. And European and North American countries are enforcing, or enacting, laws that allow for the prosecution of nationals who travel to foreign countries for sexual liaisons with child prostitutes. However, the forces that promote the sexual exploitation of children as prostitutes remain strong and are unlikely to dissipate in the foreseeable future. Muntarbhorn (1996, 7) suggests the following concerning the root causes of the problem:

> Poverty rears its head consistently in developing countries, but it also emerges in developed countries where there are pockets of the disadvantaged. Because many families are unable to support their children, the latter become easy prey for the sex trade. This is compounded by family disintegration, including incest and domestic violence, as well as migration from rural to urban areas and from one country to another in search of a livelihood. More often than not, however, it is not poverty alone which pushes children to become victims of prostitution. There are the additional factors of market demand and criminal networks, aggravated by sociocultural traditions and practices mixed with discrimination against the girl child.

Child Pornography

Pornography involving children is not new. However, it appears that the Internet has become a boon for its worldwide distribution and for increasing the opportunities for pedophiles to locate and make contact with potential victims of both genders (Bocij and McFarlane 2003). The sexual depiction of children in visual and audio form is closely linked to child prostitution and the trafficking of children for use in the sex trade. But young people appear to become engaged in the activity via a number of routes. In some cases parents force their children to appear in pornographic media for money. Runaways become models to earn a living. Sometimes children are specially procured or sold into the trade. In some instances a parent who is working as a pornographic model introduces their child to the industry (Buys 1989).

Recent widespread concern with the global dimensions of child pornography has prompted efforts to combat the use of children in pornographic materials. And media dramatized arrests of individuals around the world who have been accused of soliciting such material over the Internet have raised public concern with pedophilia and the use of children in the industry. The BBC (2005), for example, reported on a series of raids in Operation Icebreaker II carried out by the European police agency Europol in France, Italy, Denmark, the

Netherlands, Sweden, and the United Kingdom that targeted child pornography suspects and led to numerous arrests and confiscation of materials. Similarly the five largest Internet service providers have even made an unusual move to join together in blocking child pornographic images from their servers (BBC 2006).

But efforts to combat the production, distribution, and possession of pornographic materials involving children on an international scale are frustrated by legal obstacles and the near impossibility of policing the Internet (Weir and Gallagher 2004). Nevertheless, the apparent widespread revulsion against this form of victimization has prompted countries to take action. Some concrete measures appear to have been taken in some countries. In the United States, for example, federal and state laws prohibiting the production and distribution of child pornography have been enacted or strengthened. In Europe, the United Kingdom, and Australia, similar efforts to combat the trade are apparent. But little, if any, action appears to be under way in much of the rest of the world (Carr 2003; Chase and Statham 2005; Davidson 2005).

As a truly international form of child victimization, the sexual exploitation of children for pornography has not yet received significant attention from criminologists. It is, however, an area that begs for criminological theory and research.

Institutional Victimization

Juveniles are dependent individuals who lack the ability, resources, and legal standing of self-determination enjoyed and expected of adults. Typically this dependency is the responsibility of the youth's parents or guardian adults. In many instances, either temporarily or for extended periods, care of dependent juveniles is delegated to some agency, such as a school, correctional institution, or welfare agency, that has the temporary legal responsibility to attend to the care and well-being of the child, besides engaging in whatever other activity the agency is expected to pursue.

As Paul Tappan (1949) asked: "Who is to protect the child from his protectors?" The victimization of children by care-providing agencies and/or their employees is by no means unknown. Referred to by Dorne (1989) as "institutional victimization," this form of child maltreatment typically includes corporal punishment, misuse of psychotropic drugs, prolonged isolation, the use of mechanical restraints, restriction of contacts with others, and the failure to provide required services. In addition, the staff of institutions may emotionally assault a child or fail to provide proper protection from other inmates or staff.

Some cases of institutional victimization can be quite severe. In one case known to the author, a private juvenile correctional facility in the United States was sued for damages for hog-tying and slamming juveniles as a way of disciplining wards and maintaining order. Contending that such practices were necessary to protect institutional staff and property from inmates, the institution lost the suit and was required to pay substantial damages to certain inmates.

In some cases, what people might consider abusive practices by certain institutions are actually legal. As the U.S. Supreme Court ruled in *Ingraham v. Wright*, 430 U.S. 651, it is constitutional for school officials to use corporal punishment in American schools to discipline children. In other cases, it becomes very difficult to determine whether victimization has actually occurred or the agency failed in its duty to prevent it, as in the case of school bullying or providing adequate nutrition or shelter to wards. On the other hand, the routine practices of some agencies would be considered victimizing by any standard, as in the case of orphanages in countries like Albania and juvenile welfare institutions in Brazil. Frequently blamed on aberrant employees of the agency, institutional victimization is ingrained in the very fabric of the institution and goes on undetected and unchecked for decades.

Children accused of misconduct by authorities and subjected to incarceration as a consequence are, perhaps, the most readily victimized subjects of this kind of maltreatment. Because of their behavior, young people placed in correctional facilities around the world are deemed potentially dangerous and in need of correction, if not punishment. These individuals are, by definition, under the care and control of correctional authorities. In most parts of the world this care is not gentle and loving, acceptable and adequate. In some cases the custody itself is a form of victimization. Such abuse occurs in most countries.

Some societies make a practice of abusing children who come to the attention of authorities. One extreme example is Brazil. For many years Human Rights Watch and other agencies have sought to take action against authorities who run detention centers for children in Brazil. A study of detention centers in five Brazilian states during 2002 alerted the international community to the cruel and inhuman treatment of the children placed in these detention and "correctional" centers (Human Rights Watch 2003). In 2004, Human Rights Watch reported that "juvenile detention centers in Rio de Janeiro are overcrowded, filthy, and violent, failing in virtually every respect to safeguard youth's basic human rights. Beatings at the hand of guards are common" (Human Rights Watch 2004, 1). On a return visit to the same localities in 2005, it was found that, in spite of government claims to the contrary, little had changed (Human Rights Watch 2005a).

A similar situation confronts accused young offenders in Papua New Guinea. Under the guise of combating the country's serious crime problem, violent police action has become standard practice. Children, composing about one-half the country's population, appear to be especially vulnerable to this police tactic. As reported by Human Rights Watch (2005b), beatings, sexual abuse, torture, and all manner of abusive treatment are routine experiences of both boys and girls who come into police custody. In the Philippines also all manner of abuse is suffered by children tossed into detention and prison facilities and at the hands of police (Amnesty International 2006b).

Children are also subject to victimization when those charged with their care fail to protect them from harm. Conceptually a form of child neglect, this kind of victimization appears to be worldwide. In the United Kingdom, for example, a survey conducted by the chief inspector of prisons reported widespread physical violence among inmates in a juvenile correctional facility in Devon (BBC 2005b). A year after this report, a follow-up inquiry found that conditions had improved but that bullying and violence were still prevalent in the institution (BBC 2005c). In the United States, a study by the Justice Department reported that in juvenile correctional facilities sexual assaults and other illicit sexual conduct occurred at ten times the rate found for adult penal institutions (Beck and Hughes 2005).

Probably the most universal victimizing experiences suffered by children under institutional care is the pervasive, and sometime very serious, abuse children suffer at the hands of other children at or near school. Often referred to as bullying, research on this phenomenon in countries around the world suggest that the lack of or inability of school officials to take action against attacks on children by other children at school is a form of institutional victimization, which, while not exactly perpetrated by staff in the sense of police and correctional officer brutality toward juveniles, causes or allows physical and emotional harm to be experienced by young people under the school's care.

Research on bullying in societies as diverse as Brazil (DeSouza and Ribeiro 2005), Canada (Ma 2002), Hong Kong (Wong 2004), and Sweden (Erling and Hwang 2004) indicate both how prevalent this kind of victimization might be and how difficult it is to combat the problem. One study by Eslea et al. (2004) compared bullying behavior and associated risk factors in seven countries. Among other things, the study found that bullying is a universal phenomenon with some cultural variations affecting the sex and age of offenders and victims. A comparison of bullying experiences of children in England and Japan found some differences in the composition of offenders between the two countries but very similar responses on the part of victims. Of growing concern among school officials in countries across the globe, effective strategies to combat this form of victimization appear to be elusive (Rigby 2003).

Institutional victimization is—perhaps more than any other form of victimization—an indicator of a people's commitment to its young. It is also an area of inquiry much deserving of criminological inquiry.

Explaining Victimization

Criminological inquiry regarding juveniles has primarily focused its attention on the misbehavior of young people and societal response to such conduct. Although there is ample reason to believe that young people are the most vulnerable and victimized populations of any society, especially from a global perspective, little criminological attention has been directed to explaining the victimization of children and juveniles. In part this is understandable given that it is the criminality of individuals that has traditionally been the primary concern of the discipline.

Yet, virtually any form of child victimization constitutes criminal behavior and is typically so designated by international and national law. Acts that victimize young people are as legitimate subjects for criminological inquiry as any other form of criminality. The same kinds of efforts to prevent and control victimizing acts against the young are essentially those we might use to prevent and control any criminal activity. In this regard, we do actually know as much about the causes and control of child-victimizing activity as we do about crime and delinquency.

The victimization of children has a unique quality about it. Their vulnerability and dependence makes their victimizations more condemnable, especially when the acts are committed by the very people upon whom the young are dependent. However, criminology has not included youthful victimization as a separate realm of scientific inquiry. Indeed, investigations of its global nature have largely fallen outside the realm of the discipline.

Efforts to explain criminal and delinquent behavior have primarily been a matter of explaining the conduct of individuals. Criminological theory devoted to answering the question "Why do they do it?" attempts to account for why individual offenders commit the crimes they do. Epidemiological theory seeks to account for variations in the prevalence and incidence of this conduct. In the case of child victimization, however, the problem of explaining the behavior of victimizers takes on another dimension. Sexual victimization illustrates this point.

It is one thing for a father to rape his daughter. It is something else for a pedophile to seek out victims via the Internet. And it is yet another for organized criminals to actively traffic in girls and boys to supply the international sex trade. Although quite different in character, all are instances of individual criminal activity subject to the same theories used to explain any other illegal conduct.

On the other hand, it is one thing for a child to be beaten by his or her parent or guardian. It is a different matter for that child to be abducted and forced to fight for some rebel leader. And it is quite another for government-sponsored killers to systematically murder and maim children as well as adults in acts of terror or genocide. Finally, it is one thing for parents to fail in their duty as child caretakers. It is quite a different matter when the state, or some organization purporting to care, fails in its obligation to provide care.

Most forms of victimizing conduct, child or otherwise, are considered ordinary crimes. Beating one's child (whether technically legal or not) is an instance of criminal assault, like any other. Trafficking in children for economic gain is a case of criminality akin to drug trafficking or other organized crime. Soliciting a teenage boy for prostitution may be more reprehensible than patronizing an adult prostitute, but the behavior is much the same. To the extent that this conduct victimizes others, theories of criminal and delinquent behavior are also theories of criminal victimization—at the individual level. Thus, explanations of why fathers rape daughters, why guardians assault those in their care, or why parents may fail to provide proper food or shelter for their children might be found in any of the theories of criminal behavior available in criminology. The same might be said of the pedophile who seeks out victims on the Internet, and even of organized criminal activity that exploits children.

What criminology lacks, however, is any theory that might be used to explain the abduction of children as military combatants or their purposive murder by such combatants. Similarly, criminology has no theory to account for why governments or their agents purposively abuse and exploit children in their care. Nor can criminology explain why governments fail to protect, promote, and nurture all their young. There are possible answers to why some people victimize those less powerful than themselves. There is, however, no answer to why governments fail in their responsibilities to those being governed.

Criminology's concern with the misbehavior of the young is not misplaced. It is limiting. Given the overwhelming evidence that children and young people throughout the world are mistreated, maltreated, abused, neglected, and otherwise victimized, and that such treatment is none other than criminal in nature, the victimization of young people offers a challenge to criminological inquiry that demands transcending its self-imposed limitations.

Conclusion

Crime, by its very nature, is a victimizing activity. As routine activities theory (Felson and Cohen 1980) explains, the young make excellent targets for victimizing activities. The examples briefly surveyed in this chapter suggest that victimizing young people is universal and pervasive. Parents, government and school officials, older youths, and adults generally abuse their power over young people by failing to protect them from harm or by inflicting harm on those less powerful. Indeed, if one were to compare a list of victimizing experiences with a list of delinquent activity on the part of young people across the globe, the victim side of the equation would far exceed that of the delinquent side. However, criminological and governmental obsession with the misbehavior of young people far exceeds that of our concern with their victimization. Efforts to explain and control the behavior of juvenile delinquents abound. Similar efforts to explain and protect young people from being victimized are comparatively wanting.

Yet, across the globe, action to combat abuse and neglect directed to those who are dependent on their elders for nurturance and support are by no means nonexistent. Some appear to have met with considerable success. Whether that success is directly a result of combative efforts or other factors is difficult to say. However, embarrassing governments with public revelations of abusive practices, providing funds and resources for education, bringing sanctions of various kinds to bear on countries that violate international law and standards, hauling in to court correctional officials who allow abusive practices to occur on their watch, bringing legal suits for monetary damages, and the criminal prosecution of persons who commit crimes against the young are all parts of the arsenal to prevent and control child victimization. But, as with efforts to understand and control criminality on the part of the young, much more remains to be done in the understanding and control of the criminality others commit against them.

9

Some Concluding Observations

It is quite possible that criminology already has all the information it needs to understand and explain youthful misconduct everywhere and to help establish just and effective mechanisms to deal with offending and needy youth in all cultures and social systems. We may not yet realize this or know how to act on the basis of our knowledge. But, if so, expanding the present scope of criminological inquiry to other cultures and social systems would be, if not a waste of time, a mere academic exercise.

Criminological knowledge of youth crime and justice, although extensive, is simply too limited and narrow to make any definitive statements that would hold worldwide. At numerous points throughout this volume I have pointed to the lack of data—to what we do not know for want of information or research of any kind. This could, of course, simply reflect the author's own failure to exhaust the extensive literature that criminologists and others have produced on these matters. In which case, one would hope that those better informed would fill in the gaps and correct the conclusions drawn here. More likely, however, youth crime and justice have been issues to which many governments and scholars throughout the world have either been unwilling or unable to devote effort or resources. Many other matters perceived to be more important demand their attention. Also, all the obstacles and difficulties criminologists confront in conducting research of any kind are compounded when they try to undertake cross-cultural or comparative research, as has been frequently noted by criminologists who actually attempt to explore criminological questions beyond the borders of their own societies (Dammer et al. 2006; Ellis and Walsh 2000; Hartjen 1998; Hill 2005). As understandable as all this may be, the failure to actively investigate youth crime and justice on a global scale can also be interpreted as yet another way in which young people in much of the world are victimized. They, in effect, are simply not considered to be important enough to warrant much concern.

Given the wide gaps in the basic information needed to build a true global-science of criminology focusing on young people and how they are treated by agents of the state in all the world's societies, the cynical reader of this volume may conclude that we know little to nothing, or that criminological inquiry into these matters has been of little scientific or policy relevant value. I would argue quite the contrary. Although we must contend with wide gaps in our information base, much like an archeologist deciphering an ancient tablet with many missing pieces, we also have much information upon which to make some general, if only tentative, observations about the topics addressed in this volume.

What We Know

Law

Virtually all societies probably differentiate in their expectations and treatment of adult and young offenders (criminal and otherwise) based on some standard related to biological age. Their standards vary, and the extent to which they are formalized in law may differ. But it is very unlikely that any society holds young people to the same behavioral standards as adults. Nor does any society generally respond as harshly to the young as they do to adult offenders.

Besides differing in the specific age to use in distinguishing between juvenile and adult, societies also differ in the extent to which and/or the manner in which the boundary between young and adult is breached as young offenders commit what are considered to be serious crimes and/or approach the age of criminal responsibility. Some societies may employ an ad hoc approach, especially those in which the actual age of young offenders may only be surmised given the lack of birth records. Others retain the legal boundary between adults and juveniles but have formalized mechanisms (e.g., waiver proceedings) to, in effect, get around the assumptions of responsibility and competence on which that boundary was drawn. In yet other countries, formalized age-graded jurisdictions (e.g., children's vs. youth courts) have been created to apply somewhat different standards and rules to youths of varying ages.

Whatever the approach, all societies appear to be confronted with the problem of how and on what basis to determine just when a young person can be held accountable for his or her conduct to the extent that adults are held using the same judicial procedures that would apply to adults in criminal cases. In addition, all seem to register some concern with what, if any, rights apply to the young and what, if any, other forms of behavior or life situations they may be involved in warrant intervention by authorities.

In short, while the terminology and procedural approaches may differ across the globe, the idea that young people can justifiably be distinguished from adults in the eyes of the law seems to be universal.

Behavior

Why young people in any society would behave in ways that offend others and violate the law remains a question that is yet to be empirically verified by criminology. A large number of theories have been proposed by criminologists and others to account for such conduct. Given the limited cross-national research to test any of these theories, it is still unknown to what extent any of them is a truly universal explanation of delinquent behavior, even where specific theories may have received considerable testing and support concerning their validity within individual societies. However, from the evidence at hand, it appears that at least some of them may be of universal explanatory relevance. If so, we need not look for different explanations of why young people in different societies and types of societies offend. At least in broad etiological terms, whatever may compel or allow a youth in any society to offend is likely to also explain the misconduct of offending young people in any other.

The legal/social recognition that the young are to be differentiated from adults is universal. Available evidence also suggests that, if not the overall extent, the nature, forms, and relative distribution of misconduct on the part of young people are also very similar across the globe. Children and young people in all manner of society are pretty much engaged in the same kinds of behaviors of concern to adults and legal authorities. In this regard, delinquent behavior, as with its recognition, is universal.

But such behavior is not equally distributed among the young of the world's societies. Some countries appear to have much more of it than others. Whether this is the result of real differences in behavior or simply a result of variations in national efforts to respond to and record such behavior in official data is not yet known. However, it appears clear that although all youths everywhere do things that infringe the law, the problem of delinquency (its actual relative occurrence and/or the perception people have of such behavior) varies across the globe. In addition, evidence suggests that during the twenty-first century the global dimensions of this problem will likely grow.

On the other hand, although various forms of youthful misconduct appear to exist in practically any society, the exact nature and relative frequency with which youths in specific societies engage in such behavior appear to be socially and culturally variable. Drug abuse on the part of juveniles, for instance, seems to exist in just about any country. But the kinds of drugs that are abused and the extent of the problem this conduct poses is not identical in all countries. The same is probably true for just about any form of delinquency. In that regard, one can conclude that delinquency is probably universal, and the broad reasons why young people engage in this behavior are too. Cross-national factors relating to culture, social structure, and economic situation are probably responsible for the observed variations in the nature and extent of specific forms of such behavior (as well as overall rates) across societies. But, global inquiry to investigate the social/cultural/economic correlates of variations in delinquent conduct has yet to be undertaken on any scale.

Justice

Among those societies that have some recognizable form of justice system that differentiates between juveniles and adults, a wide variety of specific approaches have been taken in how young people are dealt with by the agents of the state. These range from fully separated (or dual) justice models to those that treat young people as less culpable adults. In addition, the judicial philosophies behind these varied systems include participatory models, crime-control models, welfare models, and due-process models.

Criminologists have yet to fully investigate what may account for the formation of these varied approaches to dealing with young offenders and needy children. Most likely unique cultural/historical/political factors influence why one society would develop a juvenile justice system that is essentially nothing more than a junior version of the adult system while a neighboring country (one even having few obvious social, economic, or cultural differences from its neighbor) may elect to develop a system that looks very much like a social-welfare enterprise.

What does seem to be clear, however, is that the varied approaches to juvenile justice have little to do with the actual seriousness of the delinquency problem individual societies confront, either with regard to producing the specific approach or as a result of its establishment. Heightened awareness or fear of juvenile crime created by media hype and/or politically motivated interests may lead to crackdowns on youth crime or even fundamental changes in judicial systems. But actual significant increases or decreases in delinquent behavior or types of such behavior seem to have little relationship to how societies respond to misbehaving youth. In that respect, from a policy perspective, except insofar as how the lives of various individuals caught up in juvenile justice may be impacted, how any society chooses to deal with young offenders seems to make little difference in the behavior toward which those efforts are supposedly directed.

Similarly, corresponding to the justice model found in individual societies, the correctional approaches individual societies adopt to deal with young people who pass through their justice systems are quite varied. In some societies, a restorative emphasis characterizes corrective efforts. In many countries, young offenders are defined as individuals in need, and programs are guided by a therapeutic, rehabilitative philosophy. In other societies, and apparently increasingly so in many parts of the world, a philosophy of (typically diminished) individual responsibility is the guiding principle. In such societies correctional responses are decidedly punitive in nature. In virtually all systems, however, juvenile corrections is individualistic oriented, in that programs geared to deal with individual offenders, pre-offenders, or needy youngsters dominate over those geared to changing social conditions or social/economic inequalities. Virtually everywhere it is the children of the poor and minorities that are the recipients of correctional efforts.

As with the models of justice by which those selected for correctional treatment are determined, available evidence suggests that the correctional approach taken by any society makes little difference insofar as impacting the delinquency problem of a society. Punitive crackdowns tend to produce high rates of incarceration, may transform judicial procedures for juveniles into adult-modeled "kiddy courts," and have large numbers of youths being treated as if they were adults. No evidence exists to show that such crackdowns are effective. Similarly, widespread, supposedly nonpunitive, therapeutic intervention approaches may be less onerous than punitive strategies. However, research has yet to demonstrate that adopting this kind of strategy will actually transform large numbers of delinquents, or would-be delinquents, into model citizens. The danger always exists that such efforts may widen the net of state intervention into the lives of a society's young. As with research on the impact of correctional strategies in individual countries, the collective findings of such efforts in countries across the globe suggest that individualistic-oriented correctional activities of any kind probably have little, if anything, to do with the criminality of a nation's young. In short, the implication of global research in juvenile delinquency and corrections indicates that individual pathology, need, or willful intent may not be the cause of a country's delinquency problem or the source of its solution.

Victims

Criminology has produced a sizable (if limited) body of information and knowledge about the misconduct of the world's young and the strategies and consequences of how societies have elected to deal with that conduct. As a science of crime and justice, however, it has yet to seriously undertake global inquiry of the mistreatment of young people and what to do about it. Much of what we know about such matters has resulted from the work of a handful of international agencies and several activist organizations (organizations that often have self-interest in promoting concern over various forms of mistreatment). The information produced by these efforts reveals that children throughout the world are subjected to all manner of abuse, exploitation, and victimization. Much of this victimization is either government generated or government tolerated—in effect, forms of government crime committed against the young.

This realization provides a key to combating abuse. By pressuring governments in abusive societies to take some action, or to cease their abusive practices—either directly, by threat of sanctions, or by enabling alternatives—progress can be gained (United Nations 2004a, 2004b). Child victimization and the strategies successfully used to combat it provide a mirror to dealing with the global problem of delinquent behavior. The study of delinquency has focused on the offender, the individual juvenile engaged in law-breaking behavior. But as with the victimization of children, one must go beyond the individual delinquent and look to the broader social-political contexts in which this behavior occurs to understand it and deal with it in a reasoned, effective manner.

Some Speculations

Globalization, Westernization, and the United Nations' efforts to enforce the provisions of international treaties regarding the treatment of children and juveniles are likely to influence the problem of delinquency and the nature of official mechanisms that deal with youthful misconduct in individual countries.

In spite of conservative and fundamentalist efforts in individual countries or regions to impede its inevitability, world homogenization stemming from economic globalization, along with the spread of Western cultural and technological influences, is likely not only to continue but also to accelerate in the twenty-first century. As has already occurred in many parts of the world, the behavioral impact of these forces will result in increased rates of actual and official delinquency. This will especially occur in nations rapidly modernizing and losing traditional means of social control while implementing policing and judicial systems based on Western (largely American) models. As suggested throughout this volume, this will produce a recognized youth crime problem throughout much of the world. In turn, this recognition will put pressure on governments to do something about the problem, often leading to demands to crack down on or get tough with juvenile miscreants. Some individual countries may take just the opposite approach and either attempt to ameliorate the conditions (e.g., poverty) that are assumed to be behind rising levels of juvenile crime or violence, and/or find ways to handle offenders that still resonate the ideals of the best interests of the child philosophy that originally produced the idea of juvenile justice a century ago. Many countries are likely to exhibit a schizophrenic mixture of restorative/punitive strategies. Whatever the case, youth crime will become an established global problem throughout the century.

If United Nations efforts to expand the implementation of international agreements regarding the rights of the child continue, it is possible that a broad global unanimity regarding how agents of the state treat young people accused of breaking the law will occur over the course of the century. According to Abramson (2006) there is reason to believe that United Nations agencies entrusted with the power to encourage implementation of treaty provisions have given less emphasis to youths in trouble with the law compared to other matters covered by these treaties, but at least some progress appears to have been made in curbing the most blatant and harmful of such abuses (such as housing juvenile detainees separately from adults). Combined with world homogenization, these implementation efforts will likely have a continued impact in changing the global practice of juvenile justice. Just what form of juvenile justice that may produce is still uncertain.

However, insofar as youth crime is perceived as a matter of criminal justice (as opposed to public health or social justice), these changes will emphasize questions of due process, procedural rights, remedies for abuse of power, and matters concerning the differential punishment, detention, and processing of juvenile compared to adult offenders. As such, they will ignore or downplay the root causes of offense behavior or treatment/rehabilitative strategies to benefit young people in trouble with legal authorities. Procedural justice will be enhanced, while delinquency prevention and the social protection of children will largely be of secondary concern.

Toward a Global Understanding

A small but growing number of publications in the criminological literature take a cross-national, comparative, international, or transnational approach. In many of them various suggestions have been made as to why international criminological research is desirable and what may be done to enhance that inquiry (e.g., Friday and Ren 2006; Jensen and Jepsen 2006; Muncie & Goldson 2006; Rounds 2000). The most obvious requirement is to broaden the base of information. The undeniable fact is that as far as youth crime and justice is concerned, for much of the world virtually nothing is known. The reader might try a simple exercise to illustrate this point. Draw up a list of the world's nearly two hundred countries and check off those about which any meaningful information on these matters is to be found. By doing so, one quickly realizes that for a majority of countries no information of relevance exists, no matter where one may look. In addition, it would also become clear that these countries are not randomly scattered across the globe. Just the opposite. With rare exception, little is known about most of Africa, most of Latin America, most of Asia, and most of the Middle East. Very little information exists on countries in East and Southern Europe, and even some Northern European countries are conspicuously absent from any list of substantial research. Indeed, it would be far easier to make a list of countries about which we know something at all. Thus, before we can develop a truly global criminological science of youth crime and justice, the first requirement is to broaden the knowledge base, conduct research, and assemble data from a much wider variety of societies across the globe.

Doing this would be no easy task. The few efforts made by the United Nations to acquire basic data on matters relating to topics addressed in this volume reveal just how difficult it would be to gather information of any kind, much less do so in a scientifically standardized and valid form. Many countries do not compile this information at all, nor do they have the resources to even do so. Others, for political or ideological reasons, are unwilling to cooperate. And no mechanism exists to compel any society to do so. Thus, conducting some kind of worldwide survey or even representative sample of countries to obtain reasonably accurate counts of offenders, youths in corrections, or other statistics is highly unlikely.

Yet broadening the knowledge base is not impossible. The United Nations, for instance, has had some success in compelling countries to implement minimal standards of juvenile justice in diverse societies. Similar efforts to gather criminologically relevant information on youth crime and/or justice could produce substantial results. In addition, over the past quarter century the field of criminology itself has expanded substantially to countries across the globe. Memberships in the international divisions of the field's leading professional organizations have grown to sizable numbers, with members from many parts of the world. In addition, international conferences on specific topics relating to youth crime, justice, or victimization are held almost annually in various countries. With social, cultural, and economic globalization, criminology as a discipline has also begun to take a global perspective. All of this suggests that in the decades to come the body of information available to criminologists from diverse parts of the world will expand substantially. A truly global science of youth crime and justice is very likely to be realized during this century.

REFERENCES

Abramson, Bruce. 2006. Juvenile Justice: The "Unwanted Child": Why the Potential of the Convention on the Rights of the Child Is Not Being Realized, and What We Can Do About It, pp. 15–38, in Eric L. Jensen and Jørgen Jepsen (eds.), *Juvenile Law Violators, Human Rights, and the Development of New Juvenile Justice Systems.* Oxford, UK: Hart.

Adams, Kenneth. 2003. The Effectiveness of Juvenile Curfews at Crime Prevention. *The Annals of the American Academy of Political and Social Science* 587:136–159.

Adler, Freda. 1975. *Sisters in Crime: The Rise of the New Female Criminal.* New York: McGraw-Hill.

———. 1983. *Nations Not Obsessed with Crime.* Littleton, CO: Fred B. Rothman.

Administration on Children, Youth, and Families. 2005. *Child Maltreatment. 2003.* Washington, DC: Department of Health and Human Services.

Aebi, M. F. 1997. Disruptive Family and Criminality: The Swiss Case. *Kriminologisches Bulletin de Criminologie* 23:53–80.

Agnew, Robert. 1992. Foundation for a General Strain Theory of Crime and Delinquency. *Criminology* 30:47–87.

———. 2005. *Why Do Criminals Offend: A General Theory of Crime and Delinquency.* Los Angeles: Roxbury.

Airomaih, Yousel Ahmed. 1993. *Social Control and Delinquency in Saudi Arabia.* Ann Arbor: University Microfilms International.

Albrecht, Hans-Jörg. 1997. Juvenile Crime and Juvenile Law in the Federal Republic of Germany, pp. 223–270, in John A. Winterdyk (ed.), *Juvenile Justice Systems: International Perspectives.* Toronto: Canadian Scholar's Press.

———. 2004. Youth Justice in Germany, pp. 443–494, in Michael Tonry and Anthony Doob (eds.), *Youth Crime and Youth Justice: Comparative and Cross-National Perspectives.* Chicago: University of Chicago Press.

Amnesty International. 2006a. Stop Child Executions! http://web.amnesty.org.

———. 2006b. Philippines a Different Childhood: The Apprehension and Detention of Child Suspects and Offenders. http://web.amnesty.org.

Anderson, Tammy, and Richard R. Bennett. 1996. Development, Gender, and Crime: The Scope of the Routine Activities Approach. *Justice Quarterly* 13:31–56.

Andrews, D. A., and James Bonta (eds.). 2003. *The Psychology of Criminal Conduct.* 3rd ed. Cincinnati: Anderson.

Ariès, Philippe. 1962. *Centuries of Childhood.* New York: Vintage.

Arnett, Jeffrey Jensen, and Lenne Arnett Jensen. 1994. Socialization and Risk Behavior in Two Countries: Denmark and the United States. *Youth and Society* 26:3–22.

Aromaa, Kauko. 1994. Self-Reported Delinquency in Helsinki, Finland, 1992, pp. 14–41, in Josine Junger-Tas, Gert-Jan Terlouw, and Malcolm W. Klein (eds.), *Delinquent Behavior among Young People in the Western World: First Results of the International Self-Report Delinquency Study*. Amsterdam: Kugler.

Bao, Wan Ning, Ain Haas, and Yijun Pi. 2004. Life Strain, Negative Emotions, and Delinquency: An Empirical Test of General Strain Theory in the People's Republic of China. *International Journal of Offender Therapy and Comparative Criminology* 48:281–297.

Barberet, Rosemary, Benjamin Bowling, Josine Junger-Tas, Cristina Rechea-Alberola, John van Kesteren, and Andrew Zurawan. 2004. *Self-Reported Juvenile Delinquency in England and Wales, The Netherlands, and Spain*. Helsinki: European Institute for Crime Prevention and Control.

Baron, Stephen W. 1999. Street Youths and Substance Use: The Role of Background, Street Lifestyle, and Economic Factors. *Youth and Society* 31:3–26.

———. 2004. General Strain, Street Youth and Crime: A Test of Agnew's Revised Theory. *Criminology* 42:457–483.

Baron, Stephen W., and Timothy F. Hartnagel. 1997. Attributions, Affect, and Crime: Street Youths' Reactions to Unemployment. *Criminology* 35:409–434.

———. 1998. Street Youth and Criminal Violence. *Journal of Research in Crime and Delinquency* 35:166–192.

Bartollas, Clemens. 1996. United States, pp. 301–316, in Donald J. Shoemaker (ed.), *International Handbook on Juvenile Justice*. Westport, CT: Greenwood.

Bartusch, Dawn, R. Jeglum, Donald R. Lynam, Terrie E. Moffitt, and Phil A. Silva. 1997. Is Age Important? Testing a General versus a Developmental Theory of Antisocial Behavior. *Criminology* 35:13–48.

Bazemore, S. Gordon. 1991. Beyond Punishment, Surveillance, and Traditional Treatment: Themes for a New Mission in U.S. Juvenile Justice, pp. 129–159, in Jim Hackler (ed.), *Official Responses to Problem Juveniles: Some International Reflections*. Euskadi, Spain: The Oñati International Institute for the Sociology of Law.

Bazemore, S. Gordon, and Mara Schiff. 2005. *Juvenile Justice Reform and Restorative Justice: Building Theory and Policy from Practice*. Devon, UK: Willan.

BBC. 2004. Japan Killing Comments Spark Row. http://news.bbc.co.uk/2/hi/asiapacific/3775845.stm.

———. 2005a. Crackdown on European Child Porn. http://news.bbc.co.uk/go/pr/fr/-/2/hi/europe/4267744.stm.

———. 2005b. "Horrendous" Violence at Youth Jail. http://news.bbc.co.uk/1/hi/uk/1259418.stm.

———. 2005c. Young offenders Still Suffer Violence. http://news.bbc.co.uk/1/hi/uk/1504893.stm.

———. 2006. Industry Vows Fight on Child Porn. http://news.bbc.co.uk/2/hi/technology/5123936.stm.

Beck, Allen J., and Timothy A. Hughes. 2005. *Sexual Violence Reported by Correctional Authorities, 2004*. Washington, DC: U.S. Department of Justice, Bureau of Justice Statistics.

Becker, Jo. 2004. A Gun as Tall as Me. http://www.countercurrents.org/hr-becker270104.htm.

Becroft, Judge Andrew. 2003. *Youth Justice—The New Zealand Experience: Past Lessons and Future Challenges*. Sydney: Australian Institute of Criminology with the NSW Department of Juvenile Justice. http://www.aic.gov.au/conferences/2003-juvenile/becroft.pdf.

Beddoe, Christine, Michael Hall, and Chris Ryan. 2001. *The Incidence of Sexual Exploitation of Children in Tourism*. Madrid: World Tourism Organization.

Bennett, Richard R. 1991. Development and Crime: A Cross-National, Time-Series Analysis of Competing Models. *Sociological Quarterly* 32:343–363.

Bensinger, Gad J. 1991. The Juvenile Court of Cook County: Past, Present, and Future, pp. 159–174, in Jim Hackler (ed.), *Official Responses to Problem Juveniles: Some International Reflections*. Euskadi, Spain: The Oñati International Institute for the Sociology of Law.

Berger, Ronald J. 1989. Female Delinquency in the Emancipation Era: A Review of the Literature. *Sex Roles* 21:375–399.

Bernard, Thomas J. 1992. *The Cycle of Juvenile Justice*. New York: Oxford University Press.

Bernard, Thomas J., and Jeffrey B. Snipes. 1996. Theoretical Integration in Criminology, pp. 301–348, in Michael Tonry (ed.), *Crime and Justice: A Review of Research*, vol. 20. Chicago: University of Chicago Press.

Bernburg, Jón Gunnar, and Thorolfur Thorlindsson. 1999. Adolescent Violence, Social Control, and the Subculture of Delinquency: Factors Related to Violent Behavior and Nonviolent Delinquency. *Youth and Society* 30:445–460.

Bhuiyan, Golam Kibria. 1990. Juvenile Delinquency and Justice System in Bangladesh. *Asian Journal of Crime Prevention and Criminal Justice* 8:92–98.

Bishop, Donna M. 2000. Juvenile Offenders in the Adult Criminal Justice System, pp. 81–167, in Michael Tonry (ed.), *Crime and Justice: A Review of Research*, vol. 27.

Black, Donald J., and Albert J. Reiss. 1970. Police Control of Juveniles. *American Sociological Review* 35:63–77.

Blatier, Catherine. 1999. Juvenile Justice in France: The Evolution of Sentencing for Children and Minor Delinquents. *British Journal of Criminology* 39:240–252.

Blomberg, Thomas G. 1984. *Juvenile Court and Community Corrections*. Lanham, MD: University Press of America.

Bocij, Paul, and LeRoy McFarlane. 2003. The Internet: A Discussion of Some New and Emerging Threats to Young People. *Police Journal* 76:3013.

Boehnke, Klaus, and Winkels Dagmar Bergs. 2002. Juvenile Delinquency under Conditions of Rapid Social Change. *Sociological Forum* 17:57–79.

Boehnke, Klaus, John Hagan, and Hans Merkens 1998. Right-Wing Extremism among German Adolescents: Risk Factors and Protective Factors. *Applied Psychology: An International Review* 47:1099–1126.

Booth, Tim. (ed.). 1991. *Juvenile Justice in the New Europe*. Sheffield, UK: Joint Unit for Social Services Research, Sheffield University.

Boswell, Gwyneth (ed.). 2000. *Violent Children and Adolescents: Asking the Question Why*. London: Whurr.

Bottoms, Anthony, and James Dignan. 2004. Youth Justice in Great Britain, pp. 21–184, in Michael Tonry and Anthony Doob (eds.), *Youth Crime and Youth Justice: Comparative and Cross-National Perspectives*. Chicago: University of Chicago Press.

Bowker, Lee H. 1981. The Institutional Determinants of International Female Crime. *International Journal of Comparative and Applied Criminal Justice* 5:11–28.

Boyoum, David. 1996. *Drugs and Crime: Lessons from Abroad*. Cambridge, MA: BOTEC Analysis Corporation.

Braithwaite, John, and Valerie Braithwaite. 1978. An Exploratory Study of Delinquency and the Nature of Schooling. *Australian and New Zealand Journal of Sociology* 14:25–32.

Bruinsma, Gerben. 1992. Differential Association Theory Reconsidered: An Expansion and Empirical Test. *Journal of Quantitative Criminology* 8:29–49.

Bruno, Francesco. 1984. *Combating Drug Abuse and Related Crime: Comparative Research on the Effectiveness of Socio-Legal Preventive and Control Measures in Different Countries on the Interaction between Criminal Behavior and Drug Abuse*. Rome: Fratelli Palombi Editori.

Brusten, M., J. Graham, N. Herriger, and P. Malinowski (eds.), 1984. *Youth Crime, Social Control and Prevention. Theoretical Perspectives and Policy Implications: Studies from Nine Different Countries*. Wuppertal, Germany: International Document and Study Centre for Conflicts of Youth, University of Wuppertal.

Bullock, Roger (ed.). 1992. *Problem Adolescents: An International View*. London: Whiting and Birch.

Bureau of Justice Statistics. 2003. *Criminal Victimization in the United States, 2002*. Washington, DC: Bureau of Justice Statistics.

Burgess, Robert I., and Ronald L. Akers. 1965. A Differential Association-Reinforcement Theory of Criminal Behavior. *Social Problems* 13:35–45.

Burnett, Ros, and Colin Roberts (eds.). 2004. *What Works in Probation and Juvenile Justice: Developing Evidence-Based Practice*. Cullompton, Devon, UK: Willan.

Bursik, Robert J., and Harold G. Grasmick. 2001. Defining and Researching Gangs, pp. 2–14, in Jody Miller, Cheryl L. Maxson, and Malcolm W. Klein. *The Modern Gang Reader*. 2nd ed. Los Angeles: Roxbury.

Butts, Jeffrey, Dean Hoffman, and Jancen Buck. 1999. *Teen Courts in the United States: A Profile of Current Programs*. Washington, DC: Office of Juvenile Justice and Delinquency Prevention.

Buys, H.W.J. 1989. *Report on the Sexual Exploitation of Children and Young Persons*. Strasbourg: Council of Europe.

Caalim, Divina P. 1988. Treatment and Rehabilitation of Youthful Offenders in the Philippines, pp. 134–141, in UNAFEI, *Resource Material Series No. 34*. Fuchu, Japan.

Caputo, Alicia A., Paul J. Frick, and Stanley L. Brodsky. 1999. Family Violence and Juvenile Sex Offending: The Potential Mediating Role of Psychopathic Traits and Negative Attitudes toward Women. *Criminal Justice and Behavior* 26:338–356.

Carlie, Mike. 1997. An Overview of Institutions for Juvenile Offenders in the Netherlands and Their Place within the Dutch System of Justice. *International Journal of Comparative and Applied Criminal Justice* 21:31–140.

Carr, John. 2003. *Child Abuse, Child Pornography and the Internet*. London: Children's Charity.

Casey, B. J., Nim Tottenham, Copnor Liston, and Sarah Durston. 2005. Imaging the Developing Brain: What Have We Learned about Cognitive Development? *Trends in Cognitive Science* 9:104–110.

Catalano, Richard F., and David J. Hawkins. 1996. The Social Development Model: A Theory of Antisocial Behavior, pp. 149–197, in David J. Hawkins (ed.), *Delinquency and Crime: Current Theories*. Cambridge: Cambridge University Press.

Catalano, Richard F., and Rick Kosterman. 1996. Modeling the Etiology of Adolescent Substance Use: A Test of the Social Development Model. *Journal of Drug Issues* 26:429–455.

Cernkovich, Stephen A., and Peggy Giordano. 2001. Stability and Change in Antisocial Behavior: The Transition from Adolescence to Early Adulthood. *Criminology* 39:371–410.

Cernkovich, Stephen A., Peggy Giordano, and Meredith D. Pugh. 1985. Chronic Offenders: The Missing Cases in Self-Report Delinquency Research. *Journal of Criminal Law and Criminology* 76:3, 705–732.

Chase, Elaine, and June Statham. 2005. Commercial and Sexual Exploitation of Children and Young People in the UK—A Review. *Child Abuse Review* 14:4–25.

Chesney-Lind, Meda. 1997. *Girls, Women, and Crime.* Thousand Oaks, CA: Sage.

Christiaens, Jennecke. 1999. A History of Belgium's Child Protection Act of 1912: The Redefinition of the Juvenile Offender and His Punishment. *European Journal of Crime, Criminal Law and Criminal Justice* 7:5–21.

Cloward, Richard A., and Lloyd E. Ohlin. 1960. *Delinquency and Opportunity.* New York: Free Press.

Coalition for Juvenile Justice. 1994. *No Easy Answers: Juvenile Justice in a Climate of Fear.* Washington, DC: Coalition for Juvenile Justice.

Cohen, Albert K. 1955. *Delinquent Boys: The Culture of the Gang.* New York: Free Press.

Cohen, Ben Zion, and Ruth Zeira. 1999. Social Control, Delinquency, and Victimization among Kibbutz Adolescents, *International Journal of Offender Therapy and Comparative Criminology* 43:503–513.

Cohen, Larence E., and Marcus Felson. 1979. Social Change and Crime Rate Trends: A Routine Activities Approach. *American Sociological Review* 44:588–608.

Collins, Damian C. A., and Robin A. Kearns. 2001. Under Curfew and Under Siege? Legal Geographies of Young People. *Geoforum* 32:389–403.

Community Research Associates. 1987. *A Comparative Analysis of Juvenile Codes.* Champaign, IL: Community Research Associates.

Conde, Carlos H. 2005. Philippine Death Squads Extend Their Reach. *International Herald Tribune* (March 23).

Corrado, Raymond R. 1992. Introduction, pp. 1–5, in Raymond R. Corrado, Nicholas Bala, Rick Linden, and Marc Le Blanc (eds.). *Juvenile Justice in Canada: A Theoretical and Analytical Assessment.* Toronto: Butterworths.

Corrado, Raymond R., and Alan Markwart. 1996. Canada, pp. 34–56, in Donald J. Shoemaker (ed.), *International Handbook on Juvenile Justice,* Westport, CT: Greenwood.

Corrado, Raymond R., and Susan D. Turnbull. 1992. A Comparative Examination of the Modified Justice Model in the United Kingdom and the United States, pp. 75–136, in Raymond R. Corrado, Nicholas Bala, Rick Linden, and Marc Le Blanc (eds.). *Juvenile Justice in Canada: A Theoretical and Analytical Assessment.* Toronto: Butterworths.

Corrado, Raymond R., Nicholas Bala, Rick Linden, and Marc Le Blanc (eds.). 1992. *Juvenile Justice in Canada: A Theoretical and Analytical Assessment.* Toronto: Butterworths.

Correction Bureau. 1995. *Correctional Institutions in Japan 1995.* Tokyo: Ministry of Justice Japan.

Cote, Suzette (ed.). 2002. *Criminological Theories: Bridging the Past to the Future.* Thousand Oaks, CA: Sage.

Council of European Committee on Crime Prevention. 2003. *European Sourcebook of Crime and Criminal Justice Statistics.* Strasbourg, France: Council of European Committee on Crime Prevention.

Covey, Herbert C. 2003. *Street Gangs throughout the World.* Springfield, IL: Charles C. Thomas.

Cox, Stephen M., and John J. Conrad. 1996. *Juvenile Justice: A Guide to Practice and Theory.* 4th ed. Dubuque: Brown and Benchmark.

Craig, Maria C., and Mark C. Stafford. 1997. Delinquency and Juvenile Justice in the United States, pp. 271–302, in John A. Winterdyk (ed.), *Juvenile Justice Systems: International Perspectives*. Toronto: Canadian Scholars' Press.

Cressey, Donald R. 1960. Epidemiology and Individual Conduct: A Case from Criminology. *Pacific Sociological Review* 3:47–58.

Crosson-Tower, Cynthia. 1999. *Understanding Child Abuse and Neglect*. 4th ed. Boston: Allyn and Bacon.

Crutchfield, Robert D., George S. Bridges, Joseph G. Weis, and Charis Kubrin (eds.). 2000. *Crime Readings*. 2nd ed. Thousand Oaks, CA.: Pine Forge Press.

Cullen, Francis T. 2005. The Twelve People Who Saved Rehabilitation: How the Science of Criminology Made a Difference. *Criminology* 1:147–172.

Cunneen, Chris, and Rob White. 1995. *Juvenile Justice: An Australian Perspective*. Oxford: Oxford University Press.

Curry, David G., and Scott H. Decker. 1998. *Confronting Gangs: Crime and Community*. Los Angeles: Roxbury.

Dalteg, Arne, and Sten Levander. 1998. Twelve Thousand Crimes by 75 Boys: A Twenty-Year Follow-Up Study of Childhood Hyperactivity. *Journal of Forensic Psychiatry* 9:39–57.

Dammer, Harry R., Erika Fairchild, and Jay S. Albanese. 2006. *Comparative Criminal Justice Systems*. 3rd ed. Belmont, CA: Wadsworth.

Davidson, Julia Oconnell. 2005. *Children in the Global Sex Trade*. Cambridge: Polity.

Decker, Scott H., and Barrik Van Winkle. 2001. The History of Gang Research, pp. 15–21, in Jody Miller, Cheryl L. Maxson, and Malcolm W. Klein. *The Modern Gang Reader*. 2nd ed. Los Angeles, CA: Roxbury.

DeSouza, Eros. R., and J'aims Ribeiro. 2005. Bullying and Sexual Harassment among Brazilian High School Students. *Journal of Interpersonal Violence* 20:1018–1038.

Dobbin, Shirley A., and Sophia I. Gatowski. 1996. *A Guide to Research on Juvenile Violence*. Reno, NV: National Council of Juvenile and Family Court Judges.

Donker, Andrea G., Wilma H. Smeenk, Peter H. van der Laan, and Frank C. Verhulst. 2002. Individual Stability of Antisocial Behavior from Childhood to Adulthood: Testing the Stability Postulate of Moffitt's Developmental Theory. *Criminology* 41:593–609.

Doob, Anthony, and Michael Tonry. 2004. Varieties of Youth Justice, pp. 1–20, in Michael Tonry and Anthony Doob (eds.), *Youth Crime and Youth Justice: Comparative and Cross-National Perspectives*. Chicago: University of Chicago Press.

Doob, Anthony N., and Jane B. Sprott. 2004. Youth Justice in Canada, pp. 185–242, in Raymond R. Corrado, Nicholas Bala, Rick Linden, and Marc Le Blanc (eds.), *Juvenile Justice in Canada: A Theoretical and Analytical Assessment*. Toronto: Butterworths.

Dorne, Clifford K. 1989. *Crimes against Children*. New York: Harrow and Heston.

Drakeford, Mark, and Ian Butler. 2001. Tough Enough? Youth Justice under New Labour. *Probation Journal* 48:119–124.

Duffy, Maureen. 2004. Introduction: A Global Overview of the Issues of and Responses to Teen Gangs, pp. 1–12, in Maureen P. Duffy and Scott Edward Gillig (eds.), *Teen Gangs: A Global View*. Westport, CT: Greenwood.

D'Unger, Amy V., Kenneth C. Land, and Patricia L. McCall. 2002. Sex Differences in Age Patterns of Delinquent/Criminal Careers: Results from Poisson Latent Class Analyses of the Philadelphia Cohort Study. *Journal of Quantitative Criminology* 18:349–375.

Dünkel, Frieder. 1991. Legal Differences in Juvenile Criminology in Europe, pp. 1–29, in Tim Booth (ed.), *Juvenile Justice in the New Europe*. Sheffield, UK: Joint Unit for Social Services Research, Sheffield University.

Durkheim, Emile. 1951. *Suicide*. Trans. John A. Spaulding and George Simpson. New York: Free Press.

Durrant, Joan E., and Gregg Olsen. 1997. Parenting and Public Policy: Contextualizing the Swedish Corporal Punishment Ban. *Journal of Social Welfare and Family Law* 19:443–461.

Ebbe, Obi N. I. 2006. The Juvenile Justice System in Nigeria, pp. 49–68, in Paul C. Friday and Xin Ren (eds.), *Delinquency and Juvenile Justice Systems in the Non-Western World*. Monsey, NY: Criminal Justice Press.

Eklund, Jenny M., and Brett af Kinteberg. 2003. *Criminal Behavior and Mental Health* 13:294–309.

Elliott, Delbert S., Suzanne S. Ageton, and Rachelle J. Cantor. 1979. An Integrated Theoretical Perspective on Delinquent Behavior. *Journal of Research in Crime and Delinquency* 16:3–27.

Ellis, Lee, and Anthony Walsh. 2000. *Criminology: A Global Perspective*. Boston: Allyn and Bacon.

Empey, LaMar T. 1979a. Children's Liberation: Dilemmas in the Search for Utopia, pp. 380–417, in LaMar T. Empey (ed.), *The Future of Childhood and Juvenile Justice*. Charlottesville: University Press of Virginia.

———, (ed.). 1979b. *The Future of Childhood and Juvenile Justice*. Charlottesville: University Press of Virginia.

Erling, Ann, and C. Philip Hwang. 2004. Swedish 10-Year-Old Children's Perceptions and Experiences of Bullying. *Journal of School Violence* 3:33–44.

Eslea, Mike, Ersilia Menesini, and Yohji Morita. 2004. Friendship and Loneliness among Bullies and Victims: Data from Seven Countries. *Aggressive Behavior* 30:71–83.

Estes, Richard J., and Neil Alan Weiner. 2001. *The Commercial Sexual Exploitation of Children in the U.S., Canada, and Mexico*. Philadelphia: University of Pennsylvania School of Social Work.

Estrada, Felipe. 1999. Juvenile Crime Trends in Postwar Europe. *European Journal on Criminal Policy and Research* 7:23–42.

———. 2001. Juvenile Violence as a Social Problem: Trends, Media Attention and Societal Response. *British Journal of Criminology* 41:639–655.

Fagan, Jeffrey, and Franklin E. Zimring. 2000. Editor's Introduction, pp. 1–12, in Jeffrey Fagan and Franklin E. Zimring, *The Changing Border of Juvenile Justice: Transfer of Adolescents to the Criminal Court*. Chicago: University of Chicago Press.

Farrington, David P. 1986. Age and Crime, pp. 189–250, in Michael Tonry and Norval Morris (eds.), *Crime and Justice: An Annual Review of Research*, vol. 7. Chicago: University of Chicago Press.

———. 2003. Developmental and Life-Course Criminology: Key Theoretical and Empirical Issues—The 2002 Sutherland Award Address. *Criminology* 41:221–255.

Farrington, David P., and Trever Bennett. 1981. Police Cautioning of Juvenile in London. *British Journal of Criminology* 21:123–135.

Farson, Richard. 1979. The Children's Rights Movement, pp. 35–65, in LaMar T. Empey (ed.), *The Future of Childhood and Juvenile Justice*. Charlottesville: University Press of Virginia.

Feld, Barry C. 1987. The Juvenile Court Meets the Principle of the Offense: Legislative Changes in Juvenile Waver Statutes. *Journal of Criminal Law and Criminology* 78:571–573.

———. 1991. The Transformation of the Juvenile Court. *Minnesota Law Review* 75:691–725.

Felson, Marcus, and Lawrence E. Cohen. 1980. Human Ecology and Crime: A Routine Activity Approach. *Human Ecology* 8:389–406.

Fenwick, Charles R. 1983. The Juvenile Delinquency Problem in Japan: Application of a Role Relationship Model. *International Journal of Comparative and Applied Criminal Justice* 7:119–128.

Fergusson, D. M., L. J. Horwood, and M. T. Lynskey. 1993. Ethnicity, Social Background and Young Offending: A 14-Year Longitudinal Study. *Australian and New Zealand Journal of Criminology* 26:155–170.

Finckenauer, James O. 1996. Russia, pp. 272–285, in Donald J. Shoemaker (ed.), *International Handbook on Juvenile Justice*. Westport, CT: Greenwood.

Finckenauer, James O., and Linda Kelly. 1992. Juvenile Delinquency and Youth Subcultures in the Former Soviet Union. *International Journal of Comparative and Applied Criminal Justice* 16:247–261.

Finckenauer, James O., Robert R. Weidner, and William C. Terrill. 1998. Delinquency among a Sample of Russian Youth: A Test of Power-Control Theory. *International Criminal Justice Review* 8:15–32.

Finkelhor, David, and Patricia Hashima. 2001. The Victimization of Children and Youth: A Comprehensive Overview, pp. 49–78, in Susan O. White, *Handbook of Youth and Justice*. New York: Kluwer Academic/Plenum.

Fionda, Julia. 2001. Youth and Justice, pp. 77–98, in Julia Fionda (ed.), *Legal Concepts of Childhood*. Oxford, UK: Hart.

Friday, Paul C., and Xin Ren (eds.). 2006. *Delinquency and Juvenile Justice Systems in the Non-Western World*. Monsey, NY: Criminal Justice Press.

Fried, Carrie S. 2001. Juvenile Curfews: Are They an Effective and Constitutional Means of Combating Juvenile Violence? *Behavioral Sciences and the Law* 19:127–141.

Fuller, John, and William Norton. 1993. Juvenile Diversion: The Impact of Program Philosophy on Net Widening. *Journal of Crime and Justice* 16:29–45.

Gabor, Thomas, and Mata Fernando. 2004. Victimization and Repeat Victimization over The Life Span: A Predictive Study and Implications for Policy. *International Review of Victimology* 10:193–221.

Gardner, M., and L. Steinberg. 2005. Peer Influence on Risk-Taking, Risk Preference, and Risky Decision-Making in Adolescence and Adulthood: An Experimental Study. *Developmental Psychology* 41:625–635.

Gastil, Raymond D. 1971. Homicide and a Regional Culture of Violence. *American Sociological Review* 36:412–427.

Gatti, Uberto, Giovanni Fossa, Eleonora Lusetti, Maria Ida Marugo, Gaetana Russo, and Giovanni Battista Traverso. 1994. "Self Reported Delinquency in Three Italian Cities," pp. 267–287, in Josine Junger-Tas, Gert-Jan Terlouw, and Malcolm W. Klein (eds.), *Delinquent Behavior among Young People in the Western World: First Results of the International Self-Report Delinquency Study*. Amsterdam: Kugler.

Gatti, Uberto, and Alfredo Verde. 1997. Comparative Juvenile Justice: An Overview of Italy, pp. 177–204, in John A. Winterdyk (ed.), *Juvenile Justice Systems: International Perspectives*. Toronto: Canadian Scholar's Press.

Gaylord, Mark S. 1996. Hong Kong, pp. 160–174, in Donald J. Shoemaker (ed.), *International Handbook on Juvenile Justice*. Westport, CT: Greenwood.

Gersão, Eliana, and Manuel Lisboa. 1994. The Self-Report Delinquency Study in Portugal, pp. 212–237 in Josine Junger-Tas, Gert-Jan Terlouw, and Malcolm W. Klein (eds.), *Delinquent Behavior among Young People in the Western World: First Results of International Self-Report Delinquency Study*. Amsterdam: Kugler.

Ghosh, Lipi. 2002. *Prostitution in Thailand: Myth and Reality*. New Delhi: Munshiram Manoharial.

Gillis, John R. 1981. *Youth and History: Tradition and Change in European Age Relations, 1770–Present*. New York: Academic Press.

Giordano, Peggy C., Stephen A. Cernkovich, and Donna D. Holland. 2003. Changes in Friendship Relations over the Life Course: Implications for Desistance from Crime. *Criminology* 41:293–328.

Goodwin, T. M. 1998. *Peer Justice and Youth Empowerment: An Implementation Guide for Teen Court Programs*. Lexington, KY: American Probation and Parole Association.

Gottfredson, Michael, and Travis Hirschi. 1990. *A General Theory of Crime*. Palo Alto, CA: Stanford University Press.

Goulden, Chris, and Arun Sondhi. 2001. *At the Margins: Drug Use by Vulnerable Young People in the 1998/99 Youth Lifestyle Survey*. London: Home office Research, Development and Statistics Directorate.

Graham, John, and Benjamin Bowling. 1995. *Young People and Crime*. London: Home Office.

Great Britain Office of Standards of Education. 2004. *Girls in Prison: The Education and Training of Under-18s Serving Detention and Training Orders*. London: Her Majesty's Inspectorate of Prisons.

Greenwood, Peter W. (ed.). 1986. *Intervention Strategies for Chronic Juvenile Offenders: Some New Perspectives*. New York: Greenwood Press.

Hackler, Jim. 1991a. Using Reintegrative Shaming Effectively: Why Fiji Has a Juvenile Justice System Superior to the US, Canada, and Australia, pp. 109–128, in Jim Hackler (ed.), *Official Responses to Problem Juveniles: Some International Reflections*. Euskadi, Spain: The Oñati International Institute for the Sociology of Law.

———.1991b. Confusing the Drama with the Reality in the French Juvenile Court, pp. 205–222 in Jim Hackler (ed.), *Official Responses to Problem Juveniles: Some International Reflections*. Euskadi, Spain: The Oñati International Institute for the Sociology of Law.

———, (ed.). 1991c. *Official Responses to Problem Juveniles: Some International Reflections*. Euskadi, Spain: The Oñati International Institute for the Sociology of Law.

Hagan, John, John Sampson, and A. R. Gillis. 1987. Class in the Household: A Power-Control Theory of Gender and Delinquency, *American Journal of Sociology* 92:788–816.

Hagedorn, John M. 2001. Globalization, Gangs, and Collaborative Research, pp. 41–58, in Malcolm W. Klein, Hans-Jürgen Kerner, Cheryl L. Maxson, and Elmar G. M. Weitekamp (eds.), *The Eurogang Paradox: Street Gangs and Youth Groups in the U.S. and Europe*. Dordrecht: Kluwer.

Hamersley, Richard, Louise Marsland, and Marie Reid. 2003. *Substance Use by Young Offenders: The Impact of the Normalization of Drug Use in the Early Years of the 21st Century*. London: Home Office Research, Development and Statistics Directorate.

Hareide, Bjorn. 2000. Naerpoliti Og Kriminalitetsbekjempeise, *Nordisk Tidsskrift for Kriminalvidenskab* 87:246–252.

Hartjen, Clayton A. 1977. *Possible Trouble: An Analysis of Social Problems*. New York: Praeger.

——. 1978. *Crime and Criminalization*. 2nd ed. New York: Holt, Rinehart and Winston.

——. 1995. Legal Change and Juvenile Justice in India. *International Criminal Justice Review* 5:1–16.

——. 1997. The Criminality of Women and Girls in India. *International Journal of Comparative and Applied Criminal Justice* 21:287–303.

——. 1998. Investigating Youth-Crime and Justice around the World, pp. 523–538, in Hans-Dieter Schwind, Edwin Kube, and Hans-Heiner Kühne (eds.), *Essays in Honor of Hans Joachim Schneider: Criminology on the Threshold of the 21st Century*. Berlin: Walter de Gruyter.

Hartjen, Clayton A., and Sesha Kethineni. 1996. *Comparative Delinquency: India and the United States*. New York: Garland.

Hartjen, Clayton A., and S. Priyadarsini. 1984. *Delinquency in India: A Comparative Analysis*. New Brunswick, NJ: Rutgers University Press.

——. 2003. Gender, Peers, and Delinquency: A Study of Boys and Girls in Rural France. *Youth and Society* 34:387–414.

——. 2004. *Delinquency and Juvenile Justice: An International Bibliography*. Westport, CT: Praeger.

Hauge, Ragnar. 1987. The Controversy between Self-Reporting Studies and Crime Statistics on Drug Use, pp. 22–33, in Per Stangeland (ed.), *Drugs and Drug Control*. Oslo: Norwegian University Press.

Hawkins, Gordon, and Frank E. Zimring. 1986. Western European Perspectives on the Treatment of Young Offenders, pp. 55–74, in Peter W. Greenwood (ed.), *Intervention Strategies for Chronic Juvenile Offenders: Some New Perspectives*. New York: Greenwood Press.

Hazlehurst, Kayleen, and Cameron Hazlehurst. 1998. Gangs in Cross-Cultural Perspective, pp. 1–34, in Kayleen Hazlehurst and Cameron Hazlehurst (eds.), *Gangs and Youth Subcultures: International Explorations*. New Brunswick, NJ.: Transaction.

Heaven, Patrick C. L. 1994. Family of Origin, Personality, and Self-Reported Delinquency. *Journal of Adolescence* 17:445–459.

Heitmeyer, Wilhelm, and John Hagan (eds.). 2003. *International Handbook of Violence Research*. Dordrecht: Kluwer.

Hemmens, Craig, and Katherine Bennett. 1999. Juvenile Curfews and the Courts: Judicial Response to a Not-So-New Crime Control Strategy. *Crime and Delinquency* 45:99–121.

Hendrick, Harry. 2006. Histories of Youth Crime and Justice, pp. 3–16, in Barry Goldson and John Muncie (eds.), *Youth Crime and Justice*. London: Sage.

Hérault, Georges, and Pius Adesanmi (eds.), *Youth, Street Culture and Urban Violence in Africa: Proceedings of the International Symposium Held in Abidjan 5–7 May 1997*. Ibadan, Nigeria: Institute of African Studies, 1997.

Herczog, Mária, and Ferenc Irk. 1997. Comparative Juvenile Justice: An Overview of Hungary, pp. 303–330, in John A. Winterdyk (ed.), *Juvenile Justice Systems: International Perspectives*. Toronto: Canadian Scholars' Press.

Hewitt, John D., Eric W. Hickey, and Robert M. Regoli. 1991. Dealing with Juvenile Delinquency: The Re-Education of the Delinquent in the People's Republic of China, pp. 67–82, in Jim Hackler (ed.), *Official Responses to Problem Juveniles: Some International Reflections*. Euskadi, Spain: The Oñati International Institute for the Sociology of Law.

Hindelang, Michael J., Travis Hirschi, and Joseph G. Weis. 1981. *Measuring Delinquency*. Beverly Hills, CA: Sage.

Hindman, Hugh D. 2002. *Child Labor: An American History*. Armonk, NY: M. E. Sharpe.

Hinshaw, S. Lee. 1993. Juvenile Diversion: An Alternative to Juvenile Court. *Journal of Dispute Resolution* 2:305–321.

Hirschi, Travis. 1969. *Causes of Delinquency*. Berkeley: University of California Press.

Hoffman, Allan M., and Randal W. Summers (eds.). 2001. *Teen Violence: A Global View*. Westport, CT: Greenwood.

Hoshino, Kanehiro. 1989. Community Programs for Preventing Delinquency and Internalization of the Bond to Conventional Society. *Reports of the National Research Institute of Police Science* 30:149–163.

Hughes, Lisa. 2000. Can International Law Protect Child Soldiers? *Peace Review* 12:399–405.

Huizinga, David, and Delbert Elliott. 1987. Juvenile Offender Prevalence, Incidence, and Arrest Rates by Race. *Crime and Delinquency* 33:206–233.

Huizinga, David, Karl Schumann, Beate Ehret, and Amanda Elliott. 2004. The Effect of Juvenile Justice System Processing on Subsequent Delinquent and Criminal Behavior: A Cross-National Study. Unpublished report submitted to U.S. Department of Justice.

Human Rights Watch. 2002. Hopes Betrayed: Trafficking of Women and Girls to Post-Conflict Bosnia and Herzegovina for Forced Prostitution. *Human Rights Watch* 14, no. 9 (D): 1–174.

———. 2003. *Cruel Confinement: Abuses against Detained Children in Northern Brazil*. New York: Human Rights Watch.

———. 2004. Brazil: "Real Dungeons" Juvenile Detention in the State of Rio De Janeiro. *Human Rights Watch* 16:1–68.

———. 2005a. In the Dark: Hidden Abuses against Detained Youths in Rio De Janeiro. *Human Rights Watch* 17:1–48.

———. 2005b. "Making Their Own Rules": Police Beatings, Rape, and Torture of Children in Papua New Guinea. http://hrw.org/reports/2005/png0905/.

———. 2006a. Child Domestics: The World's Invisible Workers. http://hrw.org/english/docs/2004/06/10/africa8789_tst.htm.

———. 2006b. Children Used as Soldiers in Most Major Conflicts. http://hrw.org/english/docs/2004/11/17/globa19677.htm.

———. 2006c. How to Fight, How to Kill: Child Soldiers in Liberia. http://hrw.org/reports/2004/liberia0204/.

———. 2006d. Fact Sheet on Child Soldiers in Sri Lanka. http://hrw.org/english/docs/2004/11/11/slanka9662.htm.

———. 2006e. Burma: Demobilize Child Soldiers. http://hrw.org/english/docs/2004/06/04/burma8734.htm.

———. 2006f. Street Children. http://hrw.org/children/street.htm.

———. 2006g. What Future? Street Children in the Democratic Republic of Congo. *Human Rights Watch* 18:1–72.

Humphris, Nicolas. 1991. Educational Aspects of French Cabinet Justice, pp. 223–224, in Jim Hackler (ed.), *Official Responses to Problem Juveniles: Some International Reflections*. Euskadi, Spain: The Oñati International Institute for the Sociology of Law.

Hyman, Irwin A., and James H. Wise. 1979. *Corporal Punishment in American Education: Readings in History, Practice, and Alternatives*. Philadelphia: Temple University Press.

Inciardi, James A. (ed.). 1980. *Radical Criminology*. Beverly Hills, CA: Sage.

Inciardi, James A., and Anne E. Pottieger (eds.). 1978. *Violent Crime: Historical and Contemporary Issues*. Beverly Hills, CA: Sage.

International Labor Office. 2006. *The End of Child Labor: Within Reach*. Geneva: International Labor Office.

International Prison Watch. 1998. *Enfants en Prison: Rapport d'Observation sur les Conditions de Détention des Mineurs dans 51 Pays*. Lyon, France: Observatoire International des Prisons.

International Society for Prevention of Child Abuse and Neglect. 2004. *World Perspectives on Child Abuse and Neglect*. 6th ed. Carol Stream, IL: ISPCAN.

International Tribunal for Children's Rights. 2006. *International Dimensions of the Sexual Exploitation of Children*. Montreal: International Bureau for Children's Rights.

Jacobs, Mark D. 1990. *Screwing the System and Making It Work: Juvenile Justice in the No-Fault Society*. Chicago: University of Chicago Press.

James, Oliver. 1995. *Juvenile Violence in a Winner-Loser Culture: Socio-Economic and Familial Origins of the Rise of Violence against the Person*. London: Free Association Books.

Jánson, Carl-Gunnar, and Per-Olaf Wikström. 1995. Growing Up in a Welfare State: The Social Class-Offending Relationship, pp. 191–215, in Zena Smith Blau and John Hagan (eds.), *Current Perspectives on Aging and the Life Cycle: Delinquency and Disrepute in the Life Course*. Greenwich, CT: JAI Press.

Jensen, Eric L., and Jørgen Jepsen (eds.). 2006. *Juvenile Law Violators, Human Rights, and the Development of New Juvenile Justice Systems*. Oxford, UK: Hart.

Johnston, Helen. 1995. Age in Criminal Proceedings in Europe, pp. 10–14, in Howard League for Penal Reform, *Child Offenders: UK and International Practice*. London, UK.

Jones, Suzanne P., and Patrick C. Heaven. 1998. Psychological Correlates of Adolescent Drug-Taking Behavior. *Journal of Adolescence* 21:127–134.

Junger, M. 1990. *Delinquency and Ethnicity: An Investigation of Social Factors Relating to Delinquency among Moroccan, Turkish, Surinamese and Dutch Boys*. Deventer, The Netherlands: Kluwer.

Junger, Marianne, and Ineke Haen Marshall. 1997. The Interethnic Generalizability of Social Control Theory: An Empirical Test. *Journal of Research in Crime and Delinquency* 34:79–112.

Junger-Tas, Josine. 1983. *Juvenile Delinquency and the Law*. The Hague: Ministry of Justice of the Netherlands.

———. 1991. Recent Trends in Juvenile Delinquency and Juvenile Justice, pp. 1–8, in Josine Junger-Tas, Leonieke Boendermaker, and Peter H. van der Laan (eds.), *The Future of the Juvenile Justice System*. Leuven, Belgium: Acco.

———. 1992. An Empirical Test of Social Control Theory. *Journal of Quantitative Criminology* 8:9–28.

———. 1997. Juvenile Delinquency and Juvenile Justice in The Netherlands, pp. 55–76, in John A. Winterdyk (ed.), *Juvenile Justice Systems: International Perspectives*. Toronto: Canadian Scholar's Press.

———. 2004. Youth Justice in The Netherlands, pp. 293–348, in Michael Tonry and Anthony Doob (eds.), *Youth Crime and Youth Justice: Comparative and Cross-National Perspectives*. Chicago: University of Chicago Press.

Junger-Tas, Josine, Gert-Jan Terlouw, and Malcolm W. Klein (eds.). 1994. *Delinquent Behavior among Young People in the Western World: First Results of the International Self-Report Delinquency Study*. Amsterdam: Kugler.

Justice. 1996. *Children and Homicide: Appropriate Procedures for Juveniles in Murder and Manslaughter Cases.* London: Justice.

Kane, June. 1998. *Sold for Sex.* Arena: Aldershot Hants, England.

Kanetsuna, Tomoyuki, and Peter K. Smith. 2002. Pupil Insights into Bullying and Coping with Bullying: A Bi-National Study in Japan and England. *Journal of School Violence* 1:5–29.

Kelly, Liz, Rachel Wingfield, Sheila Burton, and Linda Regan. 1995. *Splintered Lives: Sexual Exploitation of Children in the Context of Children's Rights and Child Protection.* Essex, England: Barnardos.

Kemmesies, Uwe E. 1995. *Compulsive Drug Use in The Netherlands and in Germany.* Berlin: VWB-Verlag fuer Wissenschaft und Bildung.

Kibuka, Eric. 1995. Children and Juveniles in Detention: Implementation of United Nations Standards and Norms, pp. 131–136, in United Nations Expert Group Meeting, *Children and Juveniles in Detention: Application of Human Rights Standards.* Vienna: Austrian Federal Ministry for Youth and Family.

Killias, Martin, and Denis Ribeaud. 1999. Drug Use and Crime among Juveniles: An International Perspective. *Studies on Crime and Crime Prevention* 8:189–209.

Kivivuori, Janne. 2000. Delinquent Behavior, Psychosomatic Symptoms and the Idea of Healthy Delinquency. *Journal of Scandinavian Studies in Criminology and Crime Prevention* 1:121–139.

Kivivuori, Janne, and Jukka Savolainen. 2003. *Helsingen Nuoret Rikosten Uhreina Ja Tekijoina (Violent Victimization and Delinquent Behavior among Helsinki Adolescents).* Helsinki: Oikeusppoliiittisen Tutkimuslaitoksen.

Klain, Eva J. 1999. *Prostitution of Children and Child-Sex Tourism: An Analysis of Domestic and International Responses.* Alexandria, VA: National Center for Missing and Exploited Children.

Klein, Malcolm W. 2001a. Resolving the Eurogang Paradox, pp. 7–19, in Malcolm W. Klein, Hans-Jürgen Kerner, Cheryl L. Maxson, and Elmar G. M. Weitekamp (eds.), *The Eurogang Paradox: Street Gangs and Youth Groups in the U.S. and Europe.* Dordrecht: Kluwer.

———. 2001b. Gangs in the United States and Europe, pp. 61–72, in Jody Miller, Cheryl L. Maxson, and Malcolm W. Klein, *The Modern Gang Reader,* 2nd ed., Los Angeles, CA: Roxbury.

Kline, Chris. 1998. Guatemalan Street Kids Face Hardships, Death Squads. http://www.Cnn/WORLD/9802/14/Guatemala.street.kids/ accessed 1/29/2006.

Kobayashi, Juichi, Haruo Nishimura, Yoshiaki Takahashi, Yoshifumi Tozaki, and Shingo Suzuki. 1988. Relations of School Life and Peers at the Time of Arrest to Subsequent Delinquency. *Reports of the National Research Institute of Police Science* 29:15–26.

Kouvonen, Anne. 2001. *Koululaisten Tyossakaynti Ja Ongelmakayttaytyminen.* Helsinki: Tyoministerio.

Kovats-Bernat, J. Christopher. 2000. Anti-Gang, Arimaj, and the War on Street Children. *Peace Review* 12:415–421.

Kratcoski, Peter, and Lucille Kratcoski. 1991. The Impact of Social Change on Juvenile Justice Policy in the United States, pp. 189–204, in Jim Hackler (ed.), *Official Responses to Problem Juveniles: Some International Reflections.* Euskadi, Spain: The Oñati International Institute for the Sociology of Law.

Krisberg, Barry. 2006. Rediscovering the Juvenile Justice Ideal in the United States, pp. 6–18, in John Muncie and Barry Goldson (eds.), *Comparative Youth Justice.* London: Sage.

Krisberg, Barry, and James Austin. 1978. *The Children of Ishmael: Critical Perspectives on Juvenile Justice*. Palo Alto, CA: Mayfield.

Kruissink, Maurits. 1991. The Halt Program: Evaluation of a Diversion Program for Juveniles, pp. 333–346, in Josine Junger-Tas, Leonieke Boendermaker and Peter H. van der Laan (eds.), *The Future of the Juvenile Justice System*. Leuven, Belgium: Acco.

Krukowski, Adam. 1987. The Criminological and Legal Problems of Juvenile Delinquency in Poland. *Eurocriminology* 1:113–129.

Kwan, Tsung Pui. 1988. The Correction of Young Offenders In Hong Kong, pp. 43–50, in UNAFEI, *Resource Material Series No. 34*. Fuchu, Japan.

Kyvsgaard, Britta. 2004. Youth Justice in Denmark, pp. 349–390, in Michael Tonry and Anthony Doob (eds.), *Youth Crime and Youth Justice: Comparative and Cross-National Perspectives*. Chicago: University of Chicago Press.

Lab, Steven P., and John T. Whitehead. 1998. An Analysis of Juvenile Correctional Treatment. *Crime and Delinquency* 34:600–683.

LaGrange, Teresa C., and Robert A. Silverman. 1999. Low Self-Control and Opportunity: Testing the General Theory of Crime as an Explanation of Gender Differences in Delinquency. *Criminology* 37:41–72.

Laub, John H., and Bruce K. MacMurray. 1987. Increasing the Prosecutor's Role in Juvenile Court: Expectation and Realities. *Justice System Journal* 12:196–209.

Lay, Barbara, Wolfgang Lhle, Guenter Esser, and Martin H. Schmidt. 2001. Risikofaktoren für Delinquenz Bei Jugendlichen und Deren Fortsetzung Bis in das Erwachscnenalter. *Monatsschrift fuer Kriminologie und Strafrechtsreform* 84:119–132.

Leal, César Barros. 1996. Brazil, pp. 20–33, in Donald J. Shoemaker (ed.), *International Handbook on Juvenile Justice*. Westport, CT: Greenwood.

LeBlanc, Marc. 1993. Late Adolescence Deceleration of Criminal Activity and Development of Self- and Social-Control. *Studies on Crime and Crime Prevention* 2:51–68.

———. 1997a. A Generic Control Theory of the Criminal Phenomenon: The Structural and Dynamic Statements of an Integrative Multilayered Control Theory, pp. 215–286, in Terence P. Thornberry (ed.), *Developmental Theories of Crime and Delinquency*, vol. 7 of *Advances in Criminological Theory*. New Brunswick, NJ: Transaction.

———. 1997b. Socialization or Propensity? Does Integrative Control Theory Apply to Adjudicated Boys? *Studies on Crime and Crime Prevention* 6:200–223.

———. 1997c. The Generality of Deviance: Replication over Two Decades with a Canadian Sample of Adjudicated Boys. *Canadian Journal of Criminology* 3:171–183.

Lederer, Laura. J. 2001. *Human Rights Report on Trafficking of Women and Children: A Country-by-Country Report on a Contemporary Form of Slavery*. Washington, DC: Johns Hopkins University, School of Advanced International Studies.

Lee, Francis Wing-Lin (ed.). 2005. *Working with Youth-at-Risk in Hong Kong*. Hong Kong: Hong Kong University Press.

Lee, Maggy. 1998. *Youth, Crime and Police Work*. London, UK: Macmillan.

Lee, Seong Sik. 1993. *A Cross-Population Test of Social Control and Differential Association Theories of Delinquency: Koreans, American Blacks, and American Nonblacks*. Ann Arbor: University Microfilms International.

LeRoux, Johann, and Cheryl Sylvia Smith. 1998. Causes and Characteristics of the Street Child Phenomenon: A Global Perspective. *Adolescence* 33:683–688.

Leschied, Alan. 1991. Canadian Juvenile Justice Reform: Is Fair and Equal Always Effective? pp. 83–90, in Jim Hackler (ed.), *Official Responses to Problem Juveniles: Some International Reflections*. Euskadi, Spain: The Oñati International Institute for the Sociology of Law.

Levy, Kenneth St. C. 1997. The Contribution of Self-Concept in the Etiology of Adolescent Delinquency. *Adolescence* 32:671–686.

Loyn, David. 2005. Forced Labour—Global Problem. http://news.bbc.co.uk/1/shared/spl/hi/world/05/slavery/html/1.stm.

Lunch, Michael J., and W. Byron Groves. 1986. *A Primer in Radical Criminology*. New York: Harrow and Heston.

Ma, Xin. 2002. Bullying in Middle School: Individual and School Characteristics of Victims and Offenders. *School Effectiveness and School Improvement* 13:63–89.

Markwart, Alan. 1992. Custodial Sanctions under the Young Offenders Act, pp. 229–281, in Raymond R. Corrado, Nicholas Bala, Rick Linden, and Marc Le Blanc (eds.), *Juvenile Justice in Canada: A Theoretical and Analytical Assessment*. Toronto: Butterworths.

Maxwell, Sheila Royo. 2001. A Focus on Familial Strain: Antisocial Behavior and Delinquency in Filipino Society. *Sociological Inquiry* 71:265–292.

McCarthy, Bill. 1996. The Attitudes and Actions of Others: Tutelage and Sutherland's Theory of Differential Association. *British Journal of Criminology* 36:135–147.

McNally, Roger B. 1995. Homicidal Youth in England and Wales, 1982–1992: Profile and Policy. *Psychology Crime and Law* 1:333–342.

Mehlbye, Jill, and Lode Walgrave (eds.). 1998. *Confronting Youth in Europe: Juvenile Crime and Juvenile Justice*. Copenhagen: AKF Forlaget.

Merton, Robert K. 1957. *Social Theory and Social Structure*. Rev. ed. London: Free Press of Glencoe.

———. 1964. Anomie, Anomia, and Social Interaction: Contexts of Deviant Behavior, pp. 213–242, in Marshall B. Clinard (ed.), *Anomie and Deviant Behavior*. New York: Free Press.

Messner, Steven F., Marvin D. Krohn, and Allen A. Liska (eds.). 1989. *Theoretical Integration in the Study of Deviance and Crime: Problems and Prospects*. Albany: State University of New York Press.

Miller, Jerome G. 1979. The Revolution in Juvenile Justice: From Rhetoric to Rhetoric, pp. 66–111, in LaMar T. Empey (ed.), *The Future of Childhood and Juvenile Justice*. Charlottesville: University Press of Virginia.

Miller, Jody, Cheryl L. Maxson, and Malcolm W. Klein (eds.). *The Modern Gang Reader*. 2nd. ed. Los Angeles: Roxbury.

Miller, Walter B. 1958. Lower Class Culture as a Generating Milieu of Gang Delinquency. *Journal of Social Issues* 14:5–19.

Milne, Heather A., Rick Linden, and Rod Kueneman. 1992. Advocate or Guardian: The Role of Defense Counsel in Youth Justice, pp. 313–346, in Raymond R. Corrado, Nicholas Bala, Rick Linden, and Marc Le Blanc (eds.), *Juvenile Justice in Canada: A Theoretical and Analytical Assessment*. Toronto: Butterworths.

Ministry of Law and Justice. 1986. *The Juvenile Justice Act 1986*. New Delhi: Gazette of India Extraordinary.

Moffatt, Gregory K. 2003. *Wounded Innocents and Fallen Angels: Child Abuse and Child Aggression*. Westport, CT: Praeger.

Moffitt, Terrie E. 1993. Adolescence-Limited and Life-Course-Persistent Antisocial Behavior: A Developmental Taxonomy. *Psychological Review* 100:674–701.

Moffitt, Terrie E., Donald R. Lynam, and Phil A. Silva. 1994. Neuropsychological Tests Predicting Persistent Male Delinquency. *Criminology* 32:277–300.

Montgomery, Imogene M., Patricia McFall Torbet, Diane A. Malloy, Lori P. Adamcik, M. James Toner, and Joey Andrews. 1994. *What Works: Promising Interventions in Juvenile Justice*. Pittsburgh: National Center for Juvenile Justice.

Morris, Allison, and Gabrielle Maxwell. 1991. Family Empowerment in Juvenile Justice in New Zealand: A Marriage of Indigenous and Western Processes, pp. 91–108, in Jim Hackler (ed.), *Official Responses to Problem Juveniles: Some International Reflections*. Euskadi, Spain: The Oñati International Institute for the Sociology of Law.

———. 1993. Juvenile Justice in New Zealand: A New Paradigm. *Australian and New Zealand Journal of Criminology* 20:72–90.

Mukherjee, Satyanshu, Carlos Carcach, and Karl Higgins. 1997. *Juvenile Crime and Justice: Australia 1997*. Griffith, ACT: Australian Institute of Criminology.

Muncie, John. 1999. *Youth and Crime: A Critical Introduction*. London: Sage.

Muncie, John, and Barry Goldson (eds.). 2006. *Comparative Youth Justice*. London: Sage.

Muntarbhorn, Vitit. 1994. Violence against Children: The Sale of Children, Child Prostitution and Child Pornography, pp. 54–65, in United Nations Expert Group Meeting, *Children and Juveniles in Detention: Application of Human Rights Standards*, Vienna: Austrian Federal Ministry for Youth and Family, 1995.

———. 1996. *Sexual Exploitation of Children*. New York: United Nations.

Nakhshab, Sirous. 1979. *Juvenile Delinquency in Tehran, Iran: An Examination of Sutherland's Theory of Differential Association*. Ann Arbor: University Microfilms International.

National Clearinghouse on Child Abuse and Neglect Information. 2006. What Is Child Abuse and Neglect? http://nccanch.acf.hhs.gov/pubs/factsheets/whatiscan.cfm.

National Council for Crime Prevention. 2007. http://www.bra.se/.

Nevares, Dora, Marvin E. Wolfgang, and Paul E. Tracy. 1990. *Delinquency in Puerto Rico: The 1970 Birth Cohort Study*. Westport, CT: Greenwood.

Newman, Graeme. 1999. *Global Report on Crime and Justice*. New York: Oxford University Press.

Nicol, Andrew Q. C. 1995. The Common Law Concept of *Doli Incapax*, pp. 5–9, in Howard League for Penal Reform, *Child Offenders: UK and International Practice*. London: Howard League for Penal Reform.

Nishimura, Haruo, Shingo Suzuki, and Yoshiaki Takahashi. 1982. An Analysis of the Conditions Conducive to Juvenile Delinquent Involvement among High School Students: On Their Deterioration on Inner Control. *Reports of the National Research Institute of Police Science* 23:27–50.

Nylund, Marianne. 1991. Young Offenders and the Mediation Program in Finland, pp. 257–268, in Jim Hackler (ed.), *Official Responses to Problem Juveniles: Some International Reflections*. Euskadi, Spain: The Oñati International Institute for the Sociology of Law.

Oberwittler, D., T. Blank, T. Köllisch, and T. Naplava. 2001. *Arbeitsberichte 1/2001: Soziale Lebenslagen und Delinquenz von Jugendlichen—Ergebnisse Der MIP-Schulbefragung 1999 in Freiburg und Köln*. Freiburg im Breisgau, Germany: Max Plank Institute for Foreign and International Penal Law.

O'Mahony, David, Tim Chapman, and Jonathan Doak. 2002. *Restorative Cautioning: A Study of Police Based Restorative Cautioning Pilots in Northern Ireland*. Belfast, Northern Ireland: Statistics and Research Agency.

Ortega, Suzanne T., Jay Corzine, and Cathleen Burnett. 1992. Modernization, Age Structure, and Regional Context: A Cross-National Study of Crime. *Sociological Spectrum* 12:257–277.

Osuna, Eduardo, Concepcion Alarcon, and Aurelio Luna. 1992a. Personality Traits in Juvenile Maladjustment. *Journal of Forensic Sciences* 37:228–236.

———. 1992b. Family Violence as a Determinant Factor in Juvenile Maladjustment. *Journal of Forensic Sciences* 37:1633–1639.

Otero-Lopez, Jose Manuel, Angeles Luengo-Martin, Lourdes Miron-Redondo, Maria Teresa Garrillo De La Peña, and Estrella Romero-Trinanes. 1994. An Empirical Study of the Relations between Drug Abuse and Delinquency among Adolescents. *British Journal of Criminology* 34:459–478.

Ottenhof, Reynold, and Jean-Francois Renucci. 1996. France, pp. 110–124, in Donald J. Shoemaker (ed.), *International Handbook on Juvenile Justice*, Westport, CT: Greenwood.

Paetsch, Joanne J., and Lorne D. Bertrand. 1999. Victimization and Delinquency among Canadian Youth. *Adolescence* 34:351–367.

Palmer, Ted. 1991. The Effectiveness of Intervention: Recent Trends and Current Issues. *Crime and Delinquency* 37:330–346.

Pape, Hilde, and Ingeborg Rossow. 2004. "Ordinary" People with "Normal" Lives? A Longitudinal Study of Ecstasy and Other Drug Use among Norwegian Youth. *Journal of Drug Issues* 34:389–418.

Paternoster, Raymond, and Lee Ann Iovanni. 1989. The Labeling Perspective and Delinquency: An Elaboration of the Theory and Assessment of the Evidence. *Justice Quarterly* 6:359–394.

Petoussi, Vassiliki, and Kalliopi Stavrou. 1996. Greece, pp. 146–159, in Donald J. Shoemaker (ed.), *International Handbook on Juvenile Justice*, Westport, CT: Greenwood.

Petrosino, Anthony, Carolyn Turpin-Petrosino, and John Buehler. 2003. Scared Straight and Other Juvenile Awareness Programs for Preventing Juvenile Delinquency: A Systematic Review of the Randomized Experimental Evidence. *Annals of the American Academy of Political and Social Sciences* 589:41–62.

Pfeiffer, Christian. 1998. *Juvenile Crime and Violence in European Countries*. Hanover: Kriminologisches Forschungsinstitut Niedersachsen.

Piliavin, Irving, and Scott Briar. 1964. Police Encounters with Juveniles. *American Journal of Sociology* 70:206–214.

Piquero, Alex R., and Timothy Brezina. 2001 Testing Moffitt's Account of Adolescence-Limited Delinquency. *Criminology* 39:353–370.

Piquero, Alex R., Timothy Brezina, and Michael G. Turner. 2005. Testing Moffitt's Account of Delinquency Abstention. *Journal of Research in Crime and Delinquency* 42:27–54.

Platt, Anthony. 1969. *The Child Savers: The Invention of Delinquency*. Chicago: University of Chicago Press.

Polk, Kenneth. 1984. Juvenile Diversion. *Crime and Delinquency* 30:648–659.

Pratt, John. 1989. Corporatism: The Third Model of Juvenile Justice. *British Journal of Criminology* 29:236–254.

Price, Susannah. 2005. UN "To Protect Children from War." http://news.bbc.co.uk/2/hi/americas/4719867.stm.

Queloz, Nicolas. 1991. Protection, Intervention and the Rights of Children and Young People, pp. 30–45, in Tim Booth (ed.), *Juvenile Justice in the New Europe*. Sheffield, UK: Sheffield University.

Rashid, Stephen Parvez. 2000. Comparing Studies of Youth and Violence: Towards An Integrated Approach, pp. 169–182, in Gwyneth Boswell (ed.), *Violent Children and Adolescents: Asking the Question Why*. London: Whurr.

Reichel, Philip L. 2005a. *Comparative Criminal Justice Systems: A Topical Approach*. 4th. ed. Upper Saddle River, N.J.: Pearson.

——, (ed.). 2005b. *Handbook of Transnational Crime and Justice*. Thousand Oaks, CA: Sage.

Reinarman, Craig, and Jeffrey Fagan. 1988. Social Organization and Differential Association: A Research Note from a Longitudinal Study of Violent Juvenile Offenders. *Crime and Delinquency* 34:307–327.

Reiss, Albert J. 1986. *The Police and the Public*. New Haven, CT: Yale University Press.

Ren, Xin. 1996. People's Republic of China, pp. 57–79, in Donald J. Shoemaker (ed.), *International Handbook on Juvenile Justice*. Westport, CT: Greenwood.

Research and Training Institute, Ministry of Japan. 2004. *White Paper on Crime: Treatment of Offenders*. Tokyo: Research and Training Institute, Ministry of Japan.

Rigby, Ken. 2003. Addressing Bullying in Schools: Theory and Practice. *Australian Institute of Criminology: Trends and Issues in Crime and Criminal Justice* 259:1–6.

Roberts, Julian V. 2004. Public Opinion and Youth Justice, pp. 495–542, in Michael Tonry and Norval Morris (eds.), *Crime and Justice: A Review of Research*, vol. 12. Chicago: University of Chicago Press.

Rounds, Delbert. 2000. *International Criminal Justice: Issues in Global Perspective*. Needham Heights, MA: Allyn and Bacon.

Ruchkin, Valdislav V., Roman A. Koposov, Martin Eisemann, Bruno Hägglöof. 2002. Alcohol Use in Delinquent Adolescents from Northern Russia: The Role of Personality, Parental Rearing and Family History of Alcohol Abuse. *Personality and Individual Difference* 32:1139–1148.

Sagel-Grande, Irene 1991. Looking for One Age, pp. 66–74, in Tim Booth (ed.), *Juvenile Justice in the New Europe*. Sheffield, UK: Sheffield University.

Sampson, Robert J., and John H. Laub. 1993. *Crime in the Making: Pathways and Turning Points through Life*. Cambridge: Cambridge University Press.

——. 2003. Life-Course Desisters? Trajectories of Crime among Delinquent Boys Followed to Age 70. *Criminology* 41:555–592.

Sampson, Robert J., Thomas C. Castellano, and John H. Laub. 1981. *Analysis of National Crime Victimization Survey Data to Study Serious Delinquent Behavior*. Albany, NY: Criminal Justice Research Center.

Sanborn, Joseph B. Jr., and Anthony W. Salerno. 2005. *The Juvenile Justice System: Law and Process*. Los Angeles: Roxbury.

Sanders, Wiley B. (ed.). 1970. *Juvenile Offenders for a Thousand Years*. Chapel Hill: University of North Carolina Press.

Sarnecki, Jerzy. 1990. Delinquent Networks in Sweden. *Journal of Quantitative Criminology* 6:31–50.

——. 2001. *Delinquent Networks: Youth Co-offending in Stockholm.* Cambridge, UK: Cambridge University Press.

Scheper-Hughes, Nancy, and Philippe Bourgois (eds.). 2004. *Violence in War and Peace: An Anthology.* Oxford: Blackwell, 2004.

Scheper-Hughes, Nancy, and Hoffman, Daniel. 1994. *Kids Out of Place (Part 2 of 2),* New York: North American Congress on Latin America (NACLA).

Schmidt, Bettina E., and Ingo W. Schröder (eds.). 2001. *Anthropology of Violence and Conflict.* London: Routledge.

Schwartz, Ira M. (ed.) 1992. *Juvenile Justice and Public Policy.* New York: Lexington.

Scottish Office Home Department Central Research Unit. 1998. *Main Findings from the 1996 Scottish Crime Survey.* Edinburgh: U.K. Stationary Office.

Sebba, L. 1986. Legalism versus Welfarism in the Juvenile Justice System: The Case of Israel, pp. 125–143, in M. Brusten, J. Graham, N. Herriger, and P. Malinowski (eds.), *Youth Crime, Social Control and Prevention: Theoretical Perspectives and Policy Implications: Studies from Nine Different Countries.* Wuppertal, Germany: International Document and Study Centre for Conflicts of Youth, University of Wuppertal.

Selih, A. 1996. Juvenile Criminal Law and Change: Trends in Some East- and Central-European Countries. *European Journal of Crime Criminal Law and Criminal Justice* 4:173–183.

Seymour, John. 1996. Australia, pp. 1–19, in Donald J. Shoemaker (ed.), *International Handbook on Juvenile Justice.* Westport, CT: Greenwood.

Shelley, Louise I. 1981. *Crime and Modernization: The Impact of Industrialization and Urbanization on Crime.* Carbondale and Edwardsville: Southern Illinois University Press.

——. 1986. Crime and Modernization Reexamined. *International Annals of Criminology* 24:7–21.

Sherman, Lawrence W., Denise Gottfredson, Doris L. MacKenzie, John Eck, Peter Reuter, and Shawn D. Bushway. 1998. Preventing Crime: What Works, What Doesn't, and What's Promising. *Research in Brief.* Washington, DC: U.S. Department of Justice.

Shestakov, Dmitry A., and Natalia D. Shestakova. 1997. Comparative Juvenile Justice: An Overview of Russia, pp. 205–232, in John A. Winterdyk (ed.), *Juvenile Justice Systems: International Perspectives.* Toronto: Canadian Scholars' Press.

Sheu, Chuen Jim. 1988. Juvenile Delinquency in the Republic of China: A Chinese Empirical Study of Social Control Theory. *International Journal of Comparative and Applied Criminal Justice* 12:59–71.

Shichor, David. 1990. Crime Patterns and Socioeconomic Development: A Cross-National Analysis. *Criminal Justice Review* 15:64–78.

Shine, James, and Dwight Price. 1992. Prosecutors and Juvenile Justice: New Roles and Perspectives, pp. 101–133, in Ira M. Schwartz (ed.), *Juvenile Justice and Public Policy.* New York: Lexington Books.

Shoemaker, Donald J. 1996a. Juvenile Corrections in the Philippines: The Barangay System. *Journal of Offender Rehabilitation* 24:39–52.

——, (ed.) 1996b. *International Handbook on Juvenile Justice.* Westport, CT: Greenwood.

Short, James F. Jr. 1979. Social Contexts of Child Rights and Delinquency, pp. 175–210, in LaMar T. Empey (ed.), *The Future of Childhood and Juvenile Justice.* Charlottesville: University Press of Virginia.

——, (ed.). 1968. *Gang Delinquency and Delinquent Subcultures.* New York: Harper and Row.

Shumba, Almon. 2001. Epidemiology and Etiology of Reported Cases of Child Physical Abuse in Zimbabwean Primary Schools. *Child Abuse and Neglect* 25:265–277.

———. 2003. Pupil Physical Abuse by Teachers: A Child-Rearing Practice or a Cultural Dilemma? *Journal of Aggression, Maltreatment and Trauma* 8:143–158.

Sickmund, Melissa. 2004. *Juveniles in Corrections.* Juvenile Offenders and Victims National Report Series Bulletin, June. Washington, DC: U.S. Department of Justice.

Singer, P. W. 2005/2006. Child Soldiers: The New Faces of War. *American Educator* (Winter): 28–37.

Skolnick, Arlene. 1979. Children's Rights, Children's Development, pp. 112–137, in LaMar T. Empey (ed.), *The Future of Childhood and Juvenile Justice.* Charlottesville: University Press of Virginia.

Smah, Sam O. 1997. *Juvenile Delinquency and Juvenile Violence in Jos-Nigeria.* Ibadan: Institute of African Studies, University of Ibadan.

Smith, David. J. 2005. The Effectiveness of Juvenile Justice Systems. *Criminal Justice: The International Journal of Policy and Practice* 5:181–195.

Smith, William R. 1991. *Social Structure, Family Structure, Child Rearing, and Delinquency: Another Look.* Stockholm: Department of Sociology, University of Stockholm.

Snyder, Howard N., and Sickmund, Melissa. 1999. *Juvenile Offenders and Victims: 1999 National Report.* Pittsburgh: National Center for Juvenile Justice.

Snyder, Howard N., Melissa Sickmund, and Ellen Poe-Yamagata. 1996. *Juvenile Offenders and Victims: Update on Violence: 1996.* Washington, DC: Office of Juvenile Justice and Delinquency Prevention.

Soares, Rodrigo. R. 2004. Development, Crime and Punishment: Accounting for the International Difference in Crime Rates. *Journal of Developmental Economics* 73:155–184.

Spear, L. P. 2000. The Adolescent Brain and Age-Related Behavioral Manifestations. *Neuroscience and Behavioral Reviews* 24:417–463.

Spergel, Irving A. 1990. Youth Gangs: Continuity and Change, pp. 171–275, in Michael Tonry and Norval Morris (eds.), *Crime and Justice: A Review of Research,* vol. 12. Chicago: University of Chicago Press.

Spinellis, Calliope D., Eleni Apospori, Maria Kranidioti, Yiota Symiyianni, and Nina Angelopoulou. 1994. Key-Findings of a Preliminary Self-Report Delinquency Study in Athens, Greece, pp., 288–318, in Josine Junger-Tas, Gert-Jan Terlouw, and Malcolm W. Klein (eds.), *Delinquent Behavior among Young People in the Western World: First Results of the International Self-Report Delinquency Study.* Amsterdam: Kugler.

Statistics New Zealand. 1991. *Justice Statistics 1990.* Wellington, NZ: Statistics New Zealand.

Statistics Sweden. 2002. *Statistisk Årsbok för Sverige 2002* (Statistical Yearbook of Sweden). Örebro: Statistics Sweden.

Steffensmeier, Darrell, Emilie Allan, and Cathy Streifel. 1989. Development and Female Crime: A Cross-National Test of Alternative Explanations. *Social Forces* 68:262–283.

Steffensmeier, Darrell, Jennifer Schwartz, Hua Zhong, and Jeff Ackerman. 2005. An Assessment of Recent Trends in Girls' Violence Using Diverse Longitudinal Sources: Is The Gender Gap Closing? *Criminology* 43:355–406.

Steinberg, L. 2004. Risk-Taking in Adolescence: What Changes and Why? *Annals of the New York Academy of Sciences* 1021:51–58.

Storgaard, Anette. 2004. Juvenile Justice in Scandinavia. *Journal of Scandinavian Studies in Criminology and Crime Prevention* 5:188–204.

Strasburg, Paul A. 1977. How France Treats Children in Trouble. *Judicature Chicago* 61:23–31.

Sussman, Frederick. 1959. *Law of Juvenile Delinquency*. Rev. ed. New York: Oceana.

Sutherland, Edwin H., and Donald R. Cressey. 1955. *Principles of Criminology*. 5th ed. New York: Lippincott.

Sutherland, I., and J. P. Shepherd. 2002. A Personality Based Model of Adolescent Violence. *British Journal of Criminology* 42:433–441.

Svensson, Robert. 2003. Gender Differences in Adolescent Drug Use: The Impact of Parental Monitoring and Peer Deviance. *Youth and Society* 34:300–329.

Tanioka, Ichiro, and Hiroko Goto. 1996. Japan, pp. 191–206, in Donald J. Shoemaker (ed.), *International Handbook on Juvenile Justice*. Westport, CT: Greenwood.

Tappan, Paul W. 1949. *Juvenile Delinquency*. New York: McGraw-Hill.

———. 1960. *Crime, Justice and Correction*. New York, McGraw-Hill.

Thomas, Charles W., and Shay Bilchik. 1985. Prosecuting Juveniles in Criminal Courts: Legal and Empirical Analysis. *Journal of Criminal Law and Criminology* 76:438–479.

Thornberry, Terence P. 1996. Empirical Support for Interaction Theory: A Review of the Literature, pp., 198–235, in David J. Hawkins (ed.), *Delinquency and Crime: Current Theories*. Cambridge: Cambridge University Press.

Thornberry, Terence P., and Marvin D. Krohn. 2001. The Development of Delinquency: An Interactional Perspective, pp. 289–306, in Susan O. White (ed.), *Handbook of Youth and Justice*. New York: Plenum.

———, (eds.). 2003. *Taking Stock of Delinquency: An Overview of Findings from Contemporary Longitudinal Studies*. New York: Kluwer.

Tomasevski, Katarina (ed.). 1986. *Children In Adult Prisons: An International Perspective*. New York: St. Martin's Press.

Torstensson, Marie. 1990. Female Delinquency in a Birth Cohort: Test of Some Aspects of Control Theory. *Journal of Quantitative Criminology* 6:101–115.

Tracy, Paul E., Jr. 1996. Prevalence, Incidence, Rates, and Other Descriptive Measures, pp. 27–36 in Joseph G. Weis, Robert D. Crutchfield, and George S. Bridges (eds.), *Juvenile Delinquency: Readings*. Thousand Oaks, CA: Pine Forge Press.

Traver, Harold. 1997. Juvenile Delinquency in Hong Kong, pp. 113–138, in John A. Winterdyk (ed.), *Juvenile Justice Systems: International Perspectives*. Toronto: Canadian Scholars' Press.

Trocmé, Nico M., Marc Tourigny, Bruce MacLaurin, and Barbara Fallon. 2003. Major Findings from the Canadian Incidence Study of Reported Child Abuse and Neglect. *Child Abuse and Neglect* 27:1427–1439.

UNICEF. 2006a. Haiti: Grim Reality for Street Children. http://www.unicef.org/infobycountry/haiti_30578.html.

———. 2006b. Education. http://www.unicef.org/sowc99/summary.htm.

———. 2006c. *The State of The World's Children: Excluded and Invisible*. New York: UNICEF.

———. 2006d. Fact Sheet. Commercial Sexual Exploitation. http://www.unicef.org/media/files/sexploitation_fact.doc.

United Nations. 1986. *United Nations Standard Minimum Rules for the Administration of Juvenile Justice: The Beijing Rules*. New York: Department of Public Information, United Nations.

———. 1989. United Nations Convention on the Rights of the Child, December 12. U.N. Doc. A/RES/44/25.

———. 1992. *Trends in Crime and Criminal Justice 1970–1985, in the Context of Socio-Economic Change.* New York: United Nations.

———. 1995a. *Children and Juveniles in Detention: Application of Human Rights Standards.* Vienna: Austrian Federal Ministry for Youth and Family.

———. 1995b. *Ninth United Nations Congress on the Prevention of Crime and the Treatment of Offenders.* Vienna: U.N. Crime Prevention and Criminal Justice Branch.

———. 1999. Youth and Drugs: A Global Overview. Paper presented to Commission on Narcotic Drugs, 42d sess., March 16–25, Vienna.

———. 2000. United Nations Millennium Declaration. http://www.un.org/millennium/declaration/ares552e.htm.

———. 2004a. The Seventh United Nations Survey on Crime Trends and the Operations of Criminal Justice Systems (1998–2000). http://www.unodc.org/unodc/en/crime_cicip_survey_seventh.html.

———. 2004b. *World Youth Report 2003: The Global Situation of Young People.* New York: United Nations Publications.

United Nations Expert Group Meeting. 1995. *Children and Juveniles in Detention: Application of Human Rights Standards.* Vienna: Austrian Federal Ministry for Youth and Family.

United Nations Office for Drug Control and Crime Prevention (UNODC). 1999. *The Drug Nexus in Africa.* Vienna: United Nations Office for Drug Control and Crime Prevention.

———. 2005. World Drug Report 2005. http://www.unodc.org/unodc/en/world drug-report.html.

Urbas, Gregor. 2000. The Age of Criminal Responsibility. *Trends and Issues in Crime and Justice* 181:1–60.

U.S. Department of Health and Human Services. 1993. *National Household Survey on Drug Abuse: Population Estimates 1992.* Rockville, MD: U.S. Department of Health and Human Services.

U.S. Office of National Drug Control Policy (USONDCP). 2005. *Drug Facts: Juveniles and Drugs.* Rockville, MD: Drug Policy Information Clearing House. http://www.whitehousedrugpolicy.gov/drugfact/juveniles/index.html.

Van Hees, Alma. 1991. Diversion in The Netherlands: Bureau Halt, pp. 232–312, in Josine Junger-Tas, Leonieke Boendermaker, and Peter H. van der Laan (eds.), *The Future of the Juvenile Justice System.* Leuven, Belgium: Acco.

Van Kesteren, John. 2000. *Criminal Victimization in Seventeen Industrialized Countries: Key Findings from the 2000 International Crime Victims Survey.* The Hague: Infodesk WODC.

Vazsonyi, A. T. 1996. Family Socialization and Delinquency in the United States and Switzerland. *European Journal of Criminal Policy and Research* 4:81–100.

———. 2001. An Empirical Test of a General Theory of Crime: A Four-National Comparative Study of Self-Control and the Prediction of Deviance. *Journal of Research in Crime and Delinquency* 38:91–131.

Vazsonyi, Alexander T., Lloyd E. Pickering, Lara M. Belliston, Dick Hessing, and Marianne Junger. 2002. Routine Activities and Deviant Behavior: American, Dutch, Hungarian, and Swiss Youth. *Journal of Quantitative Criminology* 18:397–422.

Wakefield, William, and J. David Hirschel. 1996. England, pp. 90–109, in Donald J. Shoemaker (ed.), *International Handbook on Juvenile Justice.* Westport, CT: Greenwood.

Walgrave, Lode. 1987. Girls in the Belgium Judicial System. EUI working paper 303/87. San Domenico, Florance, European University Institute.

Ward, David A., and Charles R. Tittle. 1994. IQ and Delinquency: A Test of Two Competing Explanations. *Journal of Quantitative Criminology* 40:189–212.

Wardhaugh, Julia. 1991. Criminalising Truancy: Legal and Welfare Responses to School Non-Attendance, pp. 133–143, in Tim Booth (ed.), *Juvenile Justice in the New Europe*. Sheffield, UK: Joint Unit for Social Services Research, Sheffield University.

Weijers, Ido (ed.). 1999. Juvenile Justice and the Origins of the Welfare State. *European Journal of Crime, Criminal Law and Criminal Justice* 7:3–78.

Weiler, Barbara Luntz, and Cathy Spatz Widom. 1996. Psychopathy and Violent Behavior in Abused and Neglected Young Adults. *Criminal Behavior and Mental Health* 6:253–271.

Weinstein, Noah, and John F. Mendoza. 1979. *Supreme Court Decisions and Juvenile Justice*. 2nd ed. Reno, NV: National Council of Juvenile and Family Court Judges.

Weir, Adele L., and Bernard Gallagher (eds.). 2004. *Child Sexual Abuse and the Internet: Tackling the New Frontier*. Dorset: Russell House.

Weis, Joseph G. 1996. Class, pp. 70–80, in Joseph G. Weis, Robert D. Crutchfield, and George S. Bridges (eds.), *Juvenile Delinquency: Readings*. Thousand Oaks, CA: Pine Forge Press.

Weitekamp, Elmar G. M. 2001. Gangs in Europe: Assessments at the Millennium, pp. 309–324, in Malcolm W. Klein, Hans-Jürgen Kerner, Cheryl L. Maxson, and Elmar G. M. Weitekamp (eds.), *The Eurogang Paradox: Street Gangs and Youth Groups in the U.S. and Europe*. Dordrecht: Kluwer.

Weitekamp, Elmar G. M., and Hans-Jürgen Kerner (eds.). 1992. *Cross-National Longitudinal Research on Human Development and Criminal Behavior*. Dordrecht: Kluwer.

Werdmölder, Hans. 1997. *A Generation Adrift: An Ethnography of a Criminal Moroccan Gang in the Netherlands*. The Hague: Kluwer Law International.

Wernham, Marie. 2001. *Background Paper on Street Children and Violence*. London, UK: Consortium for Street Children.

Wessells, Michael. 2000. How We Can Protect Child Soldiering. *Peace Review* 12:407–413.

Winterdyk, John A. 1997a. Introduction, pp. vii–xxiii, in John A. Winterdyk (ed.), *Juvenile Justice Systems: International Perspectives*. Toronto: Canadian Scholars' Press.

———. 1997b. Juvenile Justice and Young Offenders: An Overview of Canada, pp. 139–175, in John A. Winterdyk (ed.), *Juvenile Justice Systems: International Perspectives*. Toronto: Canadian Scholars' Press.

———, (ed.). 1997c. *Juvenile Justice Systems: International Perspectives*. Toronto: Canadian Scholars' Press.

———. 2005. Juvenile Justice in the International Arena, pp. 457–469, in Philip L. Reichel (ed.), *Handbook of Transnational Crime and Justice*. Thousand Oaks, CA: Sage.

Wita, Marcel. 2000. Community Policing—Das Daenische SSP-Modell. *Die Kriminalpraevention* 4:7–12.

Wolfe, Nancy Travis. 1991. Socialist Juvenile Justice: The German Democratic Republic, pp. 349–376, in Jim Hackler (ed.), *Official Responses to Problem Juveniles: Some International Reflections*. Euskadi, Spain: The Oñati International Institute for the Sociology of Law.

———. 1996. Germany, pp. 125–145, in Donald J. Shoemaker (ed.), *International Handbook on Juvenile Justice*. Westport, CT: Greenwood.

Wolfgangerler, René Bendit, and Heiner Schäfer (eds.). 2000. *Child and Juvenile Delinquency: Strategies of Prevention and Intervention in Germany and Netherlands*. Utrecht, Netherlands: Verwey-Jonker Instituute.

Wong, Dennis S.W. 2001. Pathways to Delinquency in Hong Kong and Guangzhou (South China). *International Journal of Adolescence and Youth* 10:91–115.

———. 2004. School Bullying and Tackling Strategies in Hong Kong. *International Journal of Offender Therapy and Comparative Criminology* 48:537–553.

Woodhouse, Barbara Bennett. 2001. Children's Rights, pp. 377–410, in Susan O. White (ed.), *Handbook of Youth and Justice*. New York: Klumer Academic/Plenum Publishers.

Wright, Bradley R. Entner, Avshalom Caspi, Terrie E. Moffitt, and Phil A. Silva. 2001. The Effects of Social Ties on Crime Vary by Criminal Propensity: A Life-Course Model of Interdependence. *Criminology* 39:321–352.

Xiaoming, Chen. 2000. Educating and Correcting Juvenile Delinquents: The Chinese Approaches. *Journal of Correctional Education* 51:334–346.

Yokoyama, Minoru. 1986. The Juvenile Justice System in Japan, pp. 102–113, in M. Brusten, J. Graham, N. Herriger, and P. Malinowski (eds.), *Youth Crime, Social Control and Prevention: Theoretical Perspectives and Policy Implications: Studies from Nine Different Countries*. Wuppertal, Germany: International Document and Study Centre for Conflicts of Youth, University of Wuppertal.

———. 1997. Juvenile Justice: An Overview of Japan, pp. 1–28, in John A. Winterdyk (ed.), *Juvenile Justice Systems: International Perspectives*. Toronto: Canadian Scholars' Press.

Zhang, Lening, and Steven F. Messner. 1995. Family Deviance and Delinquency in China. *Criminology* 33:359–387.

Zimring, Franklin E. 1979. Privilege, Maturity, and Responsibility: Notes on the Evolving Jurisprudence of Adolescence, pp. 312–335, in LaMar T. Empey (ed.), *The Future of Childhood and Juvenile Justice*. Charlottesville: University Press of Virginia.

INDEX

ABOUT THE AUTHOR

CLAYTON A. HARTJEN is chair of the Department of Sociology and Anthropology and a professor in the School of Criminal Justice at Rutgers University–Newark. He has conducted fieldwork on youth crime and justice in India and France. The results of his research have been published in a number of books and articles, as well as an international annotated bibliography on delinquency and juvenile justice.